RESCUE

RESCUE

The true-life drama of Royal Air Force Search and Rescue

PAUL BEAVER
AND
PAUL BERRIFF

Patrick Stephens Limited

IN ASSOCIATION WITH
SCOTTISH TELEVISION

First published in 1990

British Library Cataloguing in Publication Data
Beaver, Paul
Rescue: the true-life drama of Royal Air Force Search and Rescue.
1. Great Britain. Air rescue services
I. Title II. Berriff, Paul
363.3'48

ISBN 1-85260-291-0

Patrick Stephens Limited is part of the Thorsons Publishing Group, Wellingborough, Northamptonshire NN8 2RQ, England.

Typeset by
Harper Phototypesetters Ltd,
Northampton, England
Printed by
William Collins & Co. Ltd, Glasgow

10 9 8 7 6 5 4 3 2 1

Front Cover:
Bob Pountney is winched into Rescue 137 with a casualty during the Piper Alpha oil rig disaster.

CONTENTS

ACKNOWLEDGEMENTS

This book has been written as a companion to the television series, RESCUE. In many instances we have been assisted by the same people who co-operated with such enthusiasm in the production of the documentaries. We would therefore like to single out the following for their special assistance with the creation of this book.

Gus MacDonald and David Scott of Scottish Television are thanked for having the foresight to let us indulge our interest in helicopters, rescue and television programme-making by supporting the whole concept of RESCUE.

At the Ministry of Defence in London: Air Vice-Marshall AFC 'Sandy' Hunter AFC, Air Commodore Mike Barnes, George Munro, Michael Hill and their staffs; Group Captain Brian Pegnall and Group Captain John Lumsden, OBE, AFC (station commanders, RAF Lossiemouth).

Special thanks to the members of D Flight, especially Flight Lieutenants Paul Readfern, John Prince, Pat Thirkell and Steve Martin who read the text and, from an operational viewpoint, corrected and amended technical points. They also made useful suggestions about content and style. Former SAR pilot, Squadron Leader David Simpson, also made useful suggestions.

Additional information and data was provided by Tony Ellis (District Staff Officer, HM Coastguard, Bridlington); Josianne Middleton (HM Coastguard, Dept of Transport); Tommy Taylor (Team Leader, RAF Kinloss MRT); Andy Anderson (Director, National Outdoor Training Centre, Glenmore Lodge); Dr Alistair MacGregor (medical officer, Mountain Rescue Committee, Scotland); John Barlow (Hon Secretary, SAR Dog Association); Ray Kipling (Deputy Director, RNLI); Fiona McGhie (Public Affairs Officer, Occidental Petroleum); and Bryan Stilling (Incident Report Officer, Lake District Mountain Accidents Association).

Sarah Last (PR Manager, Westland) provided the cutaway drawing of the Sea King and we are indebted to the skilled pen of Ian Commin for the explanatory line drawings and maps used in this book. The Lossiemouth rescue helicopter team was also responsible for the critique of these illustrations to ensure accuracy. Commercial helicopter operational data was provided by Phil Strickland (Bond Helicopters) and A.P. Hopkins (Bristow Helicopter Company); the Fleet Air Arm input was checked and updated by Lieutenant Commander Peter West RN. The team at Patrick Stephens Ltd and Sue McCormack also deserve a vote of thanks.

We are also indebted to all those who assisted and to those who D Flight rescued during the making of the television series; without them there would be no book.

As usual, the authors take full responsibility for all errors which might have crept into the text despite many hours of burning the midnight oil.

Paul Beaver and Paul Berriff

THE AUTHORS

PAUL BEAVER
Paul Beaver is a professional journalist, author and broadcaster who specializes in aerospace matters, especially helicopters. In 1982 he founded *Defence Helicopter World* magazine, the first international journal dealing solely with the defence implications of rotorcraft. On leaving the magazine in 1986 he began development of *Jane's Videotape Reference Library* before joining *Jane's Defence Weekly* as a specialist editor on helicopters and naval matters. In April 1988 he was appointed Managing Editor (Defence & Aerospace) for Jane's Information Group, since when he has developed the Soviet and specialist publishing side of the Group's activities. In August 1989 he went to Moscow, the first Westerner to be shown the latest Soviet helicopter developments. In September 1989, he was appointed Publisher of *Jane's Defence Weekly*.

As an author of 30 books, including *Modern Military Helicopters* and *Encyclopaedia of the Modern Royal Navy*, he has lectured on aerospace and defence issues to service and industry groups on two continents and had his articles translated into six languages.

In 1983, Paul started working with the broadcast media, providing specialist knowledge of aerospace (civil and military), including weekly aviation input to British Forces Broadcasting. He has appeared regularly on *BBC Breakfast Time*, *Nine O'clock News* and *Newsnight*, *ITN News at Ten*, *CBC Telejournal*, *ZDF News*, *Nippon TV*, *CBS News* and *ABC Good Morning America*.

PAUL BERRIFF
Paul began his career as a photojournalist on the *Yorkshire Evening Post* before joining the BBC Television news team as a cameraman in 1968. His first award was in 1968 for sports, followed by another dozen over the next 20 years. He has worked on location in Arctic Canada, the Soviet Union and the United States for such series as *Panorama*, the *South Bank Show, Newsnight, Horizon* and *Tomorrow's World*.

He filmed and directed such memorable television documentaries as *Lonely Sea and Sky*, the life story of Sir Francis Chichester; *Pilot Royal*, about HRH Prince Charles's helicopter pilot career in the Royal Navy; and *Lifeboat*, about the crew of the Humber Lifeboat. He later developed a talent for the full gambit of television documentary production and was responsible for *Animal Squad*, about the job of an RSPCA inspector, for BBC 1; *Motorway*, about the M62 police, for ITV Network; and *Fire* at Britain's busiest fire station (during which time he undertook a fireman's training course).

Paul is a former lifeboatman and is now HM Coastguard's Auxiliary-in-Charge of the River Humber near his home in Hessle, North Humberside. When not filming or producing he is often found as coxswain of the Humber Inshore Rescue boat.

LOCATION OF INCIDENTS COVERED BY 202 SQUADRON RAF LOSSIEMOUTH

1st April 1988 to 1st April 1989

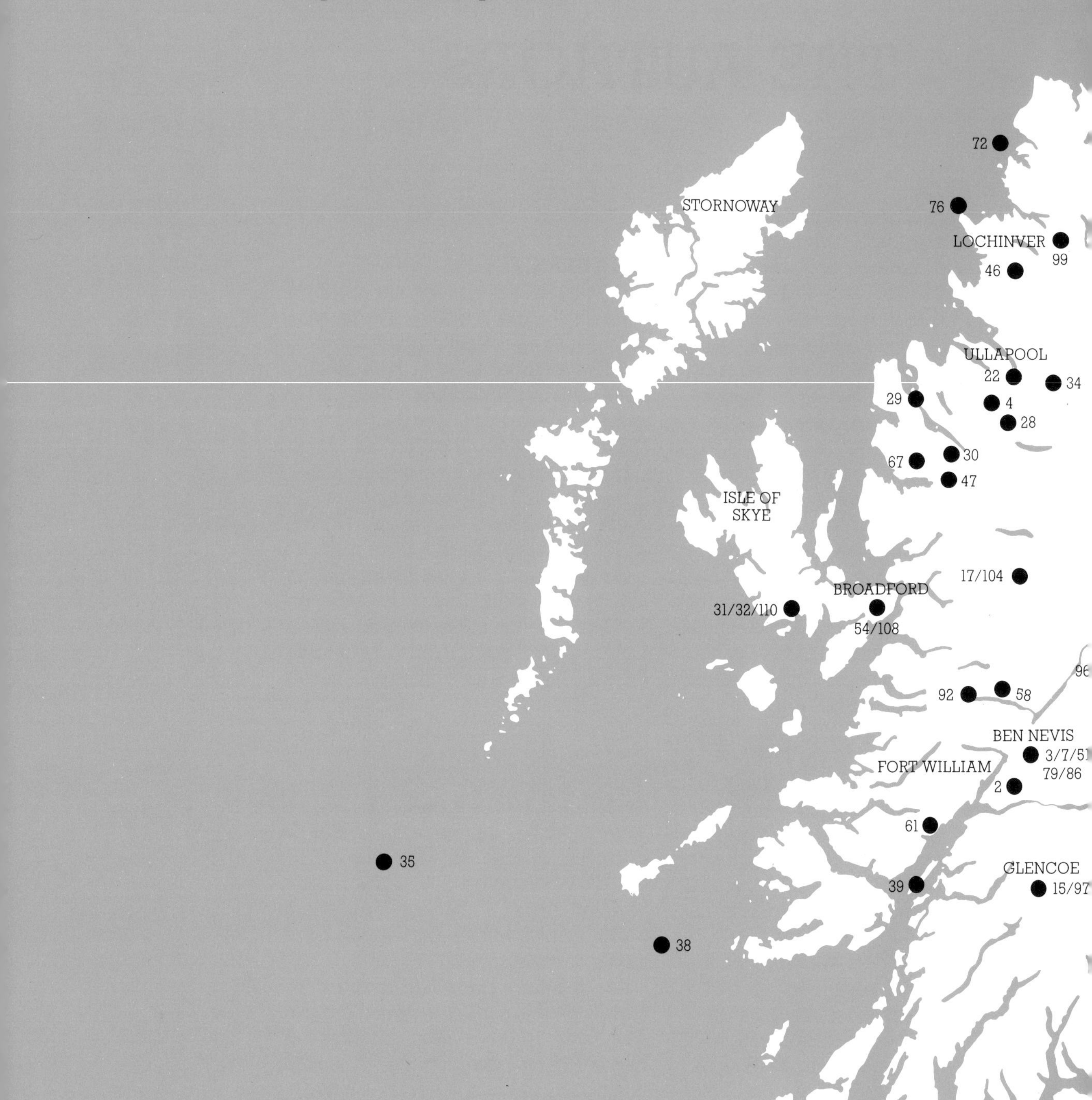

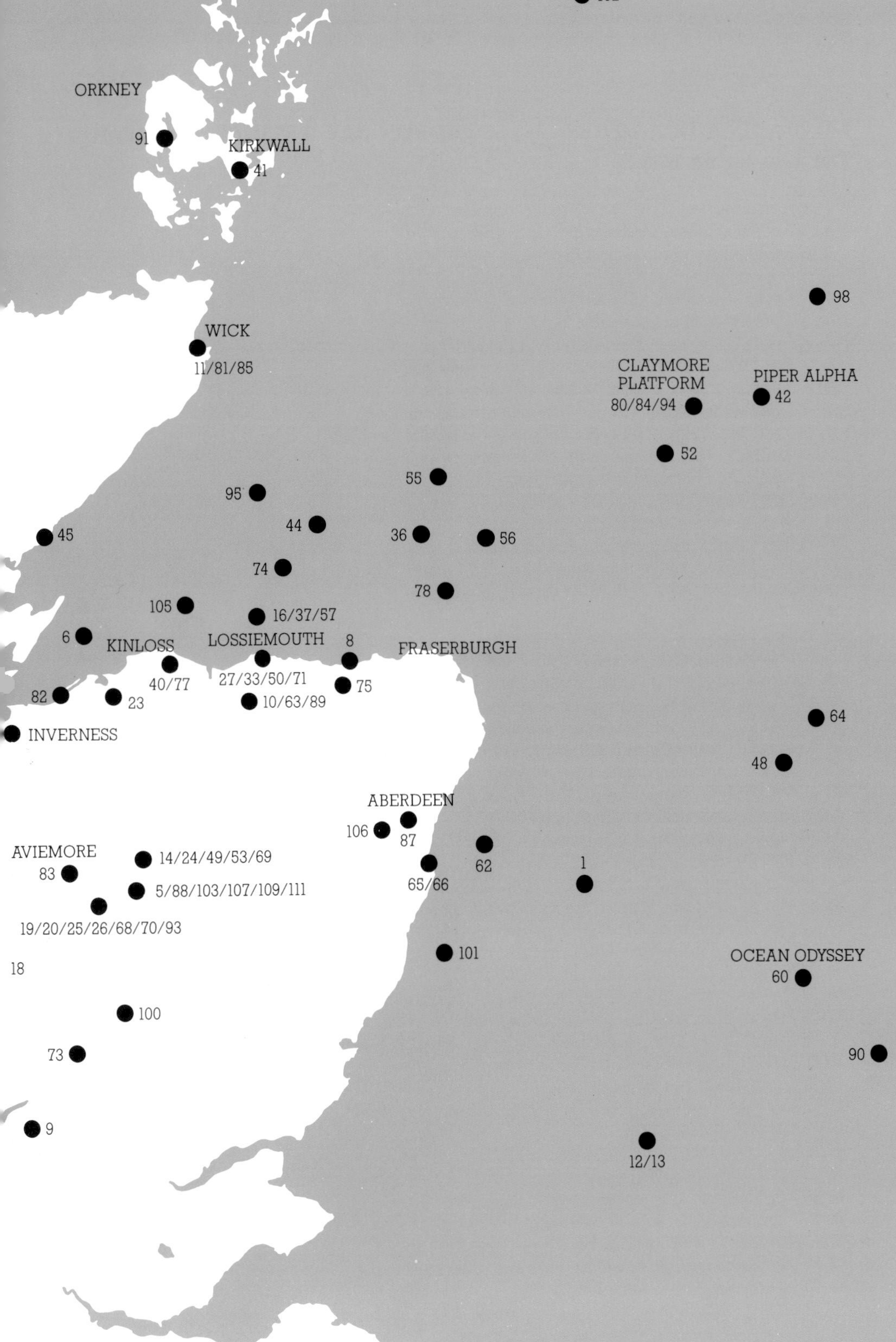
102
ORKNEY
91
KIRKWALL
41
98
WICK
11/81/85
CLAYMORE
PLATFORM
80/84/94
PIPER ALPHA
42
52
55
95
44
36
56
45
74
78
105
16/37/57
6
KINLOSS
LOSSIEMOUTH
8
FRASERBURGH
40/77
27/33/50/71
75
82
23
10/63/89
INVERNESS
64
48
ABERDEEN
106
87
62
AVIEMORE
14/24/49/53/69
83
1
5/88/103/107/109/111
65/66
19/20/25/26/68/70/93
18
101
OCEAN ODYSSEY
60
100
73
90
9
12/13

NO 202 (SEARCH AND RESCUE) SQUADRON RAF D FLIGHT, LOSSIEMOUTH

The jobs during 1988-89

1988

1 1 April Medevac from Fishing Vessel *Shieldwood*
2 3 April Two missing walkers in Glen Nevis
3 3 April Injured climber near Ben Nevis
4 8 April Injured climber taken to Stornoway
5 9 April Fallen skier collected but dead on arrival
6 13 April Two missing canoeists (NAR)
7 14 April Two missing climbers on Ben Nevis (NAR)
8 14 April Personal locator beacon operating near Banff
9 15 April Search for missing walker near Ben Lawers
10 15 April Medevac Elgin to Glasgow with burns victim
11 18 April Baby from Wick to Raigmore with breathing problems
12 20 April RAF Phantom crash, search for aircrew
13 21 April RAF Phantom crash, continued search
14 30 April Missing boy in the Cairngorms
15 1 May Recovered woman's body in Glencoe
16 2 May Boat capsized off Lossiemouth (NAR)
17 6 May Missing walker near Kintail; found OK
18 9 May Missing skier near Newtonmore; found OK
19 10 May Ill soldier in the Cairngorms
20 11 May Injured walker in the Cairngorms
21 12 May Medevac from Raigmore (Inverness) to Aberdeen
22 13 May Road traffic accident, motorcyclist at Loch Broom
23 14 May Injured canoeist in gorge at Forres
24 15 May Old lady with broken ankle near Glenmore
25 15 May Old lady with heat exhaustion near Glenmore
26 15 May Old lady with injured knees near Glenmore
27 18 May RAF Buccaneer alert (NAR)
28 24 May Injured climber at Dundonnell
29 26 May Drowning baby at Poolewe
30 27 May Overdue climbers near Torridon
31 29 May Climber with broken ankle in the Cuillins
32 29 May Injured climber and dead climber in the Cuillins
33 31 May Military aircraft in-flight emergency (NAR)
34 2 June Three missing walkers, including one Canadian
35 16 June Casevac injured seaman to Belfast
36 22 June Seaman with pain from North Sea to Aberdeen
37 22 June Windsurfer in trouble off Lossiemouth
38 22 June Casevac from submarine to Raigmore hospital
39 23 June Pregnant woman from Inner Hebrides to Glasgow
40 1 July Nimrod alert for missing boat
41 2 July Premature baby from Orkneys to Aberdeen
42 6 July *PIPER ALPHA*
43 10 July Overturned boat off Inverness
44 18 July Sinking fishing vessel
45 19 July Medevac to Aberdeen Royal Infirmary
46 20 July Scramble to mountains (NAR)
47 21 July Search with Torridon MRT for (dead) climber
48 25 July Sinking fishing vessel in North Sea, seven rescued
49 29 July Missing Dutch walker
50 4 August RAF Andover in-flight emergency
51 13 August Casevac from Ben Nevis after heart attack
52 17 August Casevac sailor with suspected heart attack
53 18 August Missing elderly couple; found (WIFA)
54 22 August Medevac Broadford to Glasgow; head injuries

55 24 August Sinking FV *Choice*; four crew rescued
56 29 August Casevac of head injuries from FV *Paramount* to Aberdeen
57 1 September Windsurfer in trouble (NAR)
58 11 September Three monks fall off waterfall; two injured, one dead
59 18 September Two missing climbers, found Lochen
60 22 September *Ocean Odyssey* fire
61 25 September Corran waterfall; injured woman
62 25 September Injured yachtsman taken to Aberdeen
63 27 September Medevac head injury Elgin to Aberdeen
64 3 October Casevac from oil rig
65 5 October Personal locator beacon in Aberdeen harbour (NAR)
66 14 October Search missing man (NAR)
67 15 October Injured climber in Torridon area
68 16 October Cairngorms search
69 16 October Two walkers taken to Glenmore Lodge (NAR)
70 17 October Missing couple at Lairig Ghru, search successful
71 17 October RAF Tornado in-flight emergency
72 17 October HMCG S-61N ditching, rescued crew
73 21 October Light aircraft crash near Aviemore; three dead
74 22 October Casevac from oil rig *Sondat* to Raigmore hospital
75 26 October Search for Spey poacher believed drowned
76 27 October Old Man of Stoer climber rescued by Paul Berriff
77 29 October Nimrod scramble to Spurn Head, two missing
78 1 November Two evacuated, boat escorted to Peterhead harbour
79 3 November Rucksack found, search for owner, Ben Nevis (WIFA)
80 10 November Helicopter crash near Claymore platform
81 13 November Premature pregnancy medevac to Raigmore hospital
82 14 November Medevac to Raigmore
83 19 November Fallen climber in Cairngorms, aborted because of blizzard
84 26 November Cargo boat fire off Claymore platform
85 26 November Premature baby from Wick to Raigmore
86 27 November Walker with suspected broken knees medevac to Fort William
87 13 December Missing man in Aberdeen area
88 18 December Missing climbers in Cairngorms
89 23 December Medevac from Elgin to Aberdeen; RTA casualty
90 24 December Drifting oil rig ship in Fulmar Field
91 28 December Search missing boy, Orkney; not found
92 30 December Search for three missing people around Loch Arkaig
1989
93 9 January Search for missing girl in Cairngorms; found OK
94 11 January Casevac from *Deep Water II* to Aberdeen
95 13 January Search for man overboard in Beatrice Oilfield
96 28 January Rescue 138 crash (film crew on board)
97 12 February Four climbers stuck in Glencoe
98 17 February Sinking FV *Armana*, 150 miles off Lossiemouth
99 18 February Fallen walkers at Assynt, very bad weather
100 19 February Casevac injured skier, Glenshee to Aberdeen
101 19 February Small FV sank; sea search at night, Stonehaven
102 25 February Evacuation of oil rig; aborted due to weather
103 27 February Casevac climber from Cairngorms to Raigmore
104 28 February Avalanche at Kintail; one dead, five saved
105 2 March Overturned boat (NAR)
106 11 March Search for PLB at Aberdeen Airport
107 17 March Fallen climber in the Cairngorms
108 20 March Evacuated meningitis case from Skye to Raigmore
109 23 March Injured climber in the Cairngorms (white out)
110 25 March Two fallen climbers on Skye to Raigmore
111 26 March Fallen climber in the Cuillins (NAR)

Baby Sam

JOB NO 41
2 JULY 1988

During the flight to Aberdeen the baby developed complications and his heart almost stopped beating

Rescue 137 scrambled in poor visibility to evacuate premature baby and mother from Kirkwall, Orkney, to Aberdeen Royal Infirmary. The weather on route deteriorated and Rescue 137 had to land in a field two miles from Kirkwall airport. Winchman Bob Pountney stopped a passing car and hitched a lift to the airport to notify the waiting ambulance containing the baby, mother and doctor that the helicopter was down the road in a field.

During the flight to Aberdeen the baby developed complications and his heart almost stopped beating. The doctor gave the baby oxygen while Bob Pountney administered cardiac massage to keep the baby alive. Steve Hodgson was the aircraft captain; Dave Lloyd, co-pilot; Pat Thirkell, radop/winch operator; Bob Pountney, winchman.

Pilot Steve Hodgson receives the call from the Rescue Co-ordinating Centre in Pitreavie.

Winchman Bob Pountney (right), assisted by the Pentland Coastguard officer and an ambulance driver, carries baby Sam Harcus in an incubator to Rescue 137.

The doctor, nurse and incubator on board Rescue 137 as they lift off from a field near Kirkwall for Aberdeen Royal Infirmary.

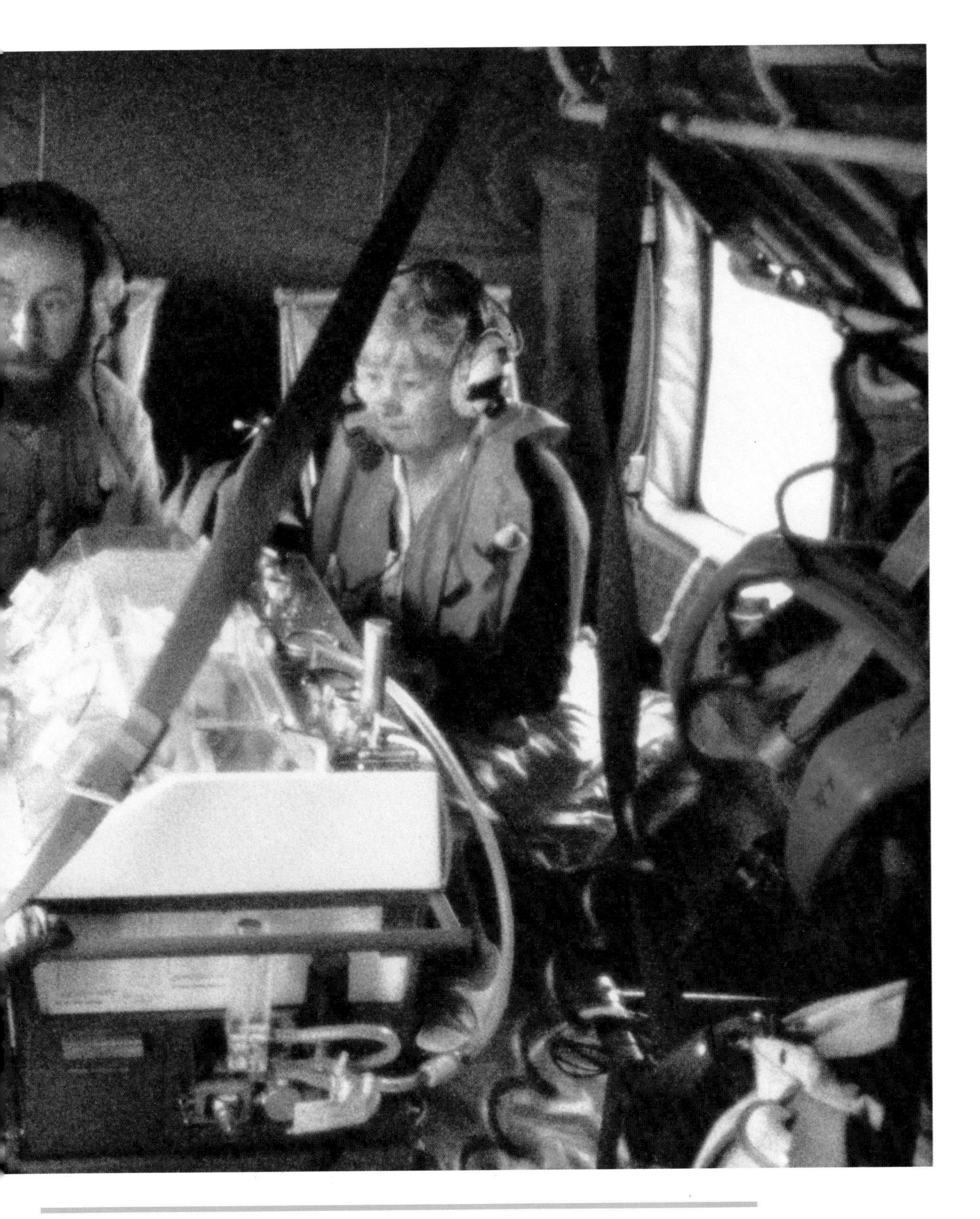

Moment of crisis; the fingers of Bob Pountney gently massage the baby's heart during the in-flight drama on board Rescue 137.

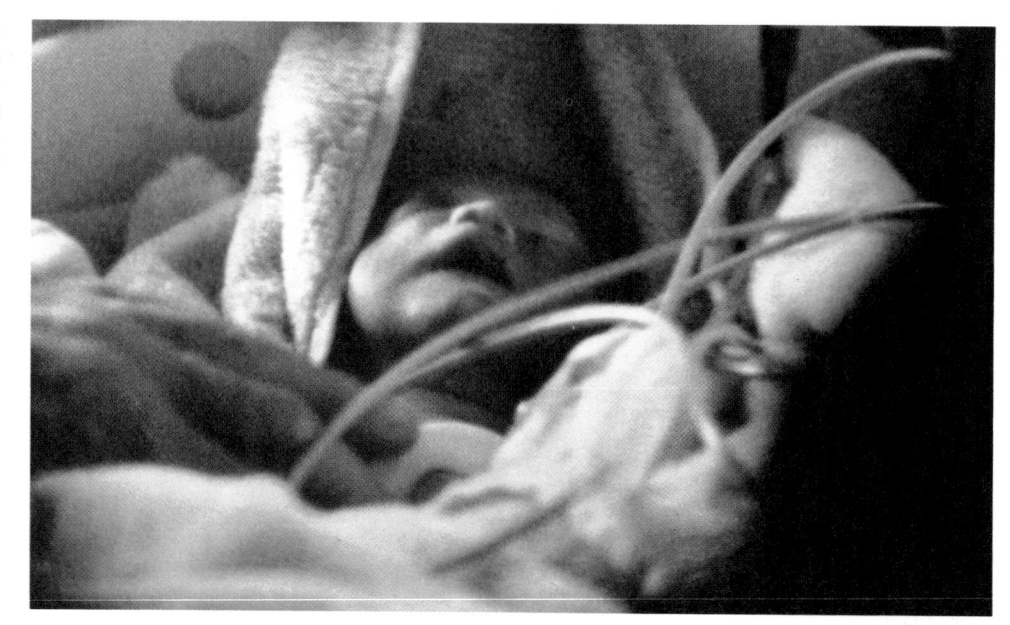

While Bob Pountney massages the baby's heart the doctor begins to administer oxygen.

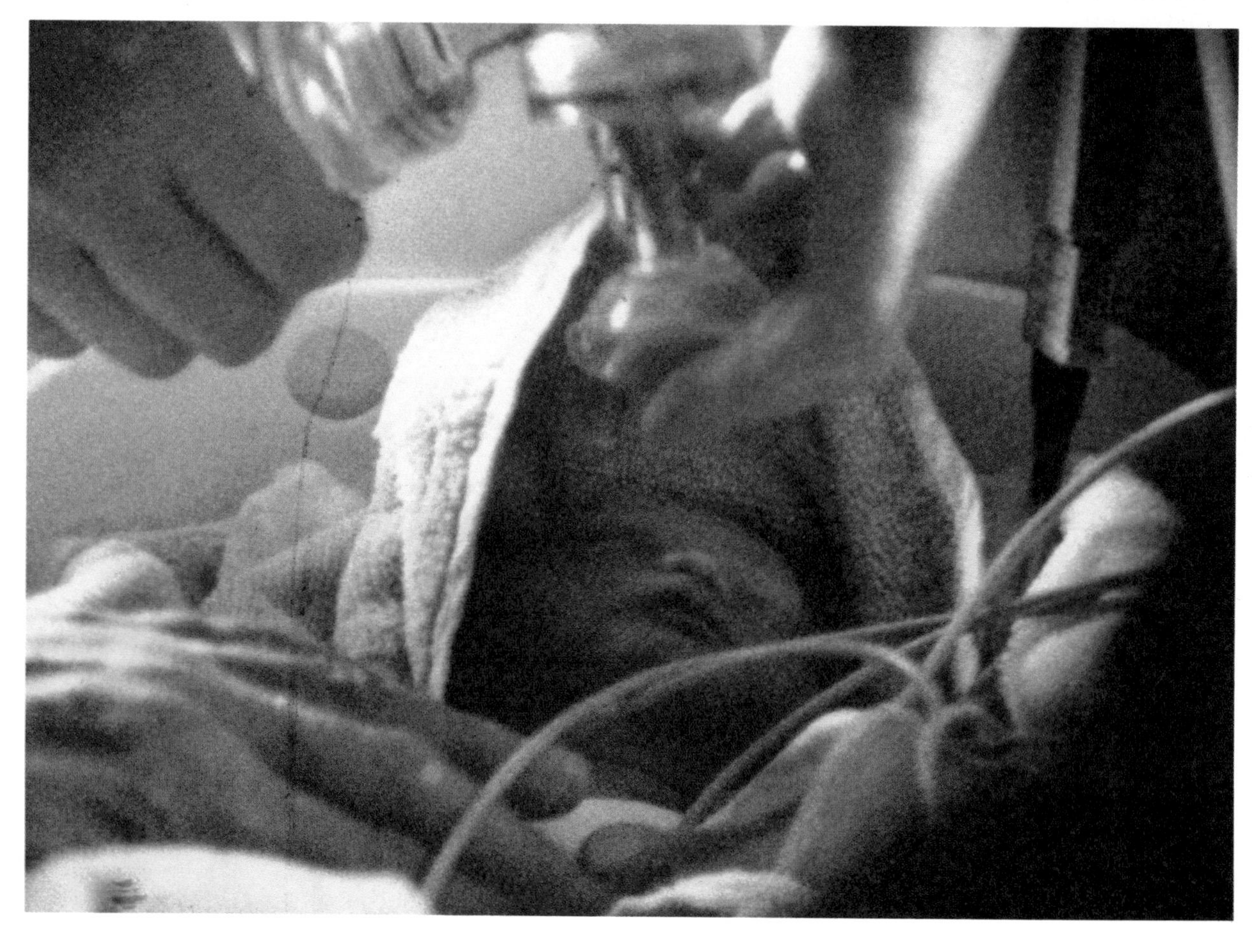

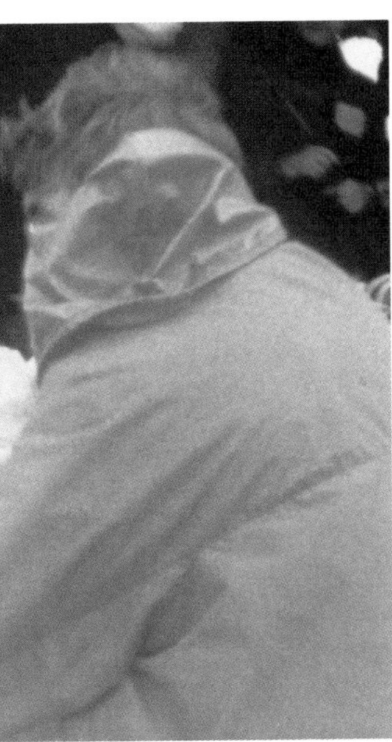

Far left *Senior consultant Alistair Matheson snatches baby Sam from Rescue 137 on the heli-pad at Aberdeen Royal Infirmary.*

Left *Bob Pountney pulls the consultant and baby Sam away from the dangerous tail rotor as they dash towards a waiting ambulance.*

Six months later: baby Sam Harcus with his mother, Gillian, and Rescue 137's co-pilot Dave Lloyd (rear), and pilot Steve Hodgson (right). Baby Sam's father is on the extreme left of the picture.

Piper Alpha

JOB NO 42
6 JULY 1988

'I crawled across the pipe-deck . . . it was white hot . . . it was slippery because the soles of our boots were melting . . .'

Right *Edinburgh Rescue to RAF Lossiemouth: 'It's Piper Alpha — there has been an explosion, they're abandoning and they're in the lifeboats. Aberdeen Coastguard would like you to proceed to the Piper Alpha and talk to them en route. The situation is a bit unclear at the moment. It looks as if it could possibly turn into a biggie.'*

'Bloody hell, it's really on fire, isn't it?' John Dean, captain of Rescue 138. 'It's a big one.' Pat Thirkell, radar and winch operator. 'I'm sweating already.' Bob Pountney, winchman.

Rescue 137 crew: Steve Hodgson (captain), David Lloyd (co-pilot), Steve Griffin (radar/winch operator), Bill Payne (winchman).

Rescue 138 crew: John Dean (captain), Paul Longdon (co-pilot), Pat Thirkell (radar/winch operator), Bob Pountney (winchman).

The horrendous events in the North Sea on 6 July 1988 developed into the worst oil platform disaster anywhere in the world. Every available helicopter, commercial and military, responsed to the call for assistance and the operation to rescue the crew and transfer the survivors to hospital. Out of 220 crew on the platform only 63 survived.

'My oh my, she's really burning. I've difficulty seeing things in this flaring light.' John Dean.

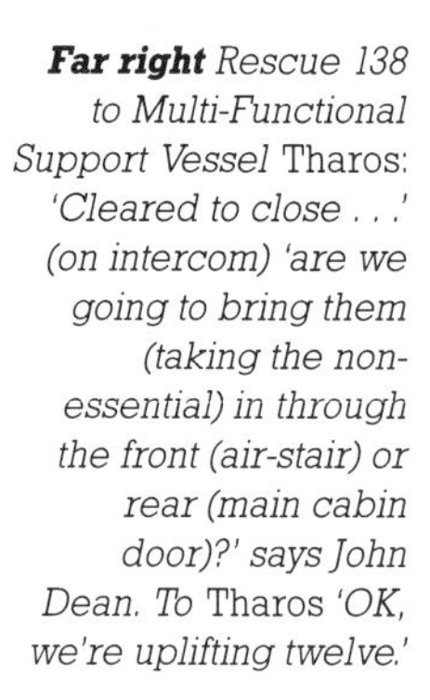

Far right *Rescue 138 to Multi-Functional Support Vessel* Tharos: *'Cleared to close . . .' (on intercom) 'are we going to bring them (taking the non-essential) in through the front (air-stair) or rear (main cabin door)?' says John Dean. To* Tharos *'OK, we're uplifting twelve.'*

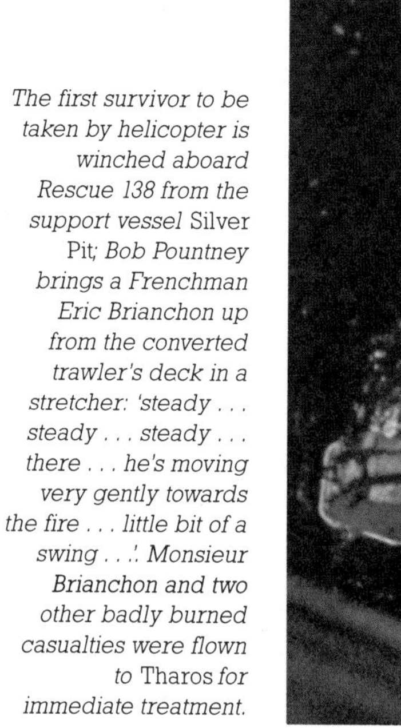

The first survivor to be taken by helicopter is winched aboard Rescue 138 from the support vessel Silver Pit*; Bob Pountney brings a Frenchman Eric Brianchon up from the converted trawler's deck in a stretcher: 'steady . . . steady . . . steady . . . there . . . he's moving very gently towards the fire . . . little bit of a swing . . .'. Monsieur Brianchon and two other badly burned casualties were flown to* Tharos *for immediate treatment.*

A badly injured survivor is rushed into Tharos*'s ultra-modern, high technology hospital. Using the helicopters, survivors were evacuated to hospital in Aberdeen.*

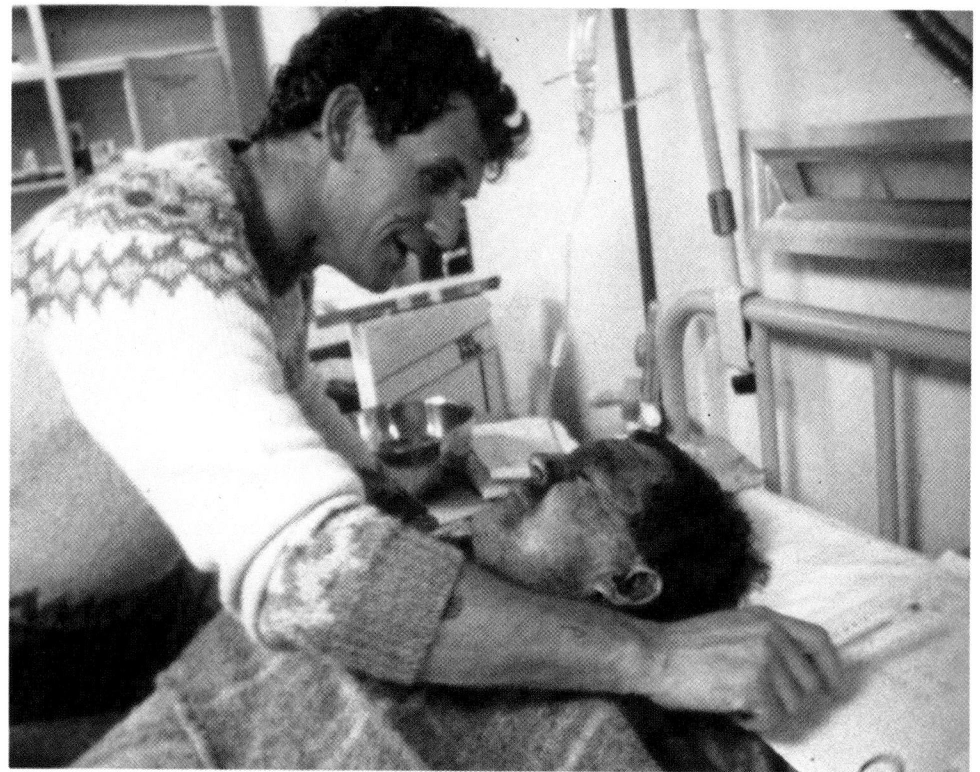

Paramedics and other medical staff from North Sea oil platforms and onshore treated the survivors in Tharos*'s hospital.*

Rescue 138 landing on Tharos *with more casualties.*

As dawn breaks, Rescue 138 returns to Tharos *with two victims found dead in the sea around Piper Alpha.*

As dawn breaks two badly burned bodies are carried across the helideck on Tharos.

In the morning, the remains of the Piper Alpha rig continued to burn. Some months later, after the accommodation block had been raised from the seabed, the remains were blown up.

THE PIPER TAPES

Taken from transcripts of actual helicopter radio conversations made at the time, here is some of the search and rescue dialogue as the tragic story of the Piper Alpha oil rig unfolds.

Rescue 137 (Sea King helicopter, on arrival): Rescue 01, Rescue 137, how do you read? Over.

Rescue 01: Rescue 137, Rescue 01 (RAF Nimrod aircraft), read you loud and clear, over.

Rescue 137: I've just called the Claymore Alpha (platform) he informs me there's a helicopter in the area already, his callsign is Yankee Bravo, and he is spotting, trying to see if there's anybody in the water. Apparently the rig (Piper Alpha) is well alight at the moment, a lot of black smoke, and he's finding it quite difficult. In terms of numbers in the water, we have no idea. Over.

Rescue 01: Rescue 137 from 01 copied all that. We're expected on the scene in two zero minutes and we have the rig visual at this time. (80 miles away)

RCC: Rescue 01, this is Edinburgh rescue, situation confused at this end. Request frequent sitreps. Over.

Rescue 01: Roger. We will pass frequent sitreps, as yet we are still in transit to the area and we can actually see the rig on fire and stand by for further transmissions.

Tharos: 01, *Tharos* (rescue platform). The situation is that the platform is completely on fire from sea level to top. We have, in fact, pulled back somewhat. The structure is collapsing and it is total fire. We are continuing to spray water on it and we wish to evacuate our non-essential personnel. We have taken and will be taking some casualties. Over.

Rescue 01: *Tharos*, Rescue 01 copied.

Tharos: One of the stand-by vessels (*Silver Pit*) has reported having 25 casualties which includes three serious burns and one injury. We wish to get rid of our non-essential staff so we can handle these casualties when we bring them on board.

Rescue 137: *Tharos*, this is Rescue 137. I'm in the area looking round. There's not a lot I can do in terms of the burning rig. Are you the rig that currently has a helicopter approximately two miles north-west of you?

Tharos: Rescue 137, that is probably Yankee Bravo, our S-76. I believe you are the yellow rescue helicopter that passed my bow five minutes ago.

Rescue 137: Roger, I've just turned round and put my lights on. I think Yankee Bravo has departed the area. If you've got casualties I can probably get to you but I cannot get any closer to the rig (Piper Alpha) because of the heat. How about the seriously injured you mentioned? Do you have the facilities to look after them or do they need moving first? Over.

Tharos: We have an intensive care hospital. The casualties are on one of the smaller boats at this time. We wish to lift them to *Tharos* and commence initial treatment.

Rescue 01: Edinburgh Rescue, this is 01. Sitrep. There is one surface vessel, semi-submersible (*Tharos*), three hundred yards on a bearing of 220 from the rig. He reports the rig is totally on fire from sea level to the very top. The structure is beginning to collapse. He is continuing to spray water. He believes that there are many casualties. He has seven survivors and another vessel in the area is believed to have 25 casualties on board; three with serious burns. This is Rescue 01.

Yankee Bravo: *Tharos*, Yankee Bravo. You have probably been told that the risers have obviously broken and the oil is now coming straight up on to the sea.

Rescue 01: All stations. The number of persons believed to be on board the Piper Alpha oil rig was two two zero. I say again two two zero (220). Intend searching around oil rig using surface vessels and helos. This is Rescue 01.

Tharos: Rescue 138, this is *Tharos*. We have no passengers at the moment. If you would like to stand by. I have made contact with the vessel. *Silver Pit*, who now has some 30 casualties. I believe 35, including some injured. I was going to contact Rescue 01 to check the feasibility of commencing winch recovery of those people to me.

Rescue 138: *Tharos*, Rescue 138. Roger, do you have a position of *Silver Pit*?

Tharos: He said he was half a mile to the east of the platform. He's moving closer to *Tharos* and is listening on this frequency. He's a converted fishing vessel with a small H landing area, no helideck.

Rescue 138: Rescue 01, we are now actually on the helideck of *Tharos* and lifting to go to *Silver Pit* to investigate winching possible casualties on to Tharos.

Silver Pit: Rescue 01, we have three seriously burned men and they will be in rescue stretchers, over.

Rescue 01: Roger that. We have Rescue 138 closing your position and Rescue 117 to follow for winching operations to remove survivors to *Tharos*.

Rescue 138: Rescue 01 and *Silver Pit*. Due to the large number of vessels in the vicinity we are having difficulty in locating *Silver Pit*. Can he illuminate himself or fire off some type of flare?

Tharos: All stations. There is a helicopter, call-sign Golf Bravo, en route from Aberdeen with four or five doctors which we wish to track straight into *Tharos*.

We will shortly begin the evacuation of walking casualties to other platforms.

Rescue 138: *Silver Pit*, this Rescue 138. Whilst you are stopped, the roll makes it extremely difficult to get stretchers safely off. Can you get underway, sir?

Tharos: Rescue 01 from *Tharos*. We are going to try and move back towards the platform (Piper Alpha) to endeavour to keep things (aboard) cool and hopefully prevent some of the underwater explosions we are afraid of.

Rescue 01: Rescue 137, request you search at low level — below 100 feet — for survivors to the west of the burning rig. Rescue 131 is searching to the east; Yankee Bravo has gone for fuel; 117 and 138 are co-ordinating our rescue operations from the *Silver Pit*.

Rescue 01: Edinburgh Rescue from Rescue 01. Sitrep. Rescue helicopters 138 and Rescue 117 are continuing their winching operations; Rescue helicopter 137 is searching an area to the west of the rig; Rescue 131 is investigating survivors in the water to the north-east of the rig. Helicopters Bristow Five Zero Yankee, Tango India Golf Bravo, Tango India Golf Oscar (both Super Pumas) and Yankee Bravo (the S-76) are either en route to the scene or holding on oil rigs. They will take over the search when other helicopters have to refuel. The rig is now believed to be emitting hydrogen sulphide and there is a high probability of an underwater explosion. There is heavy smoke and flames spreading to the north of the rig. This is Rescue 01.

Rescue 01: Rescue 01 to *Tharos*. Request the number of survivors and casualties you have accounted for so far. Over.

Tharos: I appreciate your request for casualty numbers but we are unable to pass them at this time. (*Tharos*' radio room is remote from the hospital.)

Rescue 01: Roger, understand. Rescue 01 out.

HMS Blackwater: Edinburgh Rescue, this warship Golf Delta Kilo Kilo (HMS *Blackwater*'s international call-sign). I am on my way.

Rescue 138: Rescue 01, we are currently sitting on *Tharos*, having winched off the three serious burns from *Silver Pit*. What do you wish us to do now?

Rescue 01: Rescue 138, to lift, orbit to the south and clear the helideck for incoming helicopters.

Golf Charlie: *Tharos*, Bristow's Golf Charlie (another Super Puma), good morning. Outbound to you at 3,000 feet from Aberdeen. What do you wish us to do on arrival? We are in company with Golf Sierra, which is one mile behind us.

Tharos: The Nimrod above is co-ordinating the air operations and although we have no work for you at present, we will later in the night. We will be commencing an evacuation of the casualties we have received . . . Rescue 01 can direct you to a holding position.

Rescue 01: To Rescue 138 — request you search a sector around the Piper . . . *Tharos* could you give me a sitrep on the Piper?

Tharos: We are still in a position approximately 300 to 400 metres from the platform . . . the north half of the platform has been raized to sea level . . . the southern part of the platform (the production part and the drilling rig) . . . the rig has gone, the remains of the platform are canted over and the wellheads are still burning.

Tharos: Rescue 01 from *Tharos*, I believe a Sea King is making its way to me from the Claymore with further medical staff.

Rescue 01: Negative, there is a Sea King inbound however with further medical staff from Aberdeen. She is Rescue 177, estimates the *Tharos* in about 12 minutes.

Tharos: Rescue 01 from *Tharos*, the doctor-in-charge advises me that there are two people he wishes to get to Aberdeen on an urgent basis . . . we also have four walking wounded that can travel if you would like to select an aircraft and direct it to the Tharos.

Tharos: Rescue 01, any aircraft calling at other locations for fuel could assist if they could bring spare stretchers . . . we're getting pretty short of stretchers . . . when 131 has lifted we'll task (Golf) Bravo to take two serious and seven walking to Aberdeen.

Rescue 01: Roger, it's my intention after 131 to land 177 (Sea King) who has doctors and medical stores; Golf Bravo is en route to pick up one additional doctor and he should be with you about 15 minutes.

Tharos: Roger, the two serious are, I believe, about 70 per cent burns.

Rescue 01: Roger, (the helicopters) on their way . . .

Rescue 01: Rescue 138, from Rescue 01. We have casualties and bodies to pick up from the *Devon Tail* which is approximately one mile north of the Piper at this time; please call on Channel 8 (VHF FM) and take out that task, over.

Rescue 138: Roger, the *Devon Tail*.

Rescue 01: Edinburgh Rescue, this is Rescue 01. Sitrep at this time. We intend sending helo (helicopter) call-sign Golf Tango India Golf Bravo (Super Puma) back to Aberdeen with casualties as follows: two serious with 70 per cent burns, and seven walking casualties with various walking injuries. The POB (persons on board) present on board the rig at the time of the explosion is understood to have been two two six (226), over.

Rescue 01: *Tharos*, this is Rescue 01. Do you wish us

to put another helo on standby for evacuation of casualties to Aberdeen, over.

Tharos: Yes sir, if you have one free. They can come in as soon as they like. We are ready.

Rescue 01: Ocean Victory (platform) from Rescue 01. Please make ready Five Zero Yankee (helicopter) to get airborne for casualty evacuation to Aberdeen.

Edinburgh Rescue: Rescue 01. Please relay to all helos: medical arrangements made at Aberdeen. All injured to Aberdeen RI (Royal Infirmary) and all non-injured to Aberdeen Airport, over.

Rescue 01: *Tharos*, this is Rescue 01. Request you give me an estimate of how regularly you need helicopters for medevac to Aberdeen, over.

Tharos: I'm sorry, sir. At this moment, I do not have any information as we are reviewing each case individually and they (the medical staff) are advising me as and when they decide somebody should go to Aberdeen.

Five Zero Yankee: Rescue 01, I intend lifting in five minutes, do you have any height restriction on the climb out? I intend going to 1,500 feet.

Rescue 01: I have no known inbound traffic at this time but do not go below 500 feet.

Five Zero Yankee: Roger, we shall be climbing to 1,500 feet.

Five Zero Yankee: *Tharos*, Five Zero Yankee is lifting for Aberdeen.

Tharos: Roger, thank you Zero Yankee . . . Yankee Bravo (S-76) *Tharos*, you are clear to land when ready. Your task if possible is two stretcher cases, one medical escort to Aberdeen . . . correction, if you could manage three stretcher cases? If not, maybe we should task another aircraft.

Yankee Bravo: No we won't be able to get three on board, it might be a bit crushed with the two actually.

Tharos: Roger, stand-by please. Break . . . break . . . Rescue 01, can you get us another aircraft to take three stretchers?

Rescue 01: *Tharos*, Rescue 01. Roger, we'll have one inbound shortly . . . suggest you load Yankee Bravo with as much as you can and we'll get Golf Oscar there in about 15 minutes.

Tharos: Yes, sir. We've just come to that conclusion ourselves . . . break . . . break . . . Yankee Bravo, the deck is clear.

Rescue 01: *Ben Loyal* (platform), from Rescue 01, can you get a copter airborne as soon as possible for medevac to Aberdeen.

Ben Loyal: Roger

Claymore Alpha (platform): Rescue 01, can you ask Five Zero Yankee how many casualties he's taking back to Aberdeen and the ETA at the hospital.

Five Zero Yankee: Rescue 01, for information the cloud base is 750 feet and we're current at 1,500 feet. We've three stretcher cases and one walking wounded.

Tharos: Yankee Bravo, *Tharos*. Your task is one stretcher and as many walking wounded as you can take. How many do you think that will be?

Yankee Bravo: Four.

Rescue 138: Rescue 01, Rescue 138. There is a further body on the *Provider*, if you are willing we are going to collect that and deliver it on to Tharos.

Rescue 01: Yes, that's fine.

Rescue 138: *Tharos*, this is Rescue 138, are we cleared to join your deck?

Tharos: Rescue 138, we have Golf Yankee Bravo on deck and loading; he should be clear shortly and then you are welcome to land on deck, sir . . . you are carrying one fatality, is that correct?

Rescue 138: We are now carrying two.

Tharos: Roger, that. Do you have a task after that?

Rescue 138: We're going to refuel on the *Santa Fe*.

Rescue 137: To Rescue 01, sitrep. We are currently three and half miles to the north of the burning rig and for information the debris in the water here is mostly very buoyant with high windage and there is no oil on the surface. Over.

Rescue 01: Do you require any further stretchers?

Tharos: Yes sir, we will take stretchers. If we end up with too many, we can always give them away later. Our next request is for an aircraft capable of taking stretcher cases to Aberdeen, please.

Rescue 01: Roger, Golf Oscar has just gone u/s and Golf Charlie is on the way in . . . break . . . break . . . Golf Charlie Oscar, from Rescue 01, please load as many stretchers as possible and as soon as possible, please.

Yankee Bravo: Rescue 01, Yankee Bravo is lifting *Tharos* for Aberdeen.

Tharos: We have received a telex from the Met Office advising the risk of a thunder storm and lightning strikes in this area.

Rescue 01: 01, thanks very much.

Tharos: Rescue 177 (Navy helo from Prestwick), we were expecting Golf Charlie first, if you can come first you can take his load, it is thought to be four stretchers, one medic, and some walking wounded.

Golf Charlie: Break, *Tharos* we have two miles to run to you, we are now on finals.

Tharos: Break, Break, Rescue 177 and Golf Charlie, in view of the last from Golf Charlie we'll take him first seeing he is closest and 177 immediately afterwards.

A survivor is greeted by a colleague after being lifted on to MSV Tharos *by basket crane.*

Rescue 177: Roger. We can take two stretchers comfortably, four at a pinch.

Tharos: 177 Roger understand two stretchers comfortably any more than that is a squeeze.

Tharos: Golf Charlie, our intention now is to load you with two stretchers with one medical escort and three walking wounded.

Golf Charlie: We'll be there waiting.

Rescue 131: 01 Rescue 131 we have a body on board what do you want us to do with it?

Rescue 01: 131 can you take it to *Tharos*.

Rescue 131: Roger.

Rescue 01: Rescue 138 can you give me an ETA on task with an RTB to Aberdeen without refuelling.

Tharos: 01 from *Tharos* sitrep. You are aware of all the evacuations we've done. Golf Sierra is on deck, we've loaded him with two stretchers, I believe a third stretcher case is on its way. Other than that I'm not quite sure at the moment. We are still taking casualties from the boats and they're still being assessed by the medical staff.

Rescue 01: 01 all copied.

Rescue 01: Rescue 117 and Rescue 131. 117 could you search an area three nautical miles radius west of the Piper rig and 131 search an area three nautical miles east of the Piper rig.

Rescue 117: all copied.

Rescue 131: all copied.

Rescue 01: *Tharos* we have 137 inbound to you, he requests the number of casualties you have for him.

Tharos: For Rescue 137 at this moment we have two stretchers and two accompanying doctors.

Rescue 01: 01 Roger, have you got any idea of a head count yet?

Tharos: Personally sir, no, not at all.

Rescue 137: Rescue 137 landing Tharos this time.

Tharos: Rescue 01 *Tharos*. Yes sir the *Silver Pit*, the rig stand-by boat we have been working with all night is alongside, we are taking walking wounded from him quite successfully with our crane. However, there are two serious casualties on board who we feel would be more safely winched than us trying to take them with the crane. He is rolling a lot alongside us. If you wish it 143 has a winch he could drop his materials (medical equipment) and then make his way to the *Silver Pit*. At this moment we have no casualties immediately available for evacuation.

Rescue 01: *Tharos* understand *Silver Pit* is alongside you now.

Tharos: 01 *Silver Pit* is alongside our port side completing a transfer of reasonably fit men by crane basket. But the vessel is too unstable to lift off a couple of the casualties.

Rescue 01: Rescue 117 did you copy that? Would you be able to lift these two casualties from this small vessel?

Rescue 117: 01 Rescue 117 affirm.

Tharos: Roger sir.

Rescue 137: Rescue 137 is lifting from *Tharos* and departing Aberdeen.

India Juliet: *Tharos* we are in bound with fourteen passengers, Occidental management and one doctor and two others returning from a previous helicopter trip.

Tharos: India Juliet, *Tharos*, how many would you be prepared to lift without stretching yourself sir?

India Juliet: Walking wounded, we can take eighteen/nineteen if necessary.

Tharos: India Juliet we've got eighteen walking wounded coming up now.

Tharos: Rescue 01 *Tharos*, could you call Aberdeen Coastguard and confirm to Aberdeen police that the Piper platform is still on fire please.

Rescue 01: *Tharos*, Rescue 01 will do.

Rescue 117: *Tharos* 117 we are on the way to you with some injured personnel. We shall be with you in two or three minutes.

Tharos: Rescue 117 copied, you are coming with injured personnel. Confirm you are the Coastguard helicopter (coming) from the *Silver Pit*.

Rescue 117: Affirmative.

Rescue 416: Rescue 01 this is Rescue 416.

Rescue 01: Rescue 416 from Rescue 01, request you search an area three nautical mile radius. About a datum one nautical mile north of Piper. Sector two four zero to three six zero, over.

Tharos: India Juliet from *Tharos*, that's nineteen walking wounded. We're trying to escort them in case there is any shock victims amongst them.

India Juliet: OK that's copied. They are to go direct to the hospital?

Tharos: India Juliet I believe the entire operation has been direct to the Royal Infirmary, Aberdeen.

Rescue 01: India Juliet from 01 that's affirmative. All casualties to Aberdeen Royal Infirmary.

India Juliet: 01 this India Juliet, lifting *Tharos*, twenty one on board for Aberdeen. We will be routing initially at five hundred feet. Estimating at 0630.

Tharos: Rescue 01 *Tharos*, yes sir, by my calculation we have taken off, including the last nineteen, a total of fifty one casualties.

Rescue 01: *Tharos* Rescue 01 thank you very much.

SUBSEA
OFFSHORE
SUBSEA
OFFSHORE

A shocked survivor is wrapped in a blanket onboard the Tharos.

Below *Minutes after being rescued a survivor removes his Kapok lifejacket.*

Below right *The horror of the disaster shows on the face of this casualty from Piper Alpha.*

As dawn breaks the helicopter controller on board Tharos *shows signs of exhaustion.*

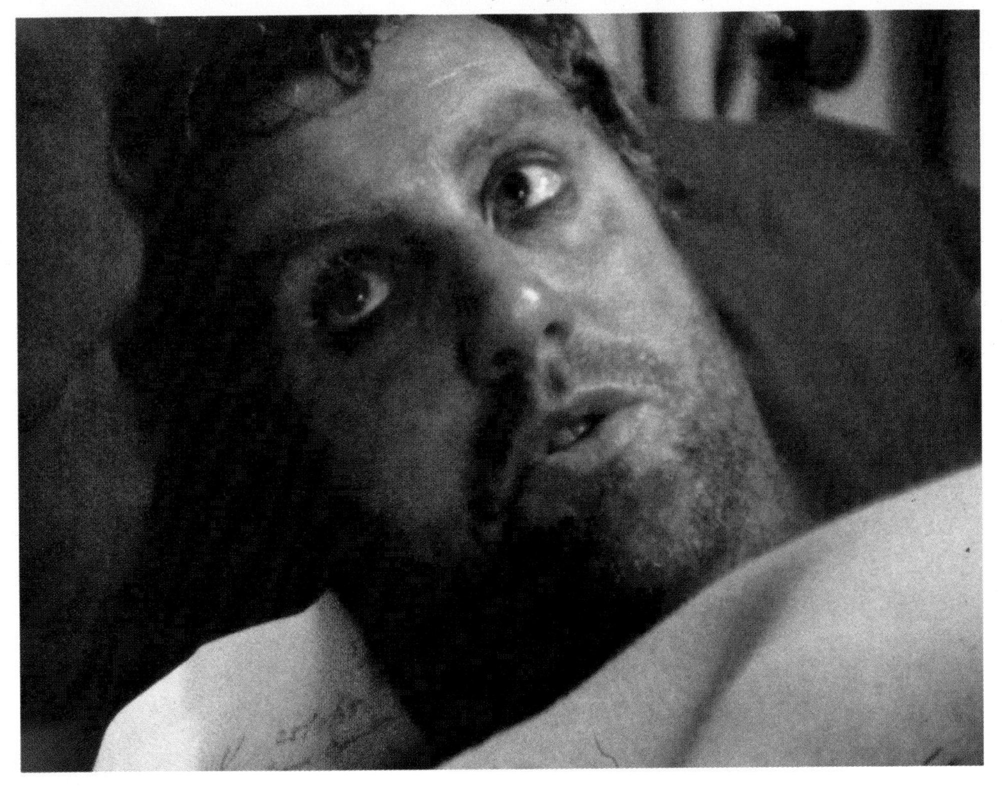

'I crawled across the pipe-deck . . . it was white hot . . . it was slippery because the soles of our boots were melting . . . I jumped about a hundred feet, climbed aboard some driftwood and it was about half-an-hour before I was picked up by a boat.'

FV *Budding Rose*

JOB NO 48
25 JULY 1988

. . . the sea has won . . . the pump has failed . . . the water is seven feet deep in the cabin . . . it's time to get off.

The Peterhead-based fishing vessel *Budding Rose* started taking on water at 0900, about 100 miles east of Aberdeen. Her pumps could not keep the engine room from flooding. With no engines in a Sea State 9, there was concern for the crew of seven and Rescue 137 was scrambled at 1230. The Sea King was captained by John Prince, with co-pilot Simon Willson, radop/winch operator Paul Challice and winchman Bob Pountney. Despite the use of a lightweight pump, the *Budding Rose* was abandoned in worsening weather, the crew taken off and flown to Longside Airfield, Peterhead. *Budding Rose* sank four hours later.

'I just want to check the height,' John Prince tells the Sea King's crew. 'There's no hurry, no one's going to be injured on this . . . I'm keeping well clear but keep an eye on those aerials . . .' he tells Paul Challice, the winch operator who is in the helicopter's main doorway.

John Prince and Simon Willson run through the pre-take-off checks to scramble Rescue 137 to the Budding Rose. *Rescue 137 to Lossiemouth Tower: 'Lifting straight off and turning straight on to track'. 'Rescue 137 you are clear to take-off . . . wind 40 gusting 60 . . .'*

Rescue 137 is on scene and prepares for a hi-line transfer by passing a weighted nylon line . . . Paul Challice, winch operator, describes the scene to John Prince: 'it's small deck area to get anyone on . . . there's a pile of nets at the back and we'll have to watch the power blocks and other tackle . . . she's got lots of whip aerials . . .'

Winchman Bob Pountney almost floating in space.

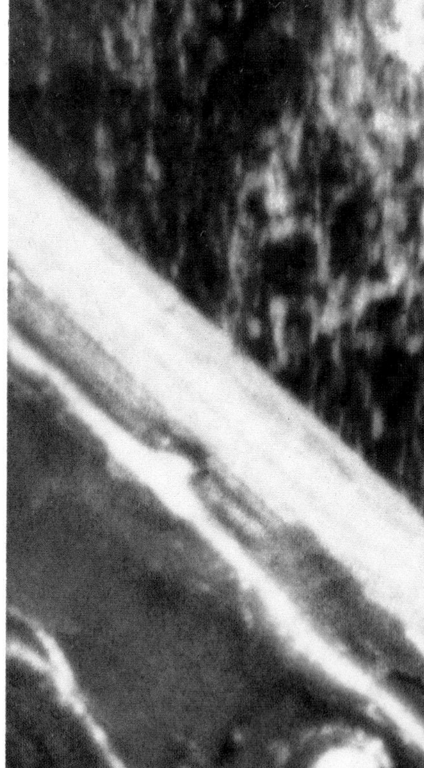

***Far right** Bob Pountney starts to swing as the* Budding Rose's *crew are tardy about pulling in the hi-line. 'Pull the bloody hi-line, you bastards . . .' shouts Paul Challice, '. . . pull you bastards . . .' He says to Simon Willson, who is in radio contact with* Budding Rose: *'Ask them to pull the hi-line, Slug (Simon Willson's nickname) . . . that's it, they've got the message . . .'*

The first two survivors are taken off Budding Rose *by a double lift . . . including (left) Justyn Llewellyn-Thomas, aged 15, on his first trip to sea.*

The moment to abandon ship. The Budding Rose's *skipper, Peter Bruce, tells Bob Pountney that the sea has won . . . the pump has failed . . . the water is seven feet deep in the cabin . . . it's time to get off.*

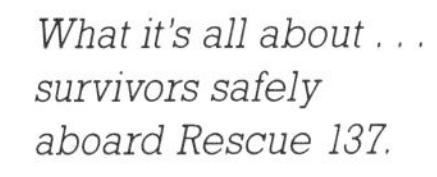

What it's all about . . . survivors safely aboard Rescue 137.

Justyn Llewellyn-Thomas safely delivered back to his mother at Longside Airfield.

Worse Things Happen at Sea

JOB NO 55
24 AUGUST 1988

'She's starting to wallow quite a bit in the water now . . . and . . . the water is gaining . . .'

Rescue 137 is scrambled to assist the Scottish fishing vessel *Choice* which is taking on water at position 58°20'N 00°20'W. The Sea King is flown by Paul Readfern (captain), Simon Willson (co-pilot), Steve Griffin (radop/winch operator) and Bob Pountney (winchman). As a result of Rescue 137's action, four fishermen were rescued before the *Choice* sank.

Choice *is dead in the water. Pilot Paul Readfern elects to take off the first two crewmen.*

Winchman Bob Pountney goes aboard the fishing vessel and with the remaining crew starts pulling the helicopter's lightweight pump aboard.

The tension of the fight to save the Choice *shows on the face of a crew member aboard the sinking fishing vessel.*

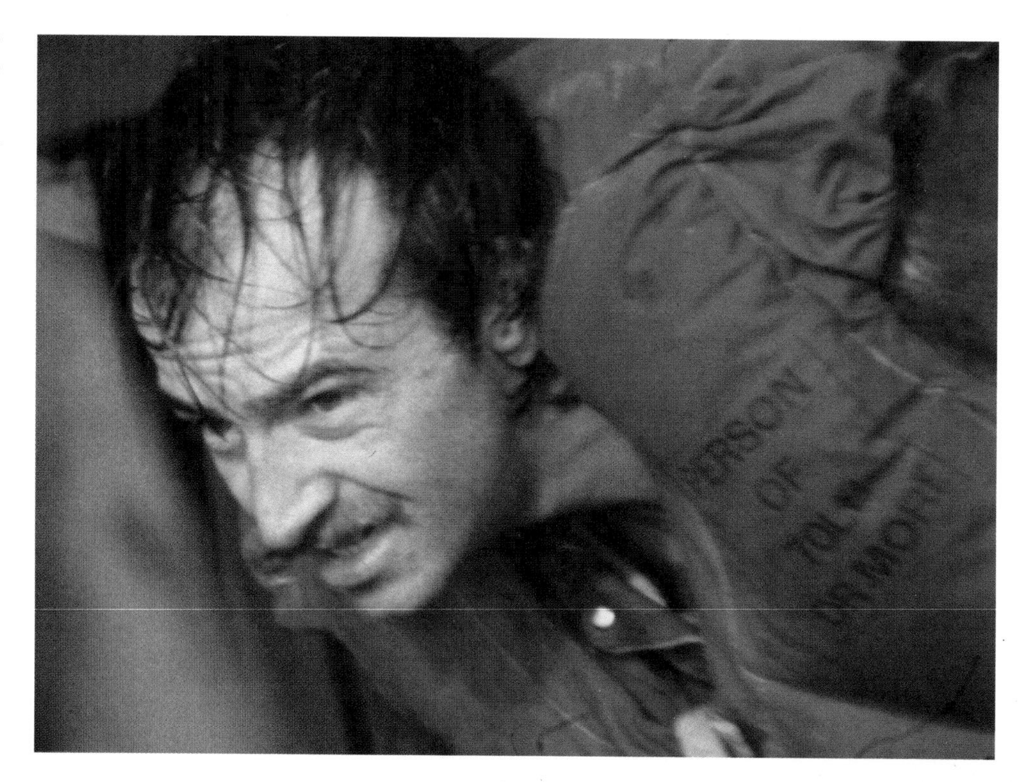

The pump fails . . . the situation deteriorates . . . the crew decide to abandon Choice *. . . they've lost the fight to keep her afloat . . .*

FPV Suliscar *to Moray Coastguard: 'She's starting to wallow quite a bit in the water now . . . and . . . the water is gaining . . .'*

Bob Pountney abandons ship with the two remaining crewmen.

'Moray Coastguard . . . the fishing vessel is now on her side. She's laying on her side.' 'Roger, is everybody off . . .?'

FPV Suliscar *to Moray CG: 'She's going fast'.*

FPV Suliscar *to Moray CG: 'The boat has now gone down . . . the boat has now gone down . . .'*

Moray CG to FPV Suliscar: *'Is everybody off? Can you please confirm that everybody is off. Over . . .'*
FPV Suliscar *to Moray CG: 'There's three in the raft . . . three men in the raft.'*

Water Falls

JOB NOS 29 & 58
26 MAY & 11 SEPTEMBER 1988

'. . . two persons fallen at Cia-Aig Falls; one fallen in the water, still missing. One on the rocks suffering numerous broken bones.'

26 May 1988 — Rescue 137 is scrambled to medevac a baby, Fraser Hughes, who has been revived after falling into a garden swimming pool at Poolewe, north-west Scotland. Baby Fraser, his mother and a district nurse were then flown to Raigmore Hospital, Inverness, where the boy made a full recovery. Steve Hodgson was the aircraft captain; Dave Lloyd, co-pilot; Steve Griffin, radop/winch operator; Bob Pountney, winchman.

'It's over there, just behind the garage.' A neighbour points out the Hughes's house to winchman Bob Pountney.

Baby Fraser's district nurse lifts him from the doctor's car to the Sea King, as Bob Pountney uses the portable radio to keep Steve Hodgson fully briefed.

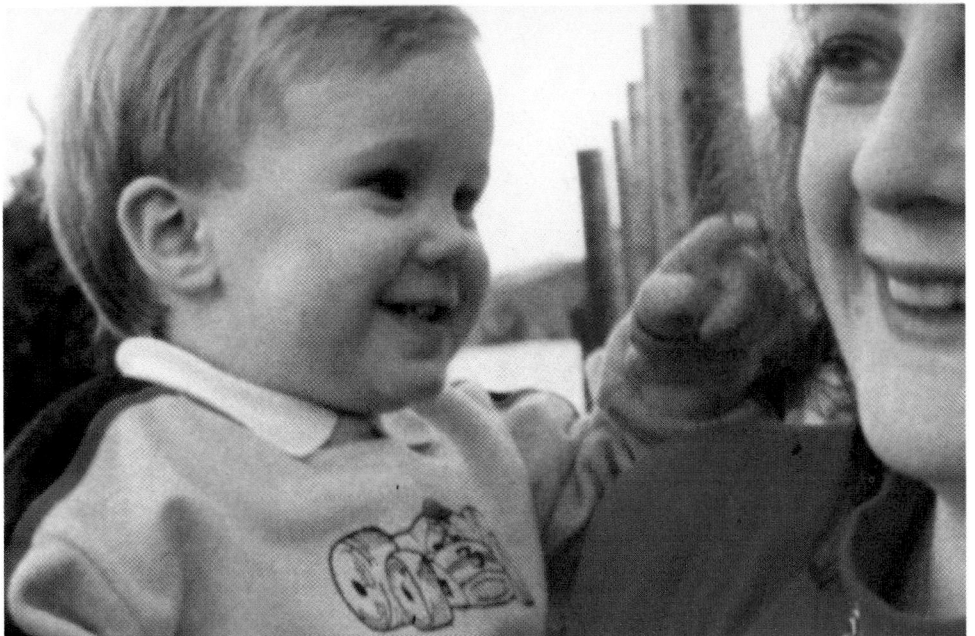

The decision is made to fly the baby to the intensive care unit at Raigmore Hospital, 45 minutes flying time away. From the helipad he is transferred into the arms of a senior ambulance officer.

Six months later and Fraser Hughes is home, fully recovered.

Edinburgh Rescue to Sea King 137: 'Change of call-sign to Rescue 137 . . . two persons fallen at Cia-Aig Falls [north-west of Fort William]; one fallen in the water, still missing. One on the rocks suffering numerous broken bones.' 'This is Rescue 137, Roger, all copied.'

'Edinburgh Rescue, Rescue 137 will be on scene in three to four minutes.'

11 September 1988 — Already airborne on a training sortie, Rescue 137 is tasked to search for three walkers who have fallen into a heavily wooded ravine in the Scottish Highlands. One of the missing walkers — all Indian monks from London — was discovered submerged in a pool. Despite urgent attempts to revive him, the monk was pronounced dead by the doctor but the other two were rescued by the Lochaber MRT. The helicopter's crew were John Prince (captain), Don Strother (co-pilot) and John Brooks (radop/winch operator) on loan from the SAR Wing. Ian Bonthrone, the Sea King's winchman, was on his first job with D Flight.

Above left *'Continue . . . your height is good . . . your tail is clear.' From the Sea King's main cabin doorway, John Brooks directs John Prince into the only available hover position for Ian Bonthrone to go down to the man in the water.*

Above *Winchman Ian Bonthrone swings out over the door frame and with a last nod to the winch operator, John Brooks, prepares to go down the winch wire.*

Left *'At the door' . . . as Ian Bonthrone arrives at helo door John Brooks prepares to bring the man on board.*

'Winch to pilot' . . . John Brooks pulls winchman Ian Bonthrone and the casualty aboard the Sea King.

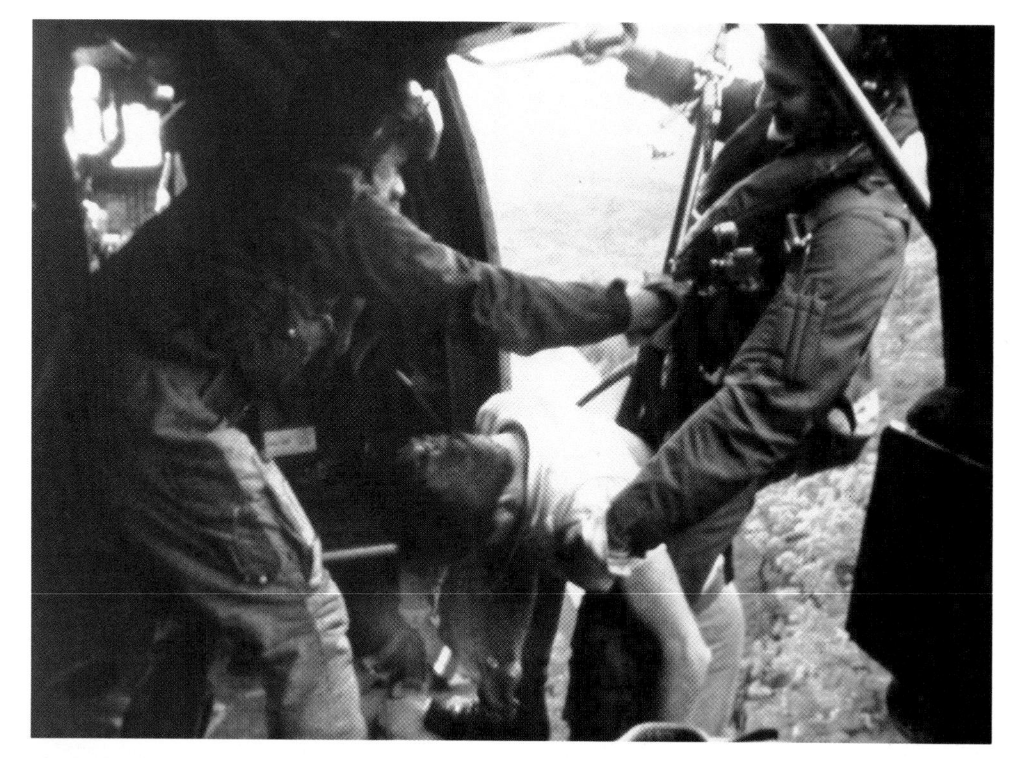

Not all rescue attempts can save a life. The monk has been underwater for too long; nevertheless valiant efforts are made to revive him. Ian Bonthrone reaches for the portable oxygen as John Prince flies the helicopter to a nearby field and waiting ambulance.

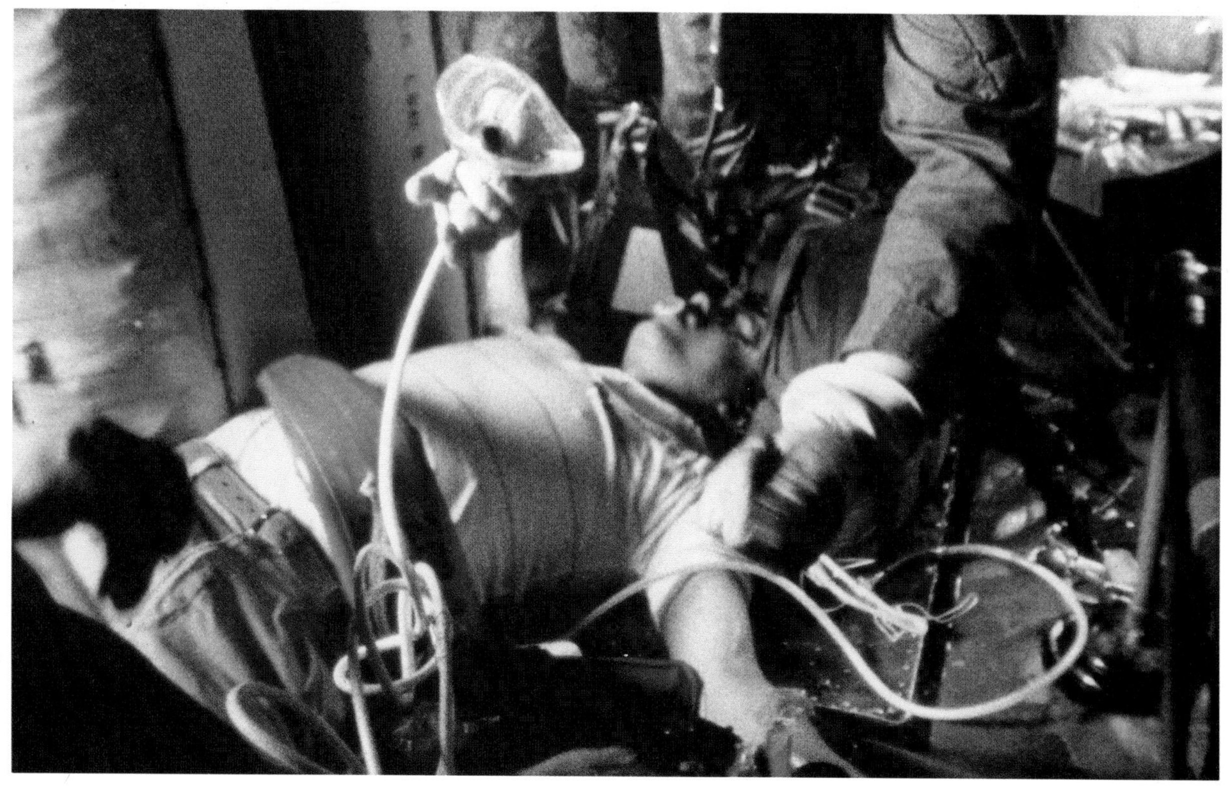

Local police on scene: 'Hi, Ian . . . any update yet?' 'Roger, we're trying to lift him up the bank and then stretcher him to the car park . . . we got one boy up, he's uninjured, just a bit cold.' Like so many rescues, the co-operation between all the emergency services (in this case police officers from Fort William) is vital.

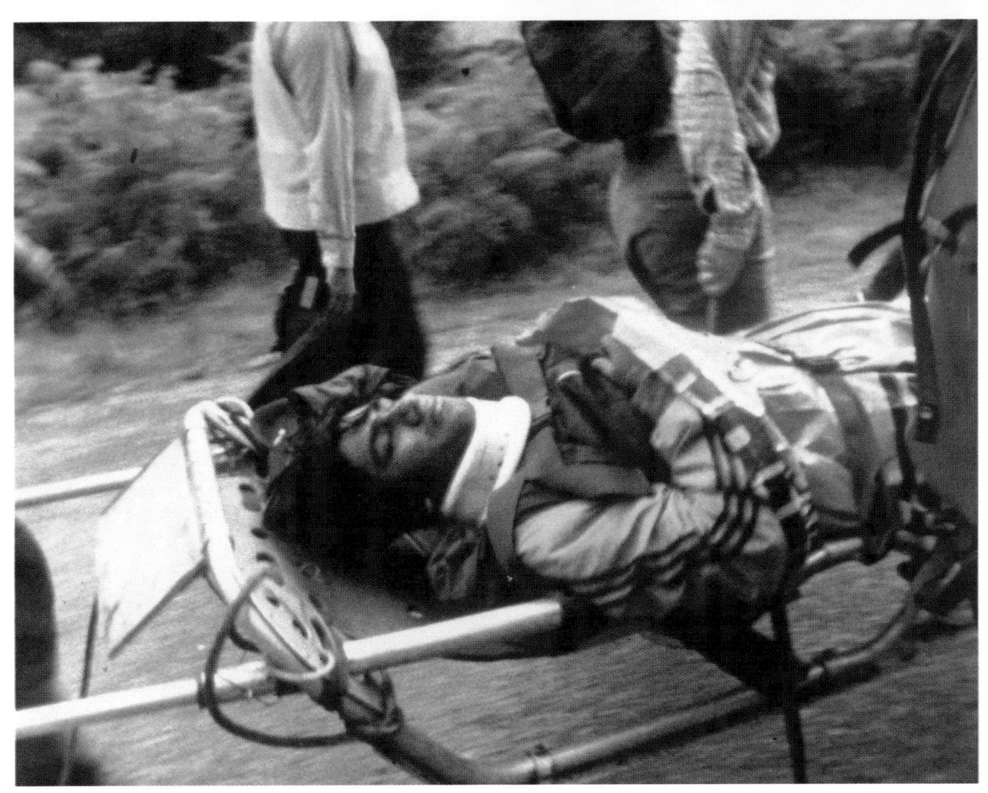

Lochaber MRT brings the third casualty down to the waiting Sea King for transfer to hospital.

Ocean Odyssey

JOB NO 60
22 SEPTEMBER 1988

'The sea all around the rig is on fire . . .'

At lunchtime Rescue 137 scrambled along with 14 other helicopters to the drilling platform *Ocean Odyssey*, 100 miles east of Aberdeen. A fire was sweeping the rig and the crew of 67 were abandoning. Ships and nearby helicopters picked up 66 men but the *Ocean Odyssey's* radio operator stayed at his post. He was found dead by firemen the following day.

The rig is ablaze as Rescue 137 closes during the search for the missing man.

'I can see debris all around . . . if there's anyone in the water I should see them . . .' Winchman Dave Walmsley keeps his eyes scanned on the sea.

Far left *Aberdeen Coastguard Maritime Rescue Control Centre co-ordinating the search and rescue.*

Coastguard Regional Controller Derek Ancona contemplates his next decision in Aberdeen MRCC during the search for the missing radio operator. Derek Ancona has since been appointed Her Majesty's Chief Coastguard.

'The sea all around the rig is on fire . . .' A coastguard radio operator receives a message from the stand-by vessel Notts Forest *alongside the blazing rig. District Controller David Foster listens in on the call.*

Ditching . . . Ditching . . . Ditching

JOB NOS 72 & 80
17 OCTOBER &
10 NOVEMBER 1988

'At this stage, I didn't panic but I didn't think I had long for this world . . . then my training took over . . .'

10 November 1988 — An oil rig support helicopter ditched in the Claymore Field and Rescue 137 scrambled to the scene. The ditched helicopter's aircrew and passengers were all rescued by passing ships and the Bond Helicopter's Dauphin. Rescue 137 transported medical personnel to various oil platforms and support vessels. Aircraft captain, Steve Hodgson; co-pilot, Don Strother; radop/winch operator, Paul Challice; winchman, Bob Pountney.

17 October 1988 — Rescue 137 was scrambled to the vicinity of Handa island in the Outer Hebrides to search for the crew of a Bristow/HM Coastguard rescue helicopter which had ditched. The Sea King's aircrew started to pick up the survivor's personal locator beacon signals about 40 miles away. Four survivors were rescued by winch from a multi-person dinghy and taken to Stornoway. The wrecked helicopter was later recovered to Aberdeen for examination. Rescue 137 was flown by John Dean, captain; Don Strother, co-pilot; Pat Thirkell, radop/winch operator; and Bob Griffiths, winchman (on loan from RAF Brawdy).

__Below__ Edinburgh Rescue to RAF Lossiemouth: 'Scramble, the Stornoway helicopter has crashed — he was searching off Handa Island and was last heard of at time 2039.' Rescue 137 was on its way. (Picture taken with a special Osprey Electronics infra-red lens in pitch black conditions.)

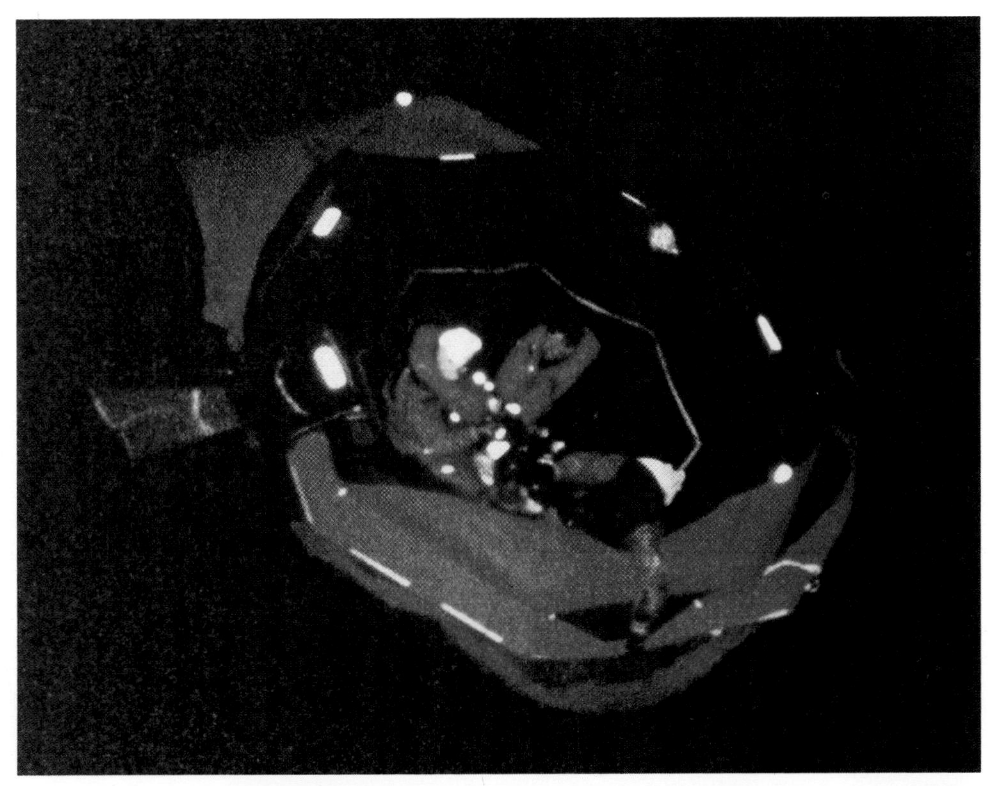

Far left *'Right one and back . . . right two and back . . . steady . . . two in the strop . . . winching in . . . two approaching the door . . .' Winch operator Pat Thirkell paints the scene of the night rescue for the pilot, John Dean.*

Two survivors, the Bristow/HM Coastguard helicopter's pilot and co-pilot, are brought into the Sea King.

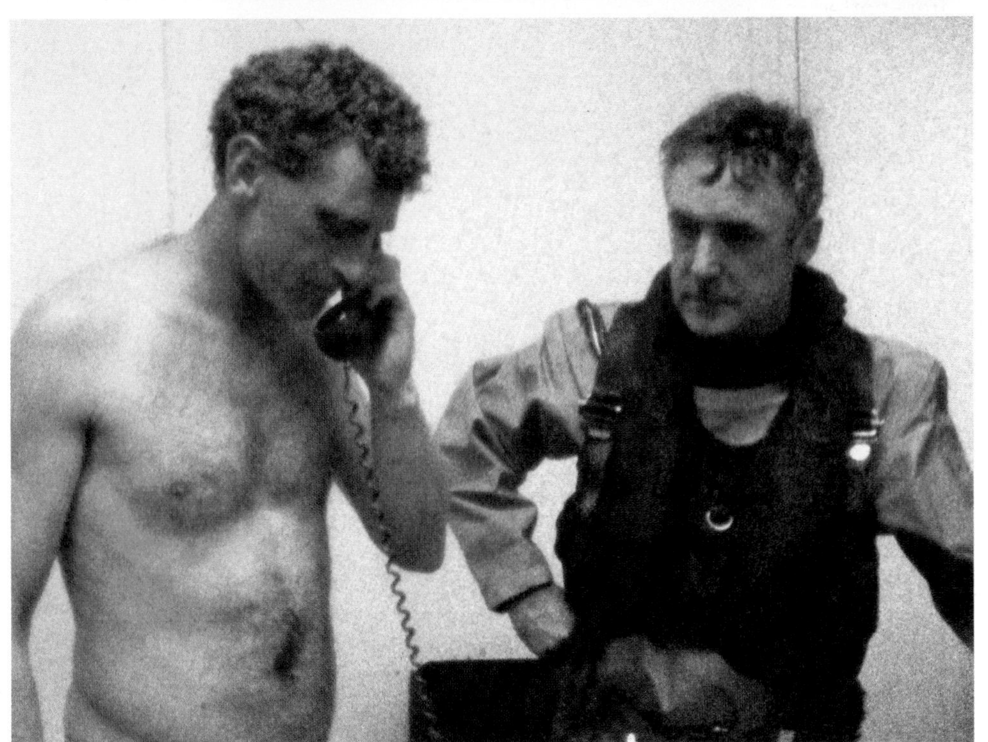

Cy Rogers, the ditched helicopter's crewman, didn't think he would live, trapped in the upturned S-61N's cabin . . . 'I tried for ten minutes to get under the water and get the emergency jettison handle. At this stage, I didn't panic but I didn't think I had long for this world . . . then my training took over . . .' Cy Rogers and Bob Griffiths (right) talk by telephone to Edinburgh Rescue.

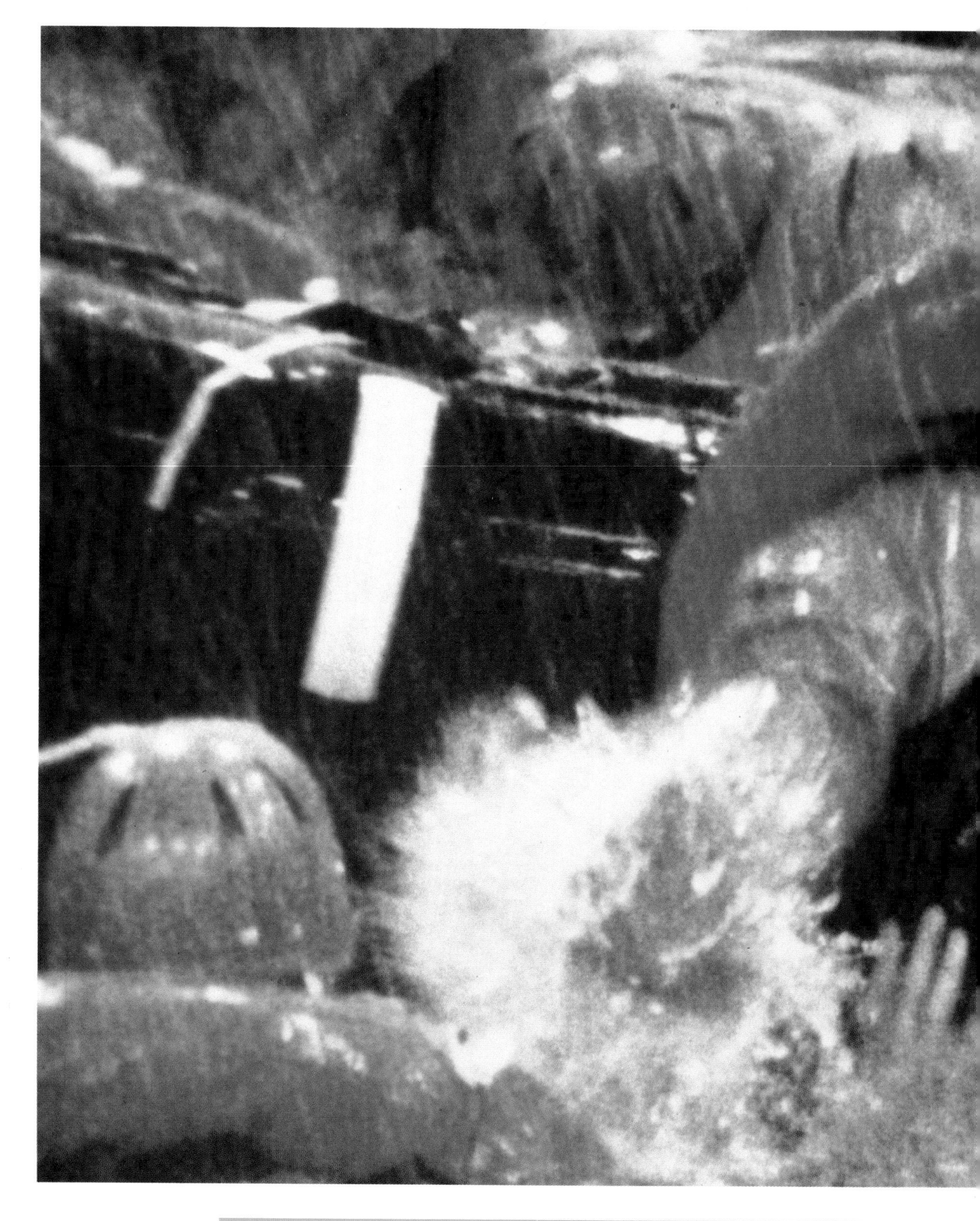

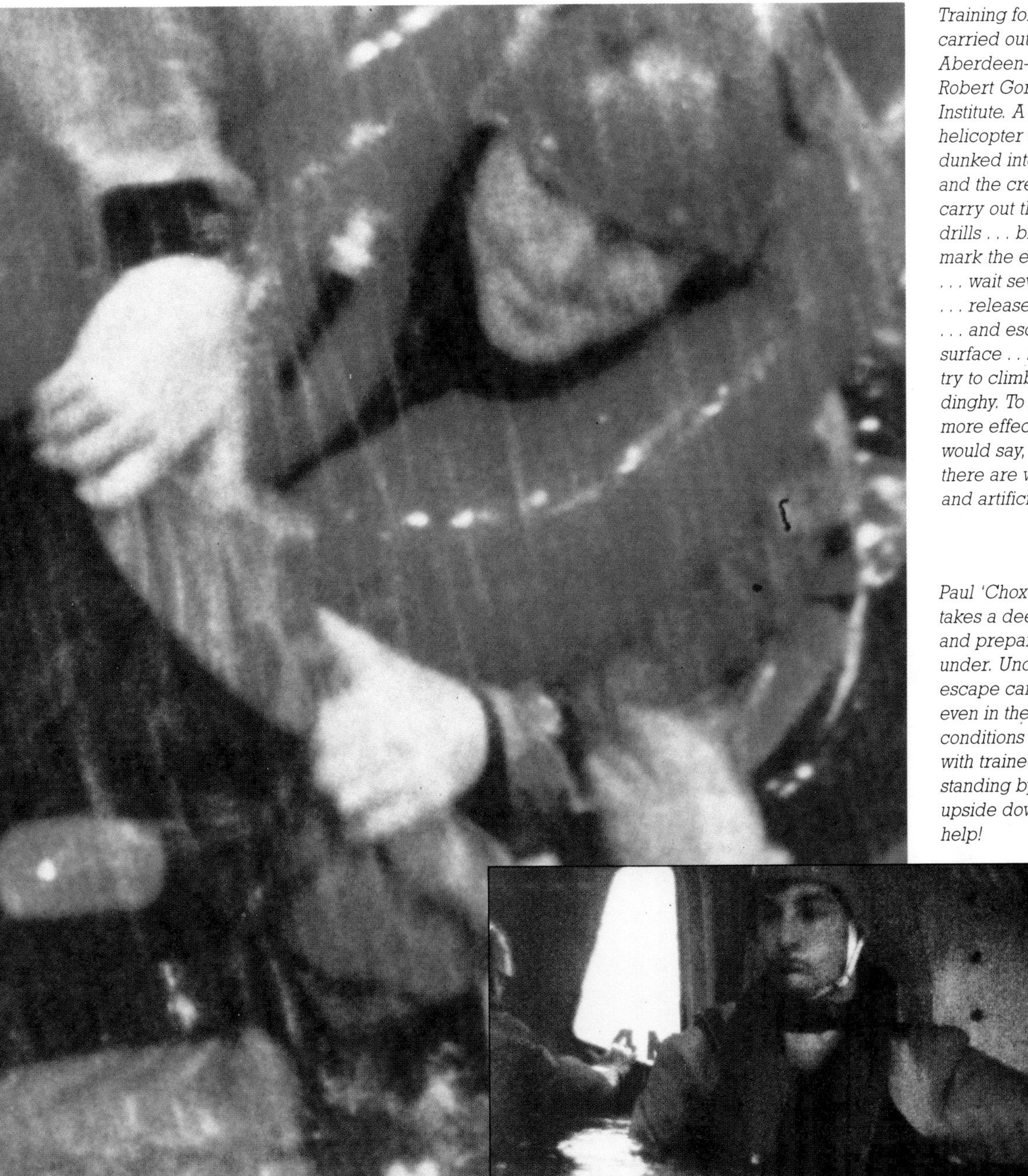

Training for ditching is carried out at the Aberdeen-based Robert Gordon Institute. A mock-up helicopter cabin is dunked into the water and the crew have to carry out the ditching drills . . . brace . . . mark the escape exit . . . wait seven seconds . . . release the harness . . . and escape to surface . . . and then try to climb into the dinghy. To make it more effective (some would say, difficult), there are waves, wind and artificial rain.

Paul 'Chox' Barton takes a deep breath and prepares to go under. Underwater escape can be difficult even in the benign conditions of a pool with trained divers standing by. Being upside down doesn't help!

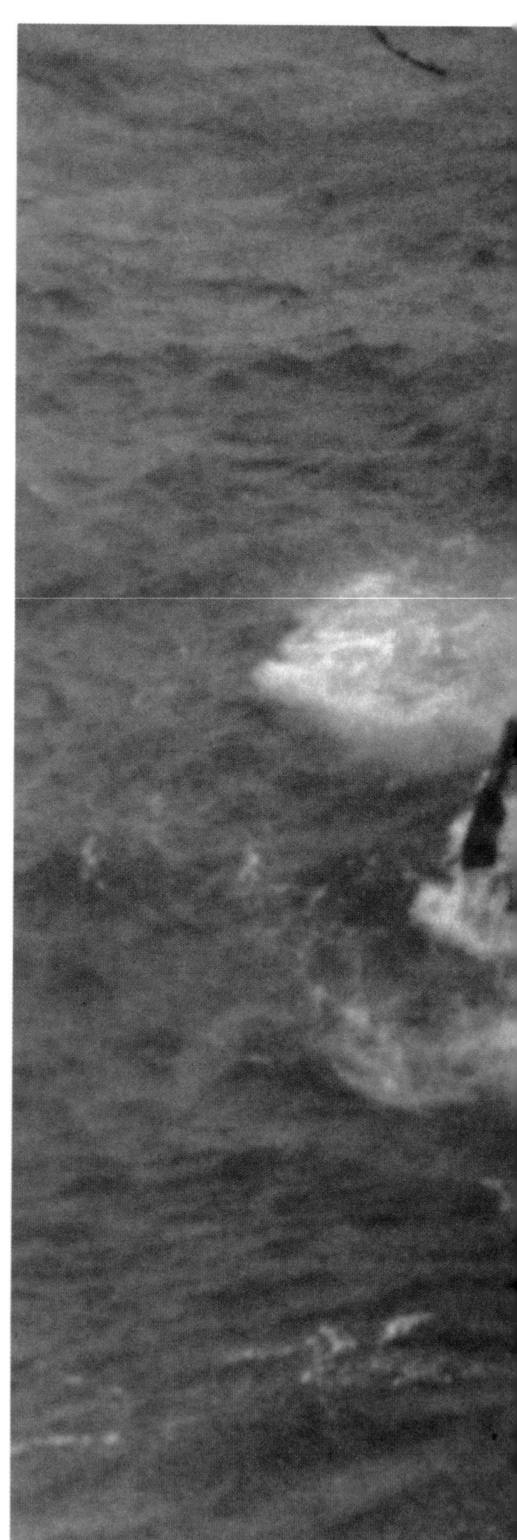

Far left *'Scramble, will you . . . an S-61 has ditched in the vicinity of the Claymore Field,' says Edinburgh Rescue on the land line from Pitreavie to RAF Lossiemouth. Within minutes, co-pilot Don Strother can report 'Rescue 137, airborne Lossie . . .'*

Main picture *'There are six passengers in the dinghy and seven people in the water, a total of 13' is the update from the Claymore local air traffic controller. They all escaped from this S-61N helicopter.*

Middle far left *A rescue vessel stands by and prepares to bring the helicopter's life raft aboard.*

Far left *The survivors tell their own individual stories . . . aboard Claymore Alpha oil production platform.*

Sea King 138 Crash

JOB NO 96
28 JANUARY 1989

'I've located the crash site and the aircraft is a complete write-off.'

At lunchtime Rescue 137 from Lossiemouth and Rescue 134 from Leuchars on a training exercise in the Cairngorms were scrambled after a report of a crash involving Lossiemouth's second stand-by helicopter, call-sign SK 138, in the mountains 25 miles north-east of Fort William.

Rescue 134, the RAF Leuchars Wessex crew, was on scene first and located the wreckage of 138 at the base of the 3,700 foot mountain Creag Meagaidh, 25 miles north-east of Fort William. Rescue 134 recovered two injured crew while Rescue 137 picked up the remaining seven survivors. Crew of Rescue 137 were John Prince, pilot; Simon Willson, co-pilot; Steve Griffin, radop/winch operator; Ian Bonthrone, winchman. Crew of Rescue 134 were George Phillips, pilot; John Prentice, navigator; Martin Ring, crewman.

Rescue 134 arrives at the crash location and a message is passed to RCC at Pitreavie, 'I've located the crash site and the aircraft is a complete write-off'.

Around mid-morning on Thursday 28 January 1989 Sea King helicopter call sign Sierra Kilo 138 took off from Lossiemouth. On board were four air crew, two film crew and members of 202 Squadron's ground crew. They were to spend the forthcoming weekend on 'detachment' in Fort William, some 90 miles south of Lossiemouth. Often the second stand-by Lossiemouth helicopter will visit a 'high casualty risk' area for a few days to familiarize crew with the terrain, local mountain rescue teams and lifeboat crews.

Thursday afternoon and Friday were spent flying around Ben Nevis, the Cuillins on Skye and carrying out winching practice on Loch Linnhe, Fort William. On Saturday morning 138 flew senior members of the Lochaber MRT on a recce around the proposed site of new ski slopes to the north of Ben Nevis. At 12.30 138 landed at Corpach near Fort William to drop off the MRT, and to collect a stretcher and other Lochaber team members for a training sortie to Creag Meagaidh. Thirty minutes later helicopter 138 was lying wrecked at the base of the mountain.

The helicopter had been making an approach to a mountain rescue post at the base of Creag Meagaidh when a mechanical problem caused a failure in one of the two engines. Sierra Kilo 138 was at a height of 80 feet and turning to approach the rescue post when pilot Steve Hodgson called over the intercom 'engine out we're going down'. Skilfully he brought the aircraft down on boggy ground, softening the impact. The helicopter skidded for 500 yards, nosedived into a ditch then turned over on to its starboard side. The main rotor blades snapped and splintered while the two sponsons were torn from the fuselage. Inside the aircraft some of the passengers were thrown around but the well-made fuselage protected everyone on board from otherwise certain death.

As soon as the aircraft had stopped moving everyone scrambled out. Two personal locator distress beacons were activated on the life-jackets of the crew and Paul Berriff, the producer/cameraman, put out a mayday call on a hand-held VHF marine radio. While the aircraft had been descending to the ground Paul 'Gramps' Challice had also sent out a mayday transmission on the HF radio, but owing to the mountainous terrain no-one received either of the mayday calls.

A passing climber, who luckily saw the crash, ran three miles to a telephone and dialled 999.

Because of a snow warning the survivors decided to walk down the mountain footpath towards the main Spean Bridge to Newtonmore road, just in case the pending weather conditions made it impossible for other rescue helicopters to reach the crash scene. At the time of the crash, Rescue 134, the Wessex rescue helicopter from 22 squadron RAF Leuchars, was on the ground at Glenmore Lodge rescue post 20 miles away in the Cairngorms, while at Lossiemouth the first stand-by Sea King, Rescue 137, was undergoing engine maintenance.

Within a few minutes of the call being received at Lossiemouth duty pilot John Prince had checked the newly serviced engine and got airborne. Rescue 134 was already on its way from the Cairngorms. No-one knew at this stage whether or not there were casualties. Twenty anxious minutes went by before Rescue 134 arrived on scene . . .

The survivors wait for rescue. The crash site can be seen in the background.

A passing nurse comforts co-pilot Paul Readfern minutes after the crash.

'Gramps' fires a distress flare to attract the attention of Rescue 134.

'Rescue 134 has now located the survivors, all OK, all OK.'

Ray Petch, Lossiemouth's ground crew, smiles with relief after escaping from the crash.

Paul Readfern and Paul Berriff are taken onboard Rescue 134 for evacuation to hospital in Fort William.

RAF

The next day the film crew recover their camera equipment from the wrecked helicopter.

Sound recordist Ross Neasham who survived the crash.

Cameramen Paul Berriff and Andrew Dearden at the crash site the following day. The wind speed was in excess of 80 mph with heavy rain. However, their Berghaus protective clothing enabled them to continue filming even in the appalling weather conditions.

Helicopter 138 showing the full extent of the damage.

Avalanche

JOB NO 104
28 FEBRUARY 1989

'Let's try and pump some air into him, but I think it's too late.'

PC Alexander Fraser, a SAR dog handler from Inverness Police, waits patiently for the signal to enter Rescue 137 with dogs Ross and Dirk. The helicopter lifted the dog team, along with the MRT, to within a few hundred feet of the avalanche.

As daylight fades Rescue 137 lowers MRT equipment on to the slopes of the Five Sisters ridge.

Probing the avalanche for the missing man. This scene was taken by a special 'night-sight' lens supplied by Osprey Electronics in Aberdeen.

Rescue 137 is scrambled to assist in the search for avalanche victims on the Five Sisters ridge in Kintail. RAF Kinloss Mountain Rescue Team and the SAR Dog Association are frequently involved in such operations, supported by rescue helicopters. On this particular occasion the Sea King's crew was Steve Martin, captain; John Tennison-Collins, co-pilot; Frank Rush, radop/winch operator; Bill Payne (winchman). Tommy Taylor, leader of the RAF Kinloss MRT, took the message from RCC Pitreavie: '. . . there is a man buried in an avalanche on the Five Sisters ridge in Kintail . . . can you go and join with Kintail MRT. There's a chopper coming to collect you from Kinloss in a few minutes.'

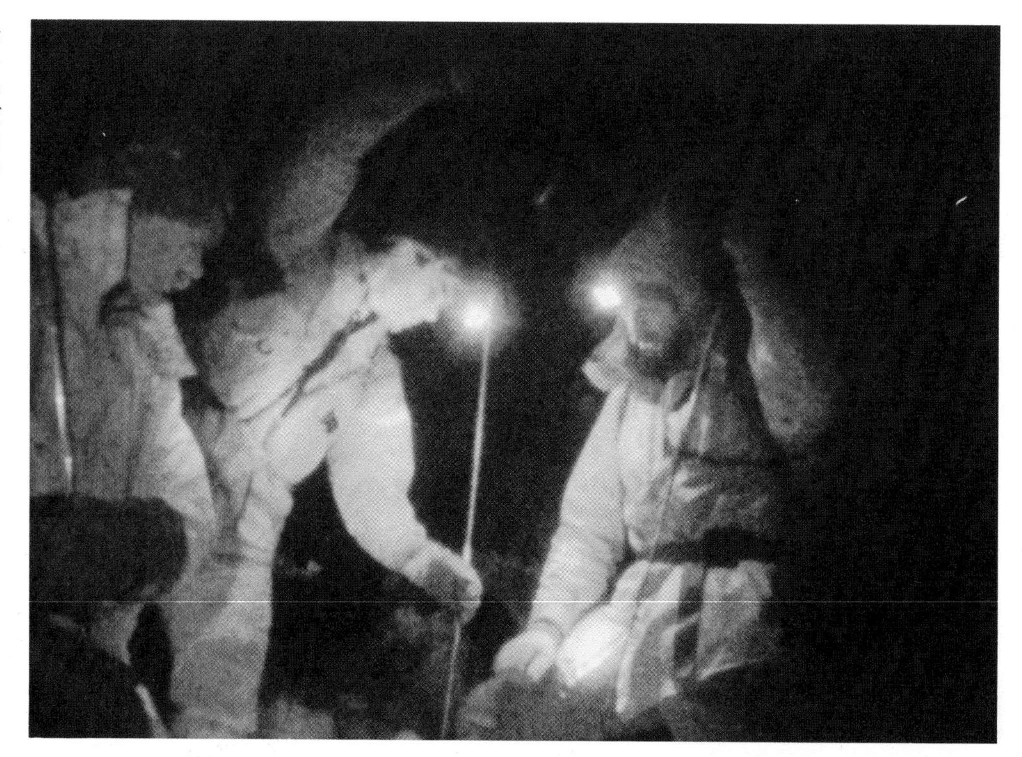

'Over here, I think we've found something . . .' The two search team leaders of Kinloss and Kintail MRT's find the missing man.

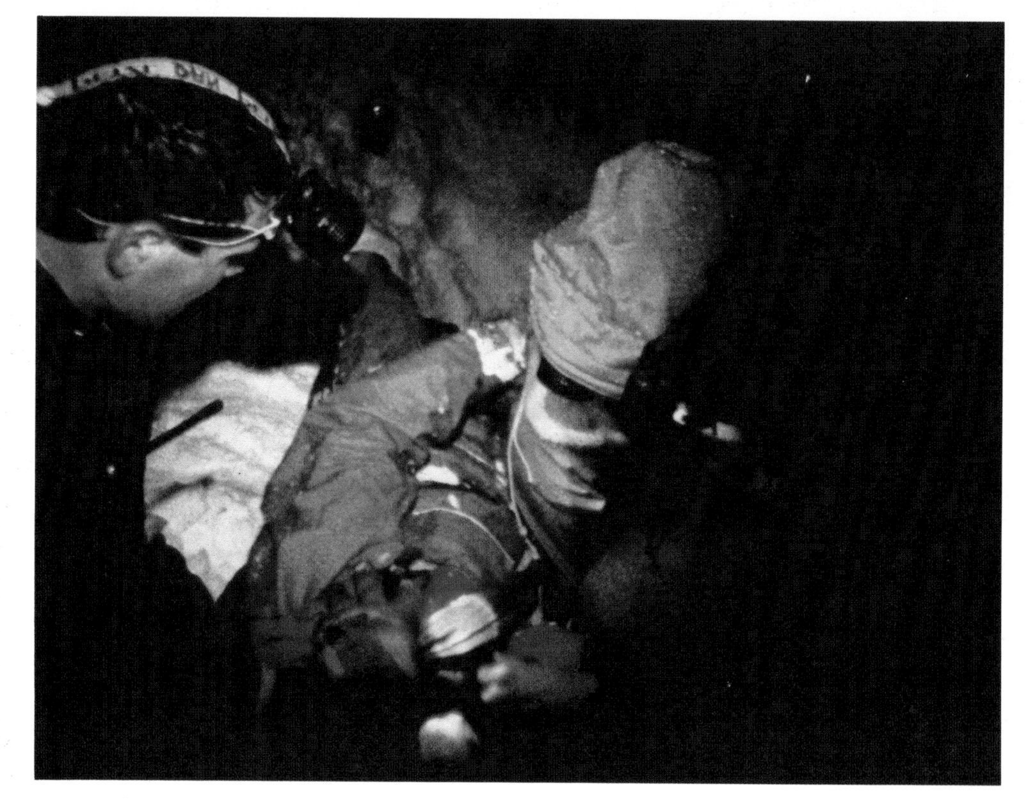

'The chances are less than 20 per cent . . . he was completely covered . . . he was lying head down under about three feet of snow. Let's try and pump some air into him but I think it's too late.' Despite all the efforts of the team's doctor, the casualty was not revived.

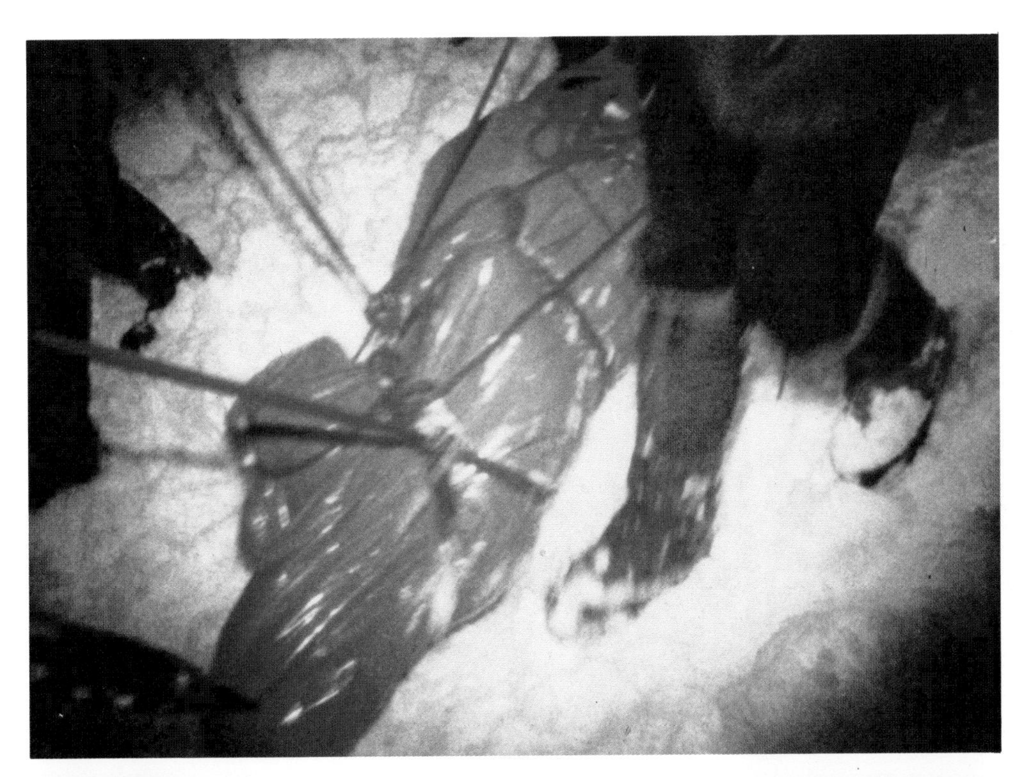

Rescue 137 could not return to the mountain owing to bad weather so the victim had to be carried three kilometers down the mountainside by the MRT.

A flare illuminates the way for the MRT as they leave the scene of the Kintail avalanche.

We never say never

JOB NO 108
20 MARCH 1989

'. . . these showers are pretty damn thick . . . you'd think it was night . . . ?

In bad weather and very heavy snow showers, Rescue 137 flies to Broadford, on the island of Skye, to evacuate a meningitis patient to hospital at Raigmore, Inverness. Normally, the Sea King takes about 30 minutes to cover the distance, but in those conditions it took Rescue 137 two-and-a-half hours — with five field landings. Despite valiant efforts by rescue helicopter aircrew, the local doctor, ambulance personnel and hospital staff, Kirsteen Campbell died. Meningitis is a killer and for 137's crew of aircraft captain, John Prince: co-pilot, John Tennyson-Collins; radar/winch operator, Pat Thirkell; and winchman, Ian Bonthrone this meant quarantine for two days. The film crew were also quarantined.

John Prince, captain of Rescue 137, flies towards RAF Kinloss, less than 10 miles from RAF Lossiemouth '. . . just to see how thick these snow showers are and it's somewhere I can just lobb-on quick if I have to . . . these showers are pretty damn thick . . . you'd think it was night . . .' Eventually, he brings the helicopter down at Kinloss.

En route again, John Prince turns out to sea '. . . there is a bit of a gap out to the right . . . just enough to go across to Cromarty . . . Pat, I'm going for it . . .' he tells Pat Thirkell, Rescue 137's radar operator as ice builds up on the windscreen wipers.

Crossing the coast, John says, 'The chances of getting to Skye are virtually nil . . . there's cloud right down on the surface in front of us . . . let alone in the hills . . . they should think about moving the patient by road . . . it's a question of just dropping into a field, then hopping from field to field'. Winchman Ian Bonthrone keeps an eye on the map.

'Forty-three miles per hour average ground speed,' says Pat Thirkell. Then suddenly the weather clears . . . Rescue 137 even finds a train. Skye seems possible, after all.

The local doctor to Ian Bonthrone: 'How long will it take to get to Inverness?' 'God only knows,' says Rescue 137's winchman, 'it has taken us about two-and-a-half hours to get here . . . landing in fields . . .'

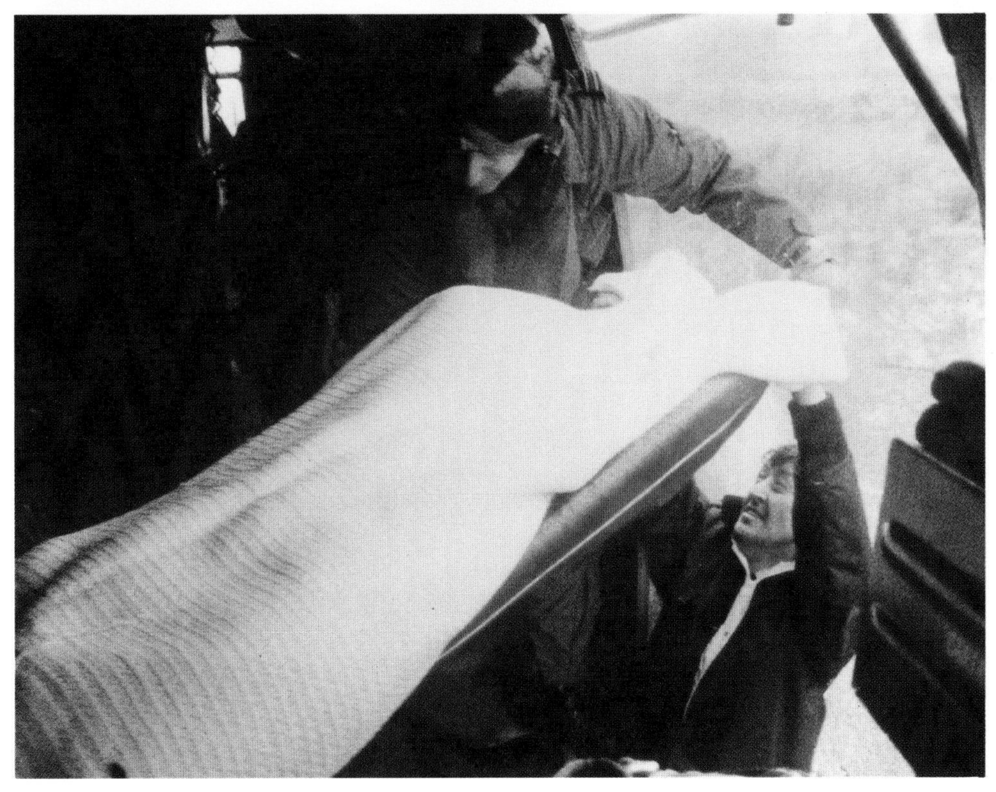

The young patient is loaded into the helicopter.

With the patient aboard, Rescue 137 sets out for Inverness, following the main road. 'One of the other considerations is that if we need to put down for any reason,' says John Prince, 'you are pretty near a road as well. Then you can get a road transfer (to an ambulance) or flag down a bloody train . . . that's not a joke. Third exit off the roundabout . . . now just follow the road signs to Inverness . . .'

The driving snow at Inverness was so bad that Rescue 137's radar operator, Pat Thirkell, had to help push the ambulance to the helicopter. 'The problem is that we are out of practice . . . we haven't had this all bloody winter,' comments John Prince.

His part in the fight to save the young girl's life complete, Ian Bonthrone radios from the hospital to the waiting helicopter: 'Rescue 137, this is 137 Mobile, patient is now in hospital, we are on our way back, over . . .'

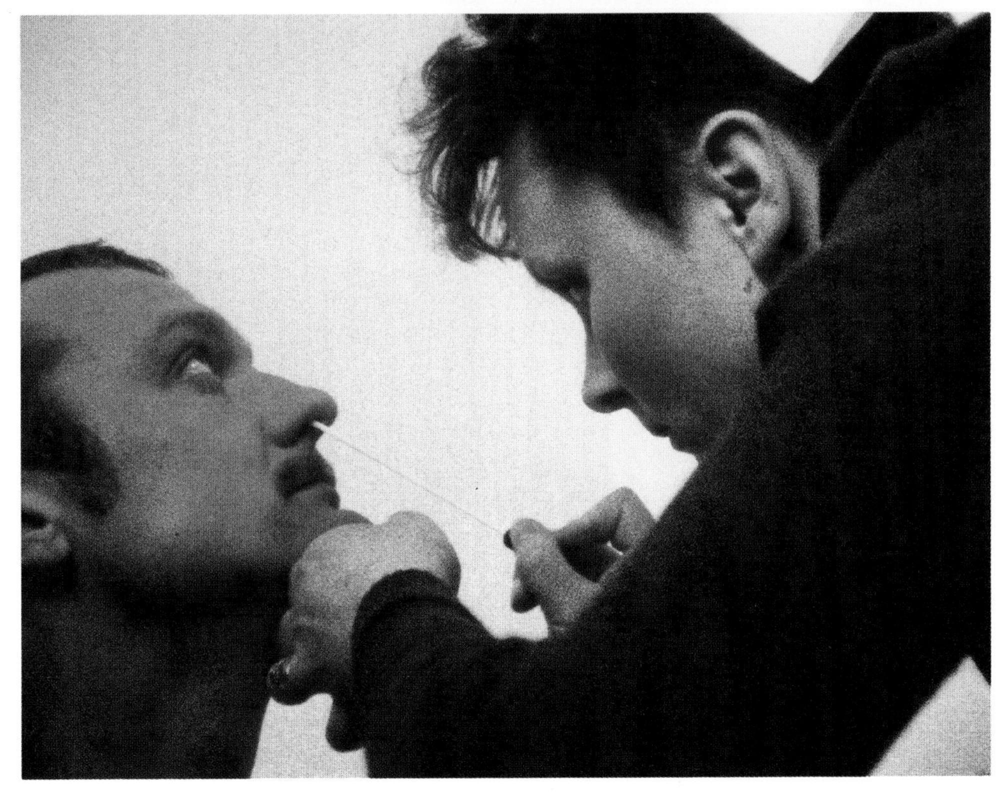

Rescue aircrew not only risk their lives in the air but a close proximity to some medical patients can also be life-threatening. Winchman Ian Bonthrone (illustrated) with three other aircrew and two film crew were swabbed by a nurse after contact with the unfortunate meningitis victim.

White Out

JOB NO 109
23 MARCH 1989

'Rescue 137 will have extreme difficulty in getting through to you.'

Rescue 137 was scrambled during a training flight into the Cairngorms to assist the Glenmore MRT search for a fallen climber with reported head, chest and arm injuries. The weather was heavy snow with 40 knots wind — a white out. The helicopter made several attempts to fly into the mountains but a snow-cat was eventually used to bring the casuality down to where the weather allowed helicopter operations. The rescue helicopter was flown by John Prince (captain), Simon Willson (co-pilot), Steve Larke (radar/winch operator) and Ian Bonthrone (winchman).

Will Rescue 137 get through? The Glenmore MRT break from their descent with the injured climber on hearing but not seeing the Sea King.

At Glenmore rescue base, the MRT co-ordinator and training centre leader, Andy Anderson, briefs the winchman of Rescue 137, Ian Bonthrone (whose blue survival jacket is just in camera to the left).

The blizzard conditions make it impossible for the helicopter to reach that location — Rescue 137 to Glenmore Richard. Apologies but due to this wind strength we'll be unable to reach you' — so the descent continues in near white-out conditions.

The snow-cat eventually gets through to the MRT and the climber's stretcher is loaded aboard, with the rescuers walking or skiing alongside. 'Rescue 137 will have extreme difficulty in getting through to you,' says Glenmore Base to the MRT on-scene leader.

HISTORIC RAF SAR HELICOPTERS

Sycamore

The Sycamore helicopter gave the Royal Air Force its first adequate performance helicopter for search and rescue operations. The initial trials with three Sycamore HR 12 variants were carried out at RAF St Mawgan, Cornwall, in February 1952 and later two HR 13s were sent for evaluation by RAF Fighter Command.

The final production variant was the Sycamore HR 14 which became the RAF's first large-scale SAR helicopter. It incorporated better throttle and power controls and featured a winch adjacent to the starboard cabin door. In total 86 were delivered to the RAF and the first entered front-line service with 275 Squadron in April 1953 for SAR, and others were used for support helicopter duties in Cyprus and the Far East.

Sycamore HR Mk 14

Manufacturer: Bristol Aeroplane Co (later Westland Helicopters): Purpose: Short-range search and rescue helicopter; Crew: 1/2 pilot(s), 1 aircrewman; Cabin: 4 survivors; Maiden flight: 1952; Service entry: April 1953; Phased out: 1971; Squadrons: 194, 275; Radius of action: 116 nm (216 km); Max speed: 110 kts (204 km/h); Operational speed: 70 kts (130 km/h); Service ceiling: 15,500 ft (4,724 m); Length: 42.0 ft (12.8 m); Height: 9.3 ft (2.83 m); Rotor diameter: 48.56 ft (14.8 m); Hover in Ground Effect: NA; Power plant: 1 × Alvis Leonides 173 piston engine (520 shp take-off power); Empty weight: 4,060 lb (1,824 kg); All-up weight: 5,600 lb (2,540 kg).

Whirlwind

The first of the US-originated helicopter designs, produced under the Sikorsky licence by Westland Helicopters, was the Whirlwind. It was based on the S-55 piston-engined aircraft and was first acquired for service with the Royal Navy.

The RAF took delivery of 32 HAR 2 variants for Coastal Command SAR operations. Later a further 31 HAR 5s were built for the Service, having an improved but not more powerful engine.

The winch arrangement on the Whirlwind, being high above the starboard cabin door, made SAR winching operations much easier, especially after modifications by Lt Cdr Sproule, the famous pioneer of SAR helicopter equipment in the Royal Navy.

The gas-turbined powered HAR 10 was ordered for squadron service in April 1960 and the production run included a number of modified airframes as well as some new build material. This series of helicopter gave UK SAR operations a mark of credibility at which previous machines had just hinted.

For a period in the early 1970s, Bristow Helicopters Ltd provided a single commercial version of the HAR 10 at RAF Manston to give an SAR service, funded by the Department of Trade and organized by HM Coastguard. Later, after a Government re-think on providing adequate military SAR, especially for heli-

copters transmitting the Channel to and from Germany, the RAF machine returned. The last Whirlwind HAR 10 retired from RAF SAR service in November 1981.

Whirlwind HAR Mk 2
Manufacturer: Westland Helicopters Ltd; Purpose: Medium-range, daylight search and rescue helicopter; Crew: 1/2 pilot(s), 1 aircrewman; Service entry: August 1954; Radius of action: 139 nm (258 km); Max speed: 86 kts (159 km/h); Operational speed: 76 kts (140 km/h); Service ceiling: 8,600 ft (2,620 m); Length: 41.71 ft (12.7 m); Height: 13.21 ft (4.03 m); Rotor diameter: 53 ft (16.15 m); Hover In Ground Effect: NA; Power plant: 1 × Pratt & Whitney Wasp R-1340-40 piston engine (600 shp take-off power); Empty weight: 5,010 lb (2,272 kg); All-up weight: 7,500 lb (3,402 kg).

Whirlwind HAR Mk 4
Data as for HAR Mk 2 but with the tropicalized Wasp R-1340-57 engine with improved supercharger.

The Whirlwind HAR Mk 10 served with the Royal Air Force for nearly 20 years and showed the way for the Sea King. The limitations of the Whirlwind in range and capacity led directly to the Sea King's service introduction.

June 1979, at the summit of Ben Nevis, the UK's highest point, and a Wessex HC Mk 2 of No 22 Squadron's flight at RAF Leuchars. The Wessex will remain in service until the mid 1990s.

Whirlwind HAR Mk 10
Manufacturer: Westland Helicopters Ltd; Purpose: Medium-range, daylight only, search and rescue helicopter; Crew: 1 pilot, 1 navigator/winch operator, 1 winchman; Cabin: 6 stretchers or 8 seated survivors; Maiden flight: February 1962 (SAR); Phased out: 30 November 1981; Squadrons: 22, 202; Radius of action: 131 nm (242 km); Max speed: 92 kts (170 km/h); Operational speed: 83 kts (153 km/h); Service ceiling: 16,600 ft (5,060 m); Length: 44.17 ft (13.46 m); Height: 13.21 ft (4.03 m); Rotor diameter: 53.0 ft (16.15 m); Hover In Ground Effect: NA; Power plant: 1 × Bristol Siddeley Gnome H1000 turboshaft engine (1,050 shp take-off power); Empty weight: 4,694 lb (2,129 kg); All-up weight: 8,000 lb (3,629 kg).

The Wessex
Although still in active service with 22 Squadron, the Wessex is now ready for retirement and replacement by the Sea King. The Wessex is based on the Sikorsky S-58 naval helicopter and is yet another example of the fruitful relationship between the design teams at Sikorsky and Westland.

The Royal Air Force did not show interest in the original single-engined piston-powered design but proceeded to order 72 of the HC 2 variant (of which several were redesignated HAR 2). In fact, the RAF led the Royal Navy in the acquisition of the gas-turbined powered helicopter.

The Wessex has a better power-to-weight ratio, although it is transmission limited. It has been described as better for cliff rescues because of a weaker downwash, but the heavier Sea King is more stable near cliffs. The Sea King, due to its heavy weight, has more inertia and so requires more anticipation to stop than the Wessex.

Overseas, the Wessex HC 2 provides search and rescue cover for the United Nations forces as well as British and NATO forces training in Cyprus under the auspices of 84 Squadron, based at RAF Akrotiri. No 28 Squadron at RAF Sek Kong, Hong Kong is also available for SAR duties.

Wessex HAR Mk 2
Manufacturer: Westland Helicopters Ltd; Purpose: Medium-range search and rescue helicopter; Crew: 1/2 pilot(s), 1 navigator/winch operator, 1 winchman; Cabin: 8 seated survivors or eight stretchers; Maiden flight: 18 January 1962; Service entry: February 1964; Squadrons: 22; Radius of action: 100 nm (185km); Max speed: 116 kts (214 km/h); Operational speed: 105 kts (195 km/h); Service ceiling: 10,000 ft (3,050 m); Length: 48.4 ft (14.7 m); Height: 14.4 ft (4.4 m); Rotor diameter: 56.0 ft (17.2 m); Hover In Ground Effect: NA; Power plants: 2 × Bristol Siddeley Gnome H1200 turboshafts (1,350 shp take-off and 900 shp continuous power); Empty weight: 8,657 lb (3,927 kg); All-up weight: 13,500 lb (6,124 kg).

RAF Finningley is the home of RAF Search and Rescue Wing. This Wessex is testing a new self-adhesive polyurethane film to protect rotor blades from damage in extreme conditions. Called Stoneguard 2000, this application is typical of the actions taken to ensure the greatest possible serviceability rates for SAR helicopters.

RAF SEARCH & RESCUE WING

The mainstay of the Royal Air Force's search and rescue helicopter force is the Westland Sea King HAR Mk 3 which is operational around the shores of the United Kingdom and the Falkland Islands. The primary role of military SAR is the search for, rescue and recovery of military personnel but in peacetime by far the greatest extent of work is in support of the civil community.

In September 1976, the Royal Air Force took the long-awaited step to form an integrated command and control organization to oversee all the RAF's UK search and rescue operations. The RAF Search & Rescue Wing took command of 22 and 202 Squadrons, as well as the specially formed Engineering squadron at RAF Finningley in South Yorkshire.

RAF Finningley is now the headquarters of the SAR Wing and coordinates the activities of the Royal Air Force Sea King Training Unit (RAFSKTU) at Royal Naval Air Station Culdrose, the home of the Royal Navy's large fleet of Sea King helicopters. Also under the aegis of the Wing is the Search and Rescue Training Unit (SARTU) at RAF Valley in Anglesey, Wales where aircrew, especially the 'back end crew' of winchman and winch radar operator, are trained in the specialization of search and rescue.

The Wing is subordinate to No 18 Group at Northwood (north-west London), which is the maritime element of RAF Strike Command, headquartered at RAF High Wycombe, Buckinghamshire. The operational tasking and coordination of SAR helicopters in the United Kingdom is the responsibility of the two Rescue Co-ordination Centres at Pitreavie Castle (with the callsign *Edinburgh Rescue*) and Mount Wise (callsign *Plymouth Rescue*). These functions are described separately.

22 Squadron RAF

A Flight	RAF Chivenor	North Devon
B Flight	RAF Valley	Anglesey, Wales
C Flight	RAF Coltishall	Norfolk
D Flight	RAF Leuchars	Fife, Scotland

202 Squadron RAF

A Flight	RAF Boulmer	Northumberland
B Flight	RAF Brawdy	Dyfed, Wales
C Flight	RAF Manston	Kent
D Flight	RAF Lossiemouth	Moray, Scotland
E Flight	RAF Leconfield	Humberside

78 Squadron RAF
B Flight RAF Mount Pleasant Falkland Islands

UK coverage

Together with the Royal Navy and HM Coastguard helicopters, Royal Air Force SAR helicopters can be scrambled to reach an emergency at any point in the United Kingdom or within 40 nm (74 km) of the coast within an hour of call-out by day. At night, the two-hour range is within 100 nm (185 km) of the coastline.

There are still two important areas of deficient coverage during daylight hours: the immediate westerly approaches to the Orkney Islands, which fall just outside the one-hour range of the HMCG S-61Ns at Sumburgh (Shetland) and Stornoway (Isle of Lewis), and a transit of about 50 minutes for the Sea King HAR3 from Lossiemouth (Morayshire).

Another deficient area is around Fort William and the Inner Hebrides which are not within the one-hour/40 nm coverage provided by the Royal Navy Sea Kings from RNAS Prestwick, the Leuchars, Wessex, the Sumburgh S-61N or the Lossiemouth Sea King, according to recent Ministry of Defence statistics.

Since 1986, the Royal Air Force and HM Coastguard have been able to improve the coverage provided by SAR helicopters in the north-west of Scotland and the Irish Sea. In the south-west approaches, the introduction in 1988 of the Sea King HAR5 helicopters of 771 Naval Air Squadron at RNAS Culdrose, Cornwall has added to the ability of RAF Brawdy's Sea Kings to cover the South-West Approaches.

With effect from October 1989, the SAR Wessex helicopter units at Chivenor (North Devon) and Leuchars (Scotland) will reduce to daylight standby only with one Wessex at readiness and a reserve helicopter available with crew. The reduction in the Wessex's capability to operate at night will not effect the total coverage of the United Kingdom.

From April 1988 the Royal Navy retired the Wessex HU5 helicopters of 772 Naval Air Squadron at Portland and replaced them with Sea King HC4s which provide a daylight-only SAR cover for the Portland/Weymouth Bay areas. In June, the Wessex Flight at RNAS Lee-on-Solent was replaced by a contract Sikorsky S-61N from Bristow on 24-hour standby, after a brief stand-in tour each by a single RAF Sea King and Wessex.

In May 1988, one of the three Sea Kings based in the Falkland Islands was returned to the United Kingdom as a result of the reduction in Phantom combat air patrols around the Islands and this allowed a fifth Sea King SAR Flight to be formed at RAF Leconfield, north of Kingston-upon-Hull. This Flight previously operated the Wessex helicopter.

Readiness

The Royal Air Force Sea King flights have a primary role of supporting operational military flying around the United Kingdom's shores and overland by providing

Flt Lt Paul Readfern, officer commanding D Flight of 202 Squadron, 1987-89, points to the location of RAF Lossiemouth on the Moray Firth; 'Lossie' is the busiest SAR helicopter base in Europe. D Flight is one of five UK units equipped with the Sea King.

Right *A Wessex HC 2 helicopter from the Search & Rescue Training Unit at RAF Valley, Anglesey, photographed during a training exercise with the winchman wearing the standard orange immersion suit.* (Paul Campbell.)

Inset *Relaxed after a difficult rescue in the Cuillins of Skye, notorious for its challenging climbing and difficult flying, the crew of Rescue 137, Lossie's first standby are (left to right) Bill Payne (winchman), Simon 'Slug' Willson (co-pilot), Harry Watt (pilot) and Paul 'Gramps' Challice (radar operator).*

a seach and rescue cover throughout the year. The most active role, however, is that of providing SAR cover as part of the UK Department of Trade and Industry obligation to provide the civilian community with this service.

In daylight hours, the 'first standby' Sea King at each flight is kept at 15 minutes readiness, which moves to 45 minutes at night. Royal Navy Sea Kings at Culdrose and Prestwick were generally on 90 minutes readiness by day or night until 1988. Today, they fit neatly into the overall UK coverage with the same 15/45 minutes day/night standby as the Royal Air Force.

When darkness falls, the SAR Sea King helicopters are generally hangared and the aircrew are able to sleep at the Flight . . . until the scramble bell sounds. Then the duty groundcrew will haul out the first standby helicopter and pre-flight the machine ready for the arrival of the duty aircrew. This might include amending the helicopter's fuel load to suit the particular needs of the sortie.

The aircrew, by the time they arrive at the helicopter, will have been briefed on the sortie and determined as much information about the emergency as is needed to launch the helicopter. Once airborne, the RCC can update the aircrew on the specifics of the operation and contact can be made with other emergency service agencies en route.

In daylight, once the first standby helicopter is airborne, the second helicopter, which has been at 60-minutes readiness, is brought forward to take the place of the first standby. If necessary, the second crew is brought into the Flight to brief themselves on the current situation, especially the weather, in case they are wanted to support the first helicopter. Or, there might be a second emergency . . .

Land operations

Although most of the attention which is directed towards the Royal Air Force's SAR operations is primarily sea-orientated, several of the Flights are well experienced in mountain rescue requirements. After all, cliff and inland

The first standby Sea King at RAF Lossiemouth is kept at 15 minutes readiness through daylight hours. The helicopter can be scrambled either from the base or whilst flying one of its regular training sorties.

ROYAL AIR FORCE
RESCUE
XT602
RAF
RESCUE

mountain rescues demand the same important skills with regard to flying and recovery techniques.

In 1988, the Royal Air Force revamped its military SAR helicopter force to meet its land, mountain and over-water considerations. In a statement from the UK Ministry of Defence, it was confirmed that the Wessex is a highly capable helicopter in mountain rescue, where its good power-to-weight ratio is important. The Sea King was also described as extremely capable and, being a more modern helicopter, is at least equal to the Wessex in terms of performance for land rescue. Unlike the Wessex, it is capable of deploying a complete mountain rescue team in one sortie.

The Sea King is also a much better performer in bad weather and at night, with the capability of carrying many more survivors — 17 as opposed to eight for the Wessex.

During the immediate aftermath of the Lockerbie disaster and the M1 plane crash, Royal Air Force SAR helicopters were immediately committed to the operations. Helicopters from Brawdy, Boulmer, Valley and Leuchars took part in the initial searches around the small Scottish border town of Lockerbie after the Pan American Airlines Boeing 747 crashed there in December 1988. Sadly, there were no survivors amongst the aircraft's crew or passengers to take to hospital, and so the helicopters concentrated on search and ferrying investigating teams instead.

The British Midland Boeing 737 crash at the East Midlands Airport was a very different operation. Television viewers from all over the world saw Wessex and Sea King helicopters from Valley, Brawdy, Leconfield and Coltishall landing on the M1 motorway to take the most critically injured passengers and aircrew to hospital. Such operations call for first-class flying skills as the aircrew need to land at a safe but convenient distance from the accident, often between the streetlights and other human-made obstacles.

The duty groundcrew ensure that the first standby helicopter (foreground) is ready for immediate scramble. In this view at RAF Lossiemouth, the second standby Sea King has already been moved out on to the helipad. Note the technician standing ready with the fire extinguisher prior to engine start.

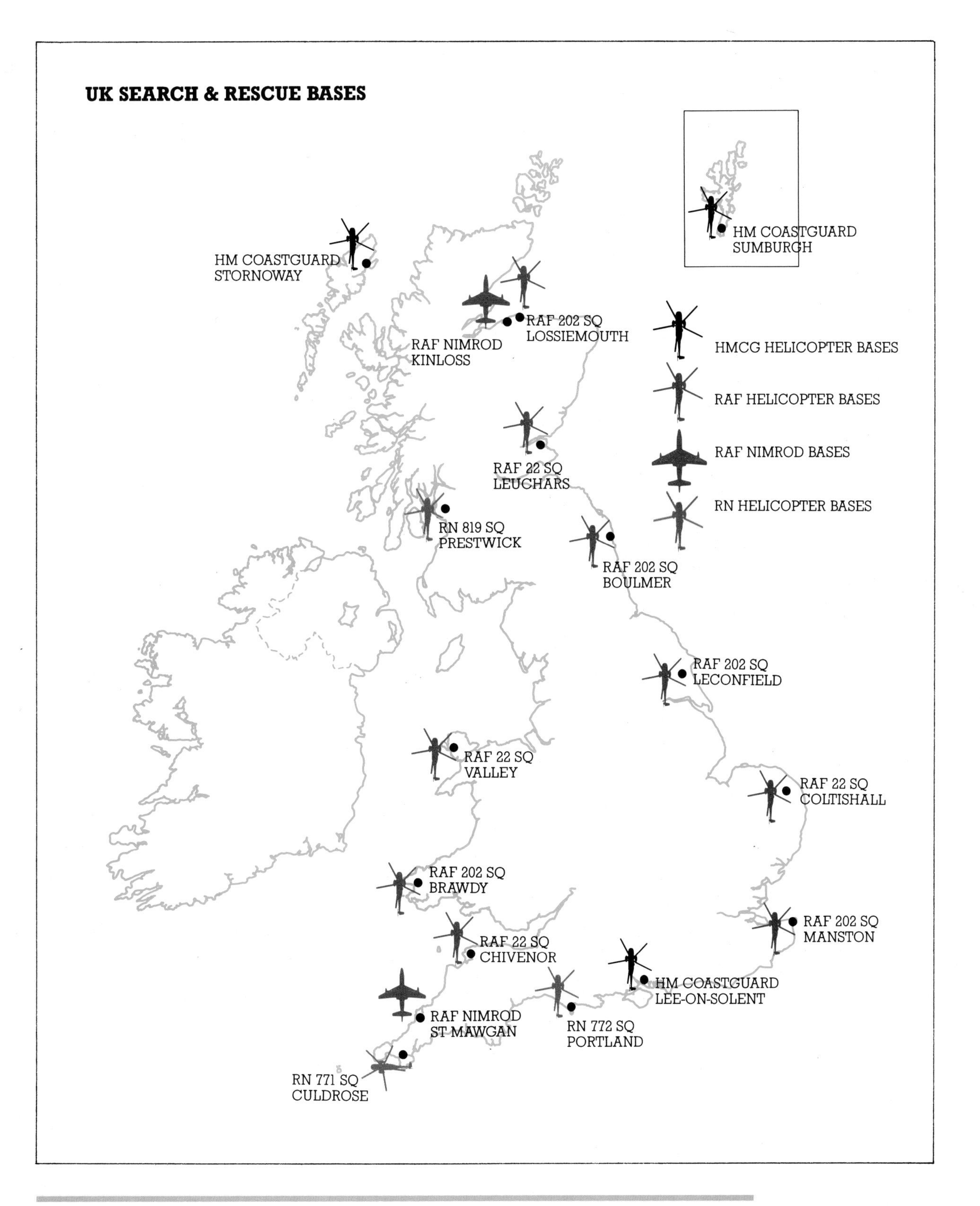
UK SEARCH & RESCUE BASES
HM COASTGUARD
SUMBURGH
HM COASTGUARD
STORNOWAY
RAF 202 SQ
LOSSIEMOUTH
RAF NIMROD
KINLOSS
HMCG HELICOPTER BASES
RAF HELICOPTER BASES
RAF NIMROD BASES
RN HELICOPTER BASES
RAF 22 SQ
LEUCHARS
RN 819 SQ
PRESTWICK
RAF 202 SQ
BOULMER
RAF 202 SQ
LECONFIELD
RAF 22 SQ
VALLEY
RAF 22 SQ
COLTISHALL
RAF 202 SQ
BRAWDY
RAF 202 SQ
MANSTON
RAF 22 SQ
CHIVENOR
HM COASTGUARD
LEE-ON-SOLENT
RAF NIMROD
ST MAWGAN
RN 772 SQ
PORTLAND
RN 771 SQ
CULDROSE

UK SEARCH & RESCUE COVER

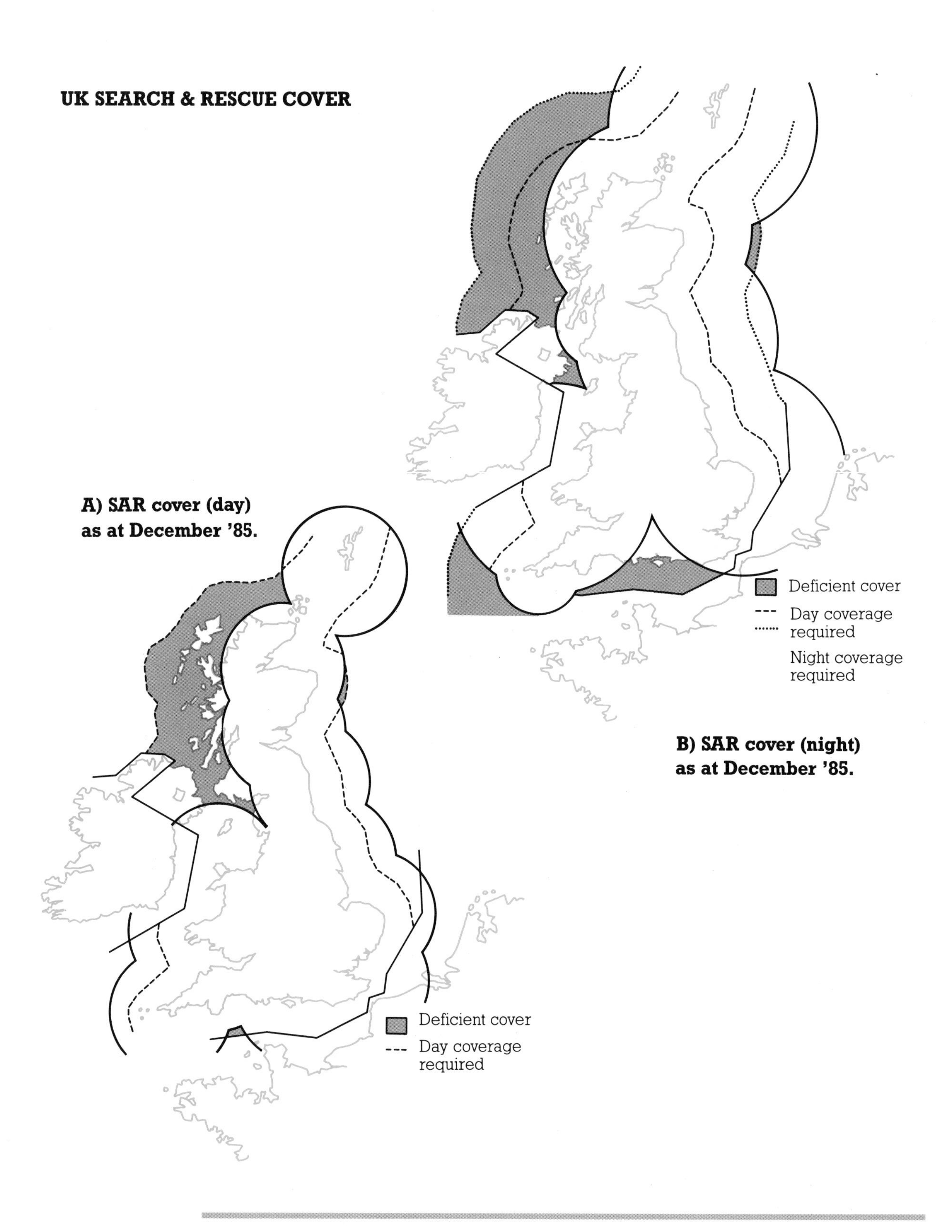

A) SAR cover (day) as at December '85.

B) SAR cover (night) as at December '85.

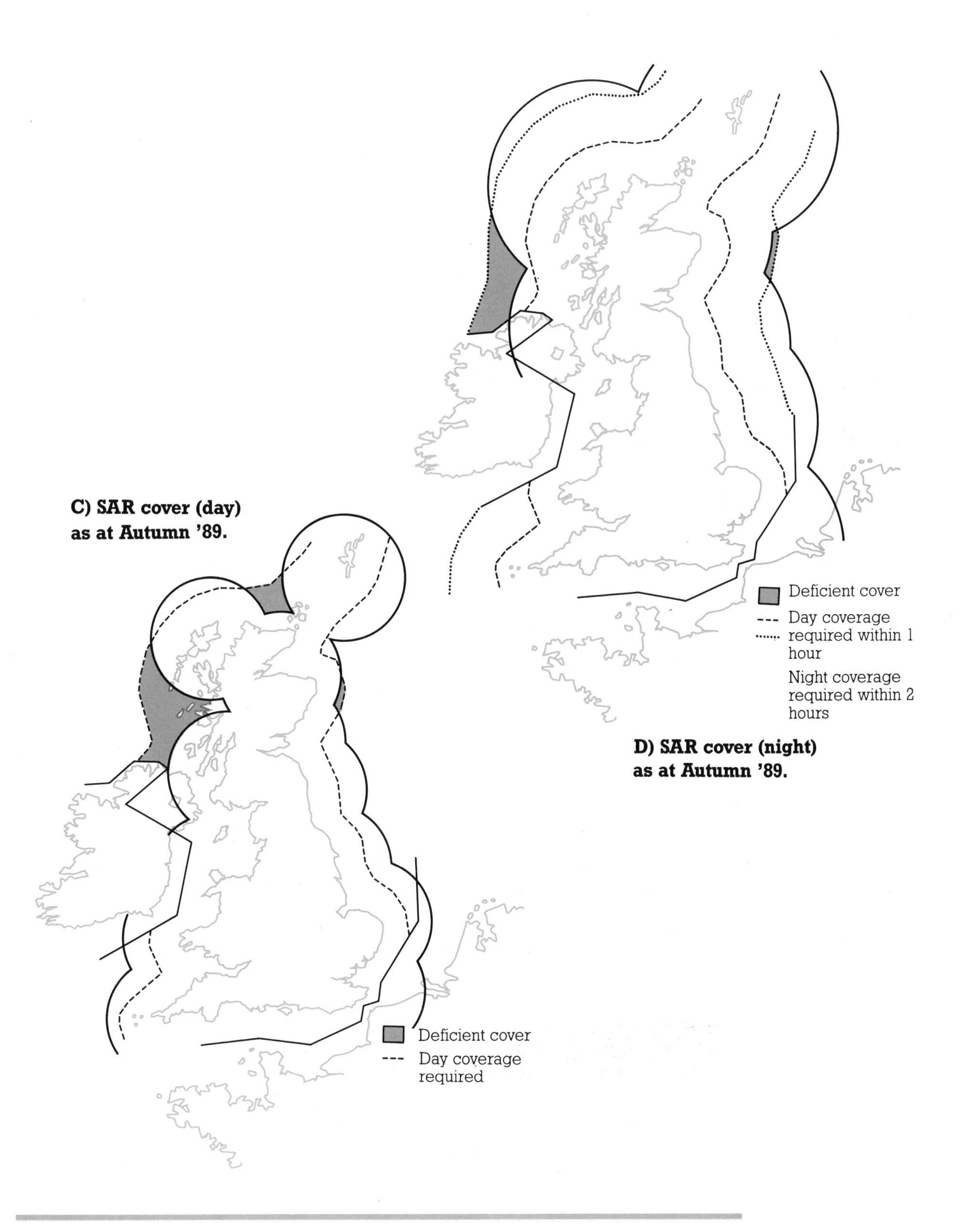

C) SAR cover (day) as at Autumn '89.

D) SAR cover (night) as at Autumn '89.

THE SEA KING

The evergreen and much-loved Sea King started life as a new generation of anti-submarine warfare helicopter for the United States Navy in the mid 1950s. Almost as soon as it had completed its maiden flight, the UK helicopter producer, Westland, took out a licence for the helicopter's production and eventual development for the British forces.

The original idea was to develop a civilian helicopter and the name Wiltshire had even been coined before the licence agreement had been signed between Sikorsky and Westland. It was not the first collaboration between the world's most important helicopter maker and Britain's only one, but it has proved to be the most important.

The Sea King remains in production in Japan (for the Japanese Maritime Self-Defence Force) and Italy (for various operators including, recently, the Argentine and Brazilian navies). In the United Kingdom, production of the Advanced Sea King continues at the Yeovil, Somerset factory of the Westland Group, with a major order from the Indian Navy for anti-submarine, vertical replenishment/support and airborne early warning.

It was ten years before the West German Navy selected the design, by

Although designed in the United States by Sikorsky, the evergreen Sea King helicopter has been developed and enhanced by Westland into one of the most versatile medium helicopters in the world.

then internally developed for European use, and ordered enough airframes to equip a complete search and rescue squadron. The Germans were followed by Belgium and Norway.

For the next 15 years, RAF aircrew in their Whirlwind and Wessex helicopters continued to soldier on without the radar, augmented flight control system, comfort and endurance of the Sea King.

The UK Ministry of Defence eventually made funds available to the RAF in 1975 for the purchase of 15 airframes based on the Royal Navy's anti-submarine helicopter but with the sonar equipment removed and accommodation for six stretchers. The powerful MEL ARI 5955 radar was retained and augmented by a Racal Decca 9447F Tactical Air Navigation System linked to a Decca Type 71 Doppler.

The radar enables the aircrew to navigate the helicopter accurately and safely in almost all weather conditions and this is certainly necessary for search and rescue operations at sea. In low cloud or driving rain the pilots can be directed towards a casualty by the radar operator giving directions. From a flight safety point of view the radar allows restricted visibility operations at sea, although over land it is very limited.

Linking the TANS system to the radar allows accurate navigation, especially over water. The computer provides accurate latitude/longitude information, waypoints can be set to provide for dog-leg navigation and drift/wind direction/wind speed data can be supplied. This is especially important to the pilots during an approach to a casualty in the water or on a mountain slope.

Earlier software problems with the TANS have been overcome in the latest versions and there has been a recent decision to upgrade the system using the US-designed Omega area navigation system. This system is also used by oil platform support helicopters around the world and especially in the North Sea. The combination provides greater flexibility in navigation.

The Racal Doppler system allows the helicopter to fly without the need to update its navigation systems from external sources. Such independence is vital for long-range SAR operations. Other navigational equipment includes the Decca Mk 19 Navigator, Racal AVQ-75 distance measuring equipment and the Marconi AD370 automatic direction finder.

Above left *The thimble radome of the MEL search and weather radar above the Sea King's cabin. In the foreground is the hydraulic rescue winch.*

Above *The Sea King is fitted with water-landing sponsons, one each side, into which the main undercarriage retracts.*

Access is through the main cabin door, from where winching operations take place. Note the blister window (one in each beam) for search operations, and the hydraulic rescue winch.

To assist the two pilots to fly the Sea King, it carries a Louis Newmark Automatic Flight Control System (AFCS) which provides three-axis stabilized flight (pitch, yaw and roll) as well as allowing for automatic transitions into a hover. At night, in a high sea state, the flying pilot can bring the helicopter into a pre-determined optimum hover and hold it for winching operations. Associated with the hover control is the Smiths Industries APN-198 radar altimeter.

The radio communications equipment aboard includes UHF (AN/ARC 116), VHF (AM), VHF (FM) Marine Band, Collins HF and Pye Olympic radios for air-to-air and air-to-ground operations, including communications with HM Coastguard, Mountain Rescue Teams and the Rescue Co-ordination Centres. It is still not possible, mainly through UK Government legislation, for the SAR helicopter force to communicate on police radio wavelengths.

The first Sea King HAR Mk 3 for the RAF flew on 6 September 1977 and was immediately involved in working up aircrew at a specially formed unit at Europe's busiest helicopter base, Royal Naval Air Station Culdrose, Cornwall, the home of the Royal Navy's Sea King fleet.

FLYING AT NIGHT

Night vision goggles have been supplied to aircrew, especially for night search operations, and all the Royal Air Force Sea King SAR fleet will be modified with blue-green filters to make the cockpit compatible with the image intensifiers. These goggles, so successfully used in the Falklands conflict to land special operations forces behind Argentine lines and now standard equipment for all advanced battlefield helicopters, demand a greater flying skill than normally required at night. The image intensifying tube gathers the available light, including starlight and semi-covered moonlight, and focuses the light for the human eye to see. Although a full spectrum of colours is not presented to the wearer, experience soon allows aircrew to fly safely at low level at night.

RAF Lossiemouth was selected by the Air Force Board, the RAF's most senior committee, as the first unit to be equipped with the Sea King. D Flight of No 202 Squadron at Lossie was then still operating the ageing single-engined Whirlwind HAR10.

For the first time, the RAF was able to provide true day/night SAR cover in most weather conditions. For the station, with its front-line operational and training aircraft, the advent of the Sea King was a significant milestone in its coverage of the world's roughest seas and some of the most difficult mountain flying anywhere.

To enhance the helicopter's navigation accuracy, the Royal Air Force is retrofitting its fleet of SAR Sea Kings with the Omega area navigation system (small blister, right) to supplement the Racal TANS and Decca Navigator. Note the identification, friend or foe transponder, aft of the Omega aerial.

Rescues 137 and 138 on standby at RAF Lossiemouth.

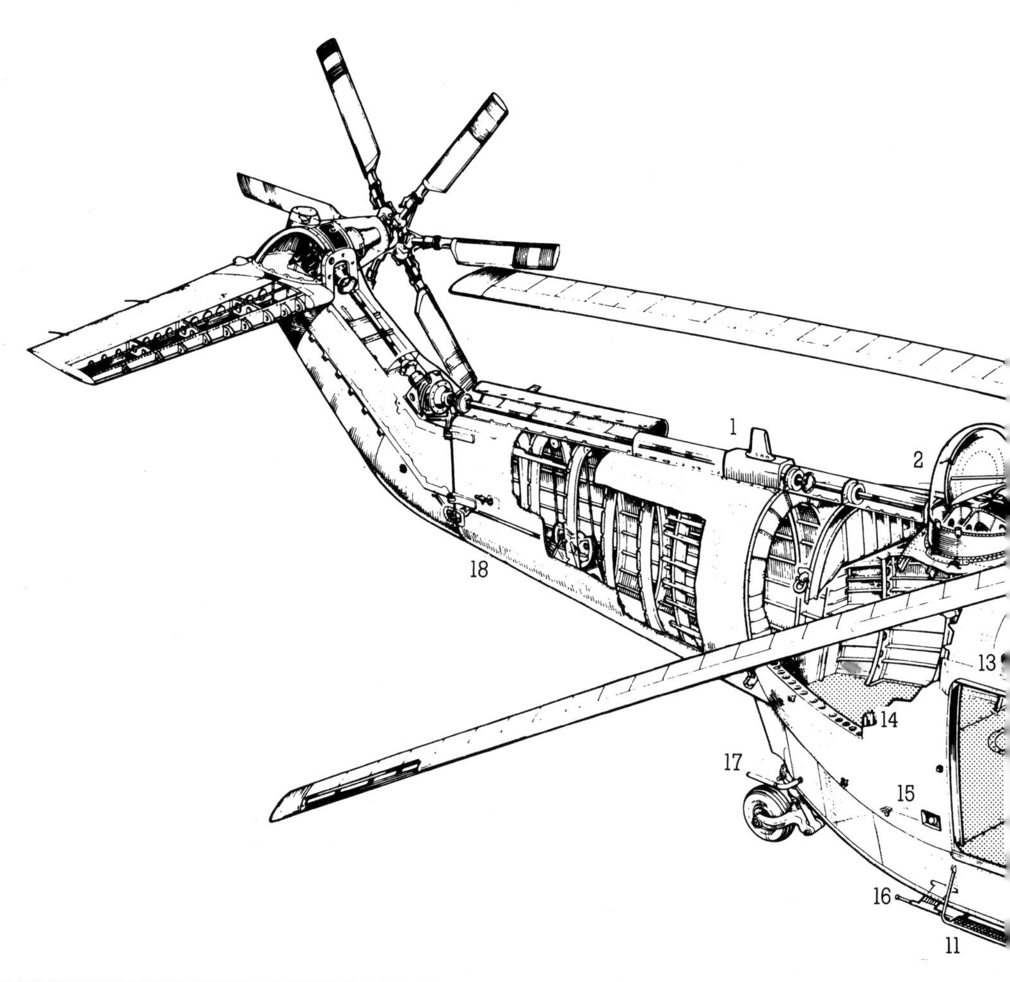

D Flight's groundcrew prepare to launch the Sea King on another training flight; note the fire extinguisher and ground power supply.

INSIDE THE SEA KING

1 Upper U/VHF radio aerial
2 MEL ARI 5944 search/weather radar inside plastic radome
3 Two Rolls-Royce Gnome H 1400-1 engines
4 FOD guard or 'barn door' to protect engine intakes
5 Co-pilot's searchlight (on door)
6 Pilot's searchlight (on nose)
7 Hover floodlights with VHF homing aerials adjacent
8 Sea King's boat hull
9 Main undercarriage

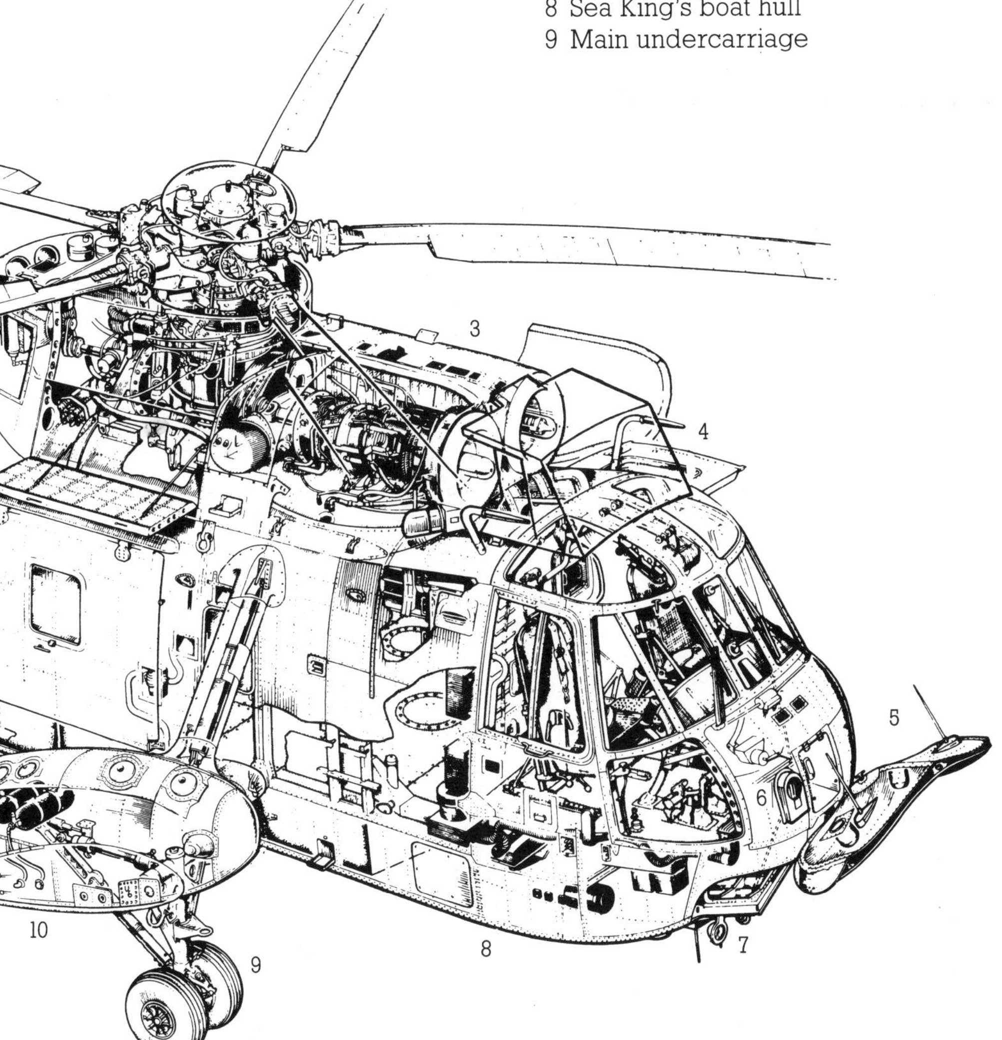

10 Flotation gear housed in stabilising floats
11 Cabin step (now removed)
12 Main cabin and life raft/rescue equipment stowage
13 Breeze hydraulic winch with spotlamp
14 Observation window (not shown) either side
15 Pressure refuelling point and Decca aerial (not shown)
16 Marine band VHF/FM radio aerial
17 Fuel jettison pipe adjacent to tail wheel
18 IFF transponder and Omega aerials (not shown)

RAF Sea King HAR Mk 3 production batches: XZ585-XZ599
ZA105
ZE368-ZE370

XZ585 was badly damaged in an accident 21 nm (40 km) north-east of Fort William, in the Scottish Highlands on 28 January 1989; the four crew, two film crew and three Mountain Rescue Team members aboard received only minor injuries. In mid-1989, work began at the Royal Naval Aircraft Yard at Fleetlands, near Portsmouth, to rebuild XZ585 for flying duties.

Sea King HAR Mk 3

Manufacturer: Westland Helicopters Ltd; Purpose: Long-range, all-weather search and rescue helicopter; Crew: 2 pilots, 1 radar/winch operator, 1 winchman; Cabin: 17 seated survivors or 6 stretchers or 3 stretchers/11 seated; Maiden flight: 6 September 1977; Service entry: September 1978; Squadrons: 78, 202, RAFSKTU; Radius of action: 275 nm (510 km) standard fuel; Max speed: 135 kts (250 km/h); Max service speed: 125 kts (232 km/h); Operational speed: 105 to 125 kts (194 to 232 km/h); Service ceiling: 10,000 ft (9,305 m); Length: 57.17 ft (17.43 m); Length (blades spread): 72.67 ft (44.3 m); Height: 16.83 ft (5.13 m); Rotor diameter: 62.0 ft (18.9 m); Hover Out of Ground Effect: 3,200 ft (975 m); Power plants: 2 × Rolls-Royce Gnome H1400-1 turboshafts (1,660 shp take-off, 1,250 shp maximum continuous power); Empty weight: 13,000 lb (5,896 kg); Max all-up weight: 21,000 lb (9,526 kg); Emergency overload weight: 21,400 lb (9,707 kg).

XZ585, badly damaged in a crash near Fort William in January 1989 during the filming of RESCUE, happily with no loss of life.

Far left *Dave Lloyd, in the co-pilot's seat, programmes the Sea King's Tactical Air Navigation System.*

Left *Paul Barton, winchman, consults with Dave Lloyd, using the Sea King's 'primary' navigation system of Ordnance Survey map and the human eye.*

En route to a rescue in Skye, Dave Lloyd checks the large scale navigation chart; just visible are the red markings of the low flying avoidance areas and the military air traffic zones around the twin RAF stations of Kinloss and Lossiemouth.

THE SCRAMBLE

In theory, Royal Air Force and Royal Navy search and rescue helicopters are scrambled by the command of the Rescue Co-ordination Centre (RCC) but often the duty standby crew are aware of the emergency from monitoring other agencies. These might include the police, HM Coastguard and other military nets. The sound of the scramble bell alerts the groundcrew and other personnel.

The procedure for the day-time scramble, with the helicopter at 15 minutes readiness, is that the captain of the aircraft (the flying pilot) will decide what extra fuel, specialist equipment or personnel to carry having been given the position and nature of the incident.

In the case of a military 'may-day' call in mid-winter and the risk of injured crew not surviving more than minutes in the water, even if they have successfully ejected, the pilot will usually decide to take immediate life-saving action and scramble with regard only for operational safety. Normally, it is expected that aircrew and passengers who have come through a military aircraft accident will survive for many hours even if only dressed in an immersion suit. Survival can be a matter of several days if there is a dinghy available. It is a case of having the right equipment and obeying the rules. Once airborne, more routine matters, such as radio checks with the RCC, can be accomplished without delaying the life-saving action.

The scramble bus pulls up alongside Rescue 137 on Lossiemouth's SAR helicopter dispersal. The bus is kept in D Flight's hangar, adjacent to the duty crew's flight and safety equipment racks.

SCRAMBLE DUTIES (RAF Sea King HAR Mk3)

The procedures followed by the RAF are not rigid but are flexible enough to accommodate all eventualities. Any member of the aircrew can take the telephone scramble message and fill out the 'scramble form'. Specialist questions can be put to the RCC by any member of the crew. The following table gives an indication of duties and responsibilities:

Crew	Responsibilities
Captain (First Pilot)	Position and nature of incident. Authorizes additional fuel, equipment, personnel. Makes decision to scramble and briefs the crew. Alerts ground crew, assigns pre-flight checks and gives briefing.
Co-pilot	Navigation duties, including a brief for the helicopter's captain after planning. Pre-flight planning.
Radar operator	Prepares navigation equipment aboard. Liaises with the RCC and will often continue the conversation with RCC after the helicopter has been launched, using the HF radio link, and liaises with HMCG on the VHF/FM radio.
Winchman	Ensures all necessary equipment aboard (including specialist kit likely to be required for the rescue, treatment and survival of the survivor).

Even the film crew scramble . . . during the filming of RESCUE the cameraman and sound recordist were part of the duty crew and scrambled with the pilots, radar operator and winchman.

As the flight crew collect the detailed information and don their protective clothing, the ground crew are already pre-flight checking Rescue 137 to ensure its readiness for immediate launch. The ground crew are a vital part of the SAR operation.

Airborne scrambles

To ensure that the SAR helicopter is always ready to divert to an incident, whenever a training or check flight is undertaken, the full crew and equip-

Right *With the pre-take-off checks complete, Rescue 137 turns into wind to launch from RAF Lossiemouth on another SAR operation.*

Far right *Rescue 137 lifts off.*

Rescue 137 passes the second standby helicopter, Sea King 138 at RAF Lossiemouth.

ment is carried. This enables the first standby aircraft to accept a request to scramble in the air and often this can save time — and lives.

The Royal Air Force has drawn up a series of practical guidelines for training operations which include the termination of the sortie if the aircraft becomes operationally unserviceable (such as losing power to the winch or if the radar ceases to function). On a training flight, the Sea King is always fully equipped and all four crew members will be carried for any flight of more than five minutes flying time away from base. These short-duration sorties are usually for engine or other equipment tests.

Whenever flying, SAR helicopters monitor the standard VHF and UHF 'guard' frequencies, on which it is possible they will hear a 'may-day' call before other stations. In addition, in coastal regions, the helicopter will monitor the HM Coastguard VHF FM radio and routinely keep in touch with the HMCG station — as well as with the RCC on the HF radio. Radio communications with the Flight's own operations room is also maintained.

It is generally held that an operation involving the rescue of survivors of a crashed British or NATO military or civilian aircraft has precedence over all other tasks.

On scene

During the transit to the incident, which may take an hour or more, the crew will

RAF
RESCUE
XZ587
RESCUE

RAF
RESCUE

During a training flight in the Scottish Highlands, Sea King 137 becomes Rescue 137 and flies to an incident on Skye, a few minutes flying time away.

On scene at the incident, the winch operator makes an initial reconnaissance as the crew discuss the best way of tackling the rescue.

have routinely contacted all the necessary emergency services with whom they can have radio contact. It is interesting to note here that, in Great Britain, military SAR aircraft do not carry radios for direct communication with the police. The aircrew can talk with police ground units on a 'phone patch' through the HF radio link.

The helicopter makes periodic 'ops normal' calls to the RCC in case it, too, becomes a victim rather than a rescuer. Such good practice is especially important in mountainous terrain and over the sea, making it routine for operations from RAF Lossiemouth and several other UK SAR locations.

Almost without exception, the SAR helicopter will make a reconnaissance of the scene of the incident before the captain, with advice from the other aircrew, makes a decision about how to conduct the rescue.

Each rescue is different. Although standard guidelines are applicable in almost all circumstances, the experience of the aircrew is vitally important. The immediate course of action is to carry out a reconnaissance of the area to assess the best method of approach to the rescue scene. In this case, the helicopter maintains a safe flight configuration and may make several passes. This is especially important in the execution of a safe winching from the deck of a ship where it is vital to understand the ship's movement or in mountains where downdraughts and turbulence can be catastrophic to helicopters.

Initial reconnaissance: what to look for
Accessibility to survivor.
Type of lift necessary.
Size, shape, surroundings, slope and surface.
Local wind, feature wind, turbulence.
Initial hover point prior to winching.

With a helicopter there are limits to its operational ability to fly in turbulent conditions and anticipation of wind is very important. Usually, the SAR helicopter's crew will use the onboard systems,

Search and rescue operations in the Cullins are difficult and often the SAR helicopter will liaise with the local police prior to a search operation. The local mountain rescue team is also on scene to assist.

Hovering over the casualty, the winch operator watches as the winchman makes an initial, immediate assessment of the fallen climber's condition.

including the TANS and Doppler to determine the direction and strength of the wind, but it is also good practice to take note of physical features such as smoke, flags and wind lanes on the surface. In some conditions, especially around mountain bowls, pyrotechnics can be launched from the main cabin door using the Very pistol. Although care has to be taken not to endanger those on the ground, especially where there is spilt fuel from a damaged aircraft, this use of smoke is very effective.

During a rescue, the pilots monitor the flight instruments and ensure that the helicopter stays within its power and weight limits for the conditions in which it is flying. The helicopter must be flown on the best possible heading to take advantage of the wind and keep good visual references available for flying. At night, this can be achieved by using the helicopter's hover and spot lights, but it is always important to keep a clear escape route in mind in case there should be an engine failure.

All the crew keep each other informed of what they, as individuals, intend to do to effect the rescue and this includes the winch operator's brief about the route to the survivor, the type of lift to be used (double, single, stretcher, etc), the method of recovery to the aircraft and any escape route for the winchman in the event of a problem on the ground or with the helicopter.

With the winchman and the rest of the crew fully briefed, a process which does not take many minutes, he is ready to launch into space on the end of the winch wire. His equipment, especially the harness, is checked by the winch operator and he goes out through the door and down.

The winch operator maintains control of the winch with a variable speed switch on the control hoist and keeps up an intercom briefing — a word picture of the

Homeward bound into RAF Lossiemouth, Rescue 137 completes another rescue. The Flight at Lossie is one of the busiest in Europe.

winchman's progress — to the rest of the crew. The winchman then deals with the situation according to its urgency and necessity.

Hand signals are used by the winchman to control his height, direction of required travel and when he and the survivor are ready to be lifted. Hoist control is only passed to the Captain for stretcher entry into the cabin or when two survivors are being lifted without a winchman. The survivor and winchman are secured in the cabin before the winch operator informs the flying pilot that he is clear to fly up and away. If the survivor has an inflated life jacket, this is removed and replaced by an uninflated one as in the event of a further emergency, with the rescue helicopter landing on the water, exit from the cabin can be impossible because the emergency exits are too small to climb through wearing a large, inflated lifejacket.

After each use of the winch the wire and system are checked thoroughly by the ground crew. This is one of many important tasks carried out by the technicians at RAF Lossiemouth.

OPERATIONAL TECHNIQUES

Special flying techniques have been developed by the aircrew of RAF Search & Rescue helicopters to cope with difficult operations. These might include searching valleys and mountain tops, looking for a small boat in a stormy sea at night or co-operating with surface ships. Some of the more common flying patterns and procedures are shown here.

1 Contour search. For mountain flying and simultaneously searching the adjacent valley area. This is considered to be the most dangerous type of search and the pilots must be experienced in mountain flying. The helicopter starts high in case cloud descends during the operation. Factors to contend with include turbulence over mountain slopes, flying around bowls and ridges, and high groundspeed flying downwind which may cause the pilot to fly low indicated airspeeds with high power settings.

2 Combined search. For co-operation between surface ships and helicopters. Considered to be relatively easy.

3 Parallel track search. Commonly used to cover a large area in conjunction with the aircraft's radar.

4 Sector search. Used when the helicopter can be positioned on an accurate datum point. A similar pattern, called the clover leaf, is used to clear an area close to the datum before beginning an expanding square search.

5 Expanding square search. The helicopter's pattern expands from the datum point into an area search regime. This is used where the likelihood of finding the object of the search is equal in all directions.

6 Creeping line ahead search. This is carried out with the prevailing wind, usually either side of the presumed track of the object being sought.

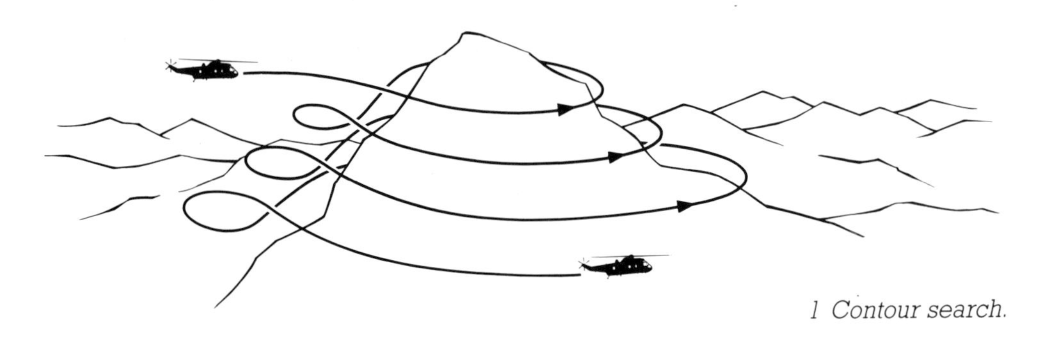

1 Contour search.

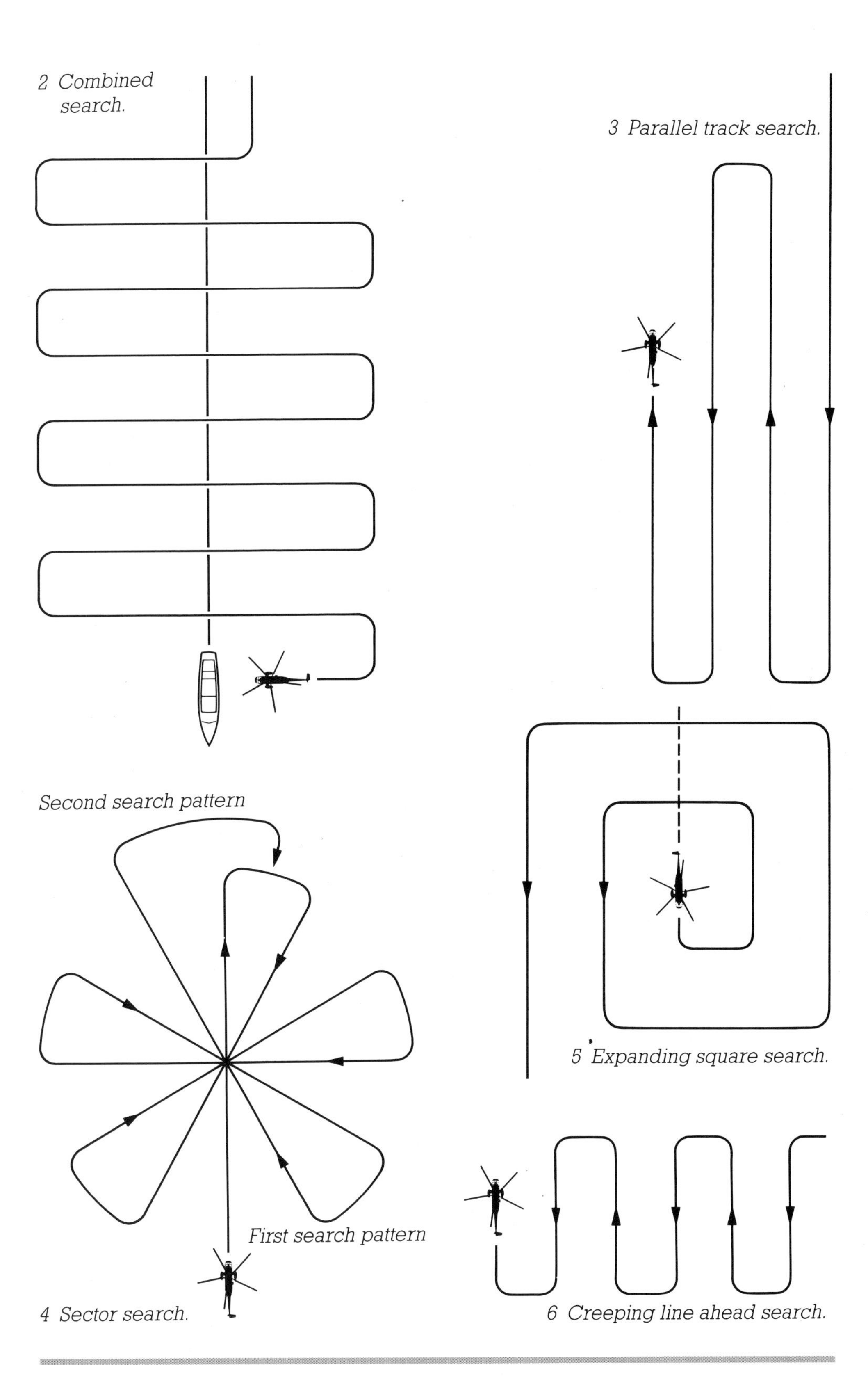

2 Combined search.

3 Parallel track search.

4 Sector search.

5 Expanding square search.

6 Creeping line ahead search.

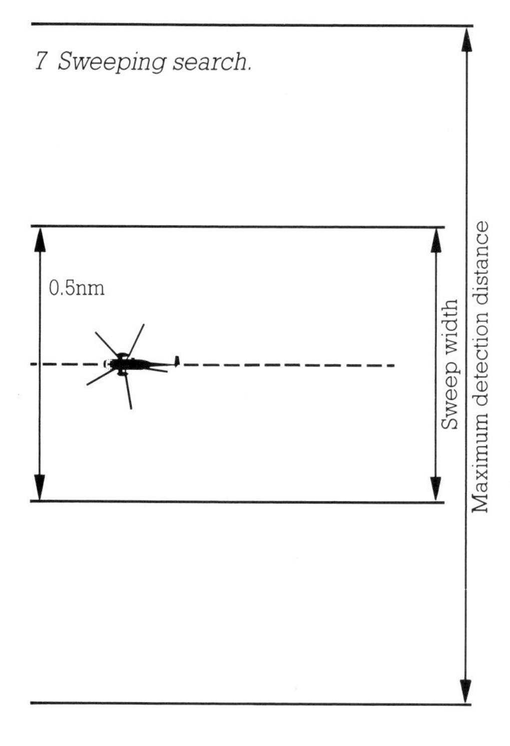

7 Sweeping search.

7 Sweeping search. A mathematical compromise calculated to produce a reduced range, within which the probability of detection is significantly higher than looking out to the maximum distance (outer lines). The sweep width (inner lines, typically 0.5 nm) is changed with the varying sea state, cloud cover and/or location aids carried by the helicopter.

HI-LINE TRANSFER

For use in badly obstructed locations, such as the decks of fishing vessels, search and rescue helicopter crews have developed a technique called the hi-line transfer. This uses a line attached to the winch hook and allows the ship's crew to assist in guiding the winchman safely to the vessel's deck. It also allows the rescue of survivors from the ship or a large airliner-type dinghy.

The helicopter does not have to hover precisely above the survivors, but can stand off in relative safety and still effect a very successful rescue of survivors. This is especially useful during long-range operations and for the passing of specialist equipment between the helicopter and the survivors below — for example, the portable pumps which can be carried aboard the Sea King during sinking ship incidents and transferred to the ship.

Because the use of the hi-line system is potentially hazardous, the helicopter's crew will brief the survivors on the vessel below about the technique involved.

There are three methods of passing the hi-line to a vessel and, following the initial reconnaissance, the aircrew will assess which is the most practical solution. These are:

Manual lowering: the hi-line is lowered vertically to the deck of the boat or dinghy;

Trawling: the hi-line is trailed in the water and dragged towards the vessel or dinghy.

Winchman assisted: the winchman is lowered with the hi-line to the deck of the vessel or to such a position that he can pass the hi-line to the vessel's crew.

Once the hi-line is securely held aboard the vessel, the winchman is lowered to the deck and can be assisted there by the vessel's crew. Survivors can then be brought into the helicopter using the single or double strop lift techniques under the supervision of the winchman on the deck and the winch operator aboard the helicopter.

While the winchman is working on the deck, the flying pilot (on the starboard side of the helicopter) positions the helicopter to maintain visual contact with the vessel at all times. The winch operator also keeps a close watch on the

HI-LINE TECHNIQUE

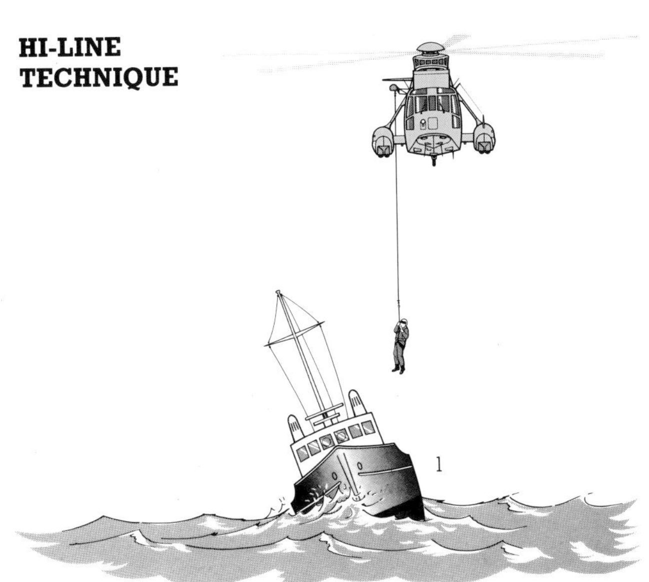

1 The winchman is lowered to the sinking craft. Generally the SAR helicopter would be in the overhead position as shown. It is possible to deploy the hi-line prior to the winchman being lowered, when the crew of the sinking craft are fishermen used to working with ropes and there is good two-way communication.

2 The winchman is collected on the sinking craft's deck by the boat's crew. Note that the winchman is wearing a bosun's chair harness.

3 The winchman pays out the hi-line for a single recovery of a survivor to the helicopter, which would normally be in the overhead position for winching down and recovery. In some circumstances the winch operator would direct the pilot away from the overhead for ease of flying or if safety considerations dictated. These could include the proximity of masts, aerials and wires on the sinking craft, especially in heavy sea conditions.

4 Winchman and survivor are winched aboard the helicopter with a member of the boat's crew paying out the hi-line. Normally the helicopter would be vertically above the fishing vessel.

vessel, especially any masts and rigging which could damage and hazard the helicopter.

With multiple-lift operations, the Sea King can stand off with the winchman in sight, during the recovery of survivors to the cabin. The single or double strops are returned to the winchman by the pilot using the winch controls while the winch operator secures the survivors in the cabin.

Cliff winching

Many of the more dramatic rescues which have been performed around the coasts of the United Kingdom by helicopters have involved cliff winching. It is a difficult and dangerous technique and one for which SAR helicopter crews train regularly. The main hazard is the proximity of the helicopter's main rotor disc to the cliff face.

The most usual technique used to place the winchman close to the survivor on a cliff face is cliff walking. This is basically a modified extended cable-lift technique which allows the helicopter to hold the winchman on to the cliff face. For a free-air descent, the helicopter remains away from the cliff during the winching operation.

Cliff walking

Described by the Royal Air Force as being preferable to a free-air descent because it allows the winchman to maintain stability during the winching operation, cliff walking can be undertaken from the top or base of a cliff, depending on the individual circumstances of each rescue. A general rule is that the descent takes place several metres away from the direct overhead line so that the survivor is not put at risk by stones and

FREE AIR DESCENT OR CLIFF WINCHING

The SAR helicopter hovers over the cliff and the winchman is lowered. The height is the lowest possible taking into consideration the proximity of the cliff and the effects of rotor downwash. Ideally the helicopter's cabin door would be facing the cliff.

CLIFF WALKING

This operation is used to put the winchman in a safe position. Normally, the helicopter's captain would prefer to have the cabin door (starboard side of the aircraft) facing the cliff but wind direction and emergency escape route considerations may necessitate another hover position, as shown.

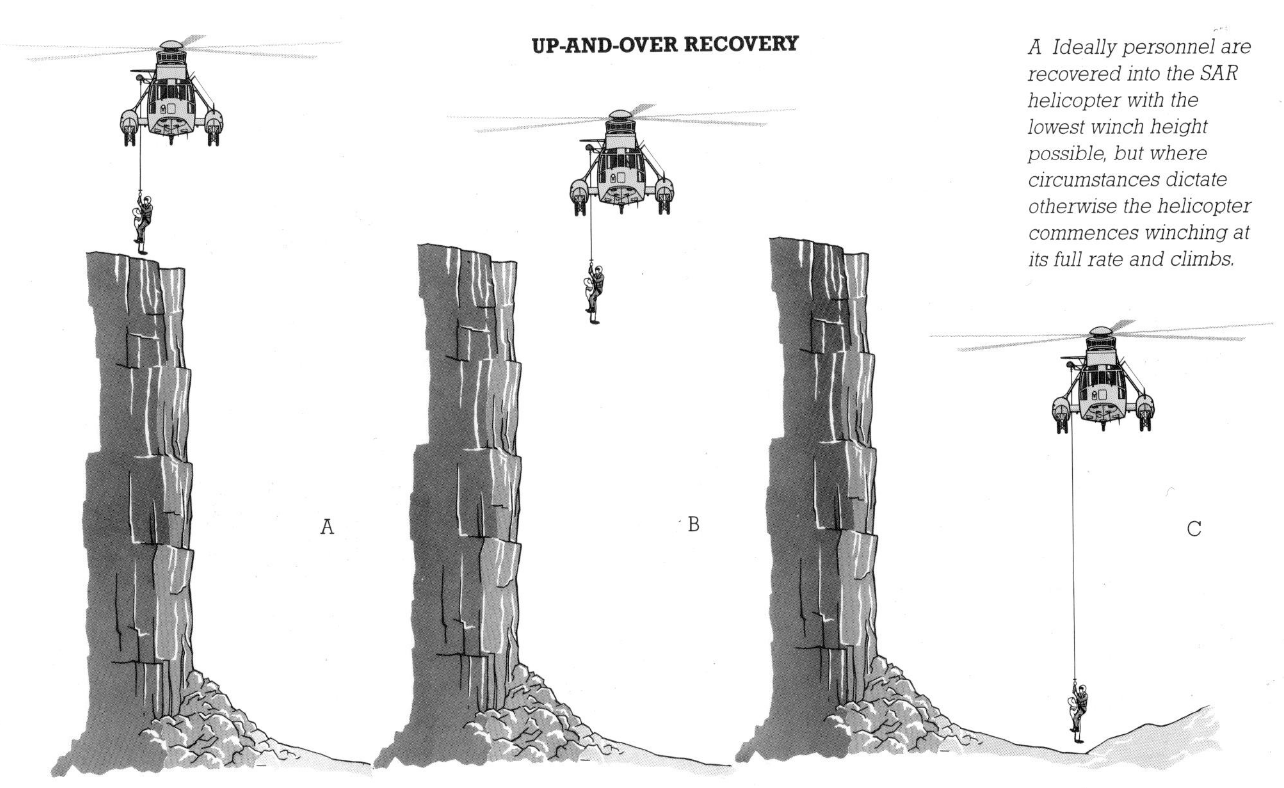

A Ideally personnel are recovered into the SAR helicopter with the lowest winch height possible, but where circumstances dictate otherwise the helicopter commences winching at its full rate and climbs.

B At the call 'height good', the pilot manoeuvres the helicopter to the cliff top overhead for maximum safety. The helicopter could alternatively move out from the cliff, over the sea, to complete the winching.

C Normal recovery is made on the cliff top; alternatively the winchman and survivor are lowered to the surface or a recovery is made via the main cabin door. As usual with all rescue situations it is not possible to generalize.

earth dislodged by the rotor down-draught nor by the winchman walking down the cliff face. For this reason, it is usual to avoid cliff walking as a technique on crumbling cliff faces and above over-hangs where there is also a risk of damaging the winch wire itself. This would, of course, prejudice the safety of the rescue.

The procedure begins with the winchman on the wire at the top of the cliff and the winch operator paying out cable to allow the winchman freedom of movement, while supporting him with the winch. The helicopter is usually positioned slightly 'into' the line of the cliff to give the winchman a better hold of the cliff face during the descent to the survivor.

Up-and-over recovery

Another technique used by SAR helicopters to take the winchman and survivor to a place of safety as quickly as possible. The reasoning is that they will be in potential 'danger' for less time. The winchman and survivor are winched clear of the ground at the full rate of 200 ft/min and the flying pilot climbs the helicopter until the winchman indicates that the 'height is good'. The helicopter is then flown smartly over a flat area where it descends to bring the winchman and survivor aboard at a height of 15 ft by conventional winching.

The technique was invented for the older generation of rescue helicopter with a limited power supply to the rescue hoist and it is not favoured by modern aircrew because the flying pilot loses his steady visual references as he climbs. It is rarely used for Sea King operations.

Winching techniques

The basic method of winching for Royal Air Force helicopter crews, although often modified by the situations in which rescue helicopters and their crews find

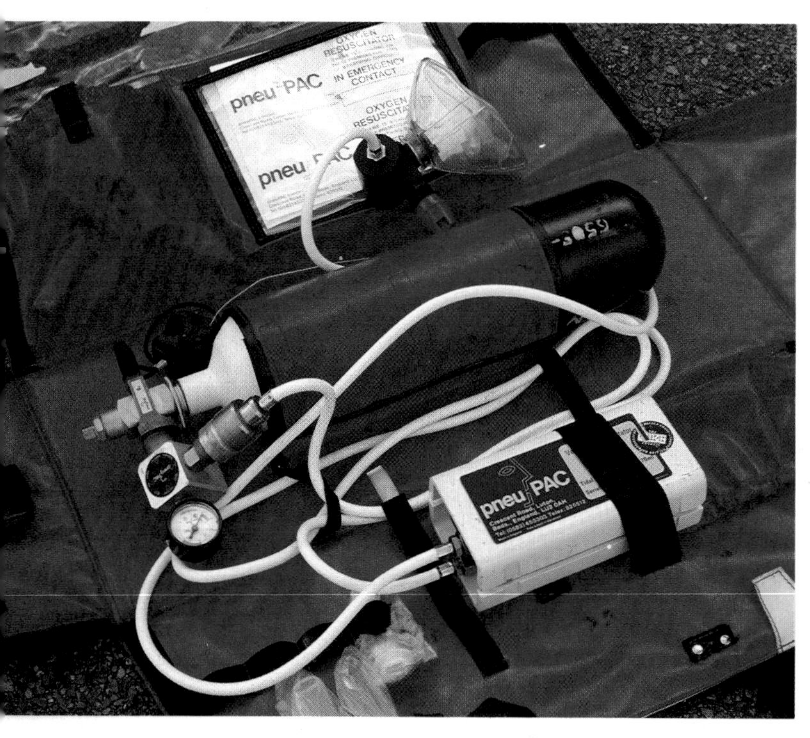

Above *Emergency oxygen unit carried at all times aboard all SAR helicopters.*

Above right *Bosun's chair style safety harness, worn by the helicopter's winchman.*

themselves, adheres to some basic principles.

The helicopter is always positioned to prevent the rescue winch wire from swinging the winchman and/or survivors with the load directly under the winch-arm. In the case of overhangs, the crew must make a value-judgement on the risk to the occupant(s) of the winch wire striking other objects if it is necessary to winch away from the overhead. For example, by extracting a winchman and survivor from a mountain crag, it might be necessary because of the cliff overhang, the rescue position and the risk to the helicopter's rotor disc to extract them with the helicopter positioned away from the vertical. In this case, the winch operator and flying pilot ensure that there are no other obstructions in the way, with which the winchman and his survivor might collide.

When commencing winching-in the winchman and/or survivors, the winch operator controls the operation from the helicopter's main cabin door by means of the hoist control. RAF crews never send down an empty strop because experience has shown it is dangerous: it could catch on an obstruction and even aircrew do not know exactly what to do with it! The Royal Navy and other rescue services occasionally send down an empty, weighted strop for single, aircrew lifts.

The flying pilot must be conscious of the winching operation and would have to modify the 'escape headings' used for an emergency. The winch operator reports 'winching in' to the pilots over the intercom. The operator continues to keep up a patter over the intercom to give the pilots a word picture of the winchman's progress. The pilots are seated some 30 ft (10 m) in front of the winch and, of course, cannot see the rescue being carried out below the helicopter.

Winching training and live recoveries, other than in exceptional circumstances,

take place at a safe height for the operation under way. The RAF has found over the years that the maximum safe heights for recovering the winchman and/or survivors into the helicopter's cabin are 15 to 20 ft (4.6 to 6 m) above a land surface and 40 to 50 ft (12 to 15 m) above the sea.

After the winchman and/or survivor leave the ground, deck of a ship or water, the winch operator will call 'clear of the ground (or deck or water)' and it is frequently necessary to move the helicopter away from the immediate overhead. This is particularly true for water rescues where there are others still to be picked up or where there is a risk of injuring further survivors with dust and debris on a mountainside. On a mountain, the Mountain Rescue Team will not want to be blown over the edge either!

To obtain this clearance, the winch operator will call 'move forward' or 'move left' as briefed during the initial reconnaissance of the site.

The Royal Air Force teaches its search and rescue aircrew seven basic rescue lifts to recover the winchman and/or survivors from land or sea environments. The basic techniques are flexible, not rigidly applied because the circumstances of every rescue or training exercise will be different and the techniques are modified to fit individual situations.

RESCUE LIFTS

The seven types of rescue lift mentioned earlier are:

- the single lift
- the double lift
- the single lift with two strops
- the stretcher lift
- the open-ended strop lift
- the physical grip lift
- the aircrew lift

All require skill and training to achieve safely and without putting the aircrew and survivors in peril. That is why the

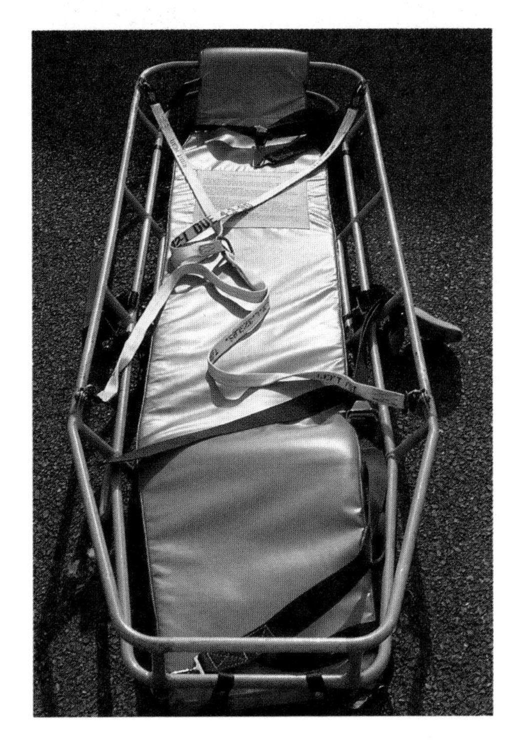

Below left *Another helicopter stretcher is the Stokes Litter.*

Below *The crew of a Sea King demonstrate the single lift technique during a training exercise.*

Royal Air Force, Royal Navy and HM Coastguard helicopter crews spend a considerable time flying training sorties rather than sitting on the ground waiting for the 'scramble' bell to sound.

The single lift. This method of recovery into the helicopter's cabin is principally used for training aircrew and other personnel. It can be carried out over land (dry winching) or over the water (wet winching) and both venues require a thorough briefing to the exercise survivor. It is now procedure to ensure that the practice survivor has undergone dry winching before being cast adrift in the water for exercise. The major concern must always be the risk that he will be hit and injured by the winch hook being lowered from the helicopter.

The basic method is very simple and includes some standard techniques which can be applied to all rescue lifts, including the earthing of the rescue strop by making it touch the surface prior to completing the final approach to the survivor. During normal flying a helicopter will create considerable static electricity and this must be discharged prior to any part of it touching anyone on the ground. When Mountain Rescue Teams and groundcrew operate with a helicopter, they are taught to earth it prior to attaching an underslung load.

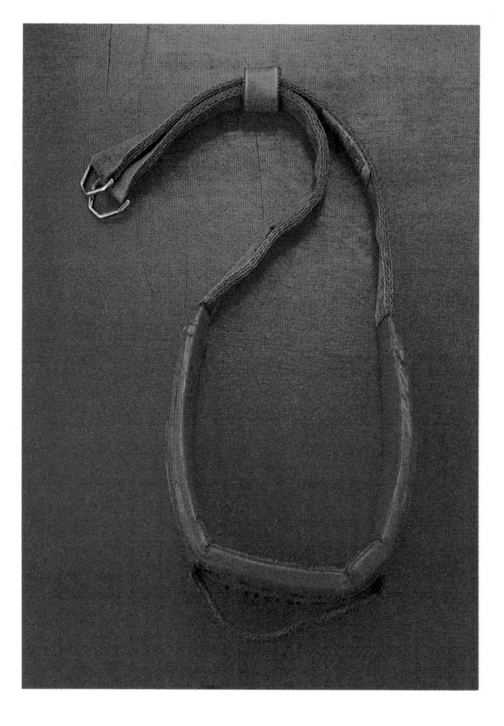

The standard rescue strop for winching survivors aboard the helicopter. The survivor puts his head and arms through the strop, with the padded section coming up under his armpits, and pulls the rubber toggle down as far as possible. Keeping his arms by his side, he is winched up to the helicopter and pulled aboard by the winch operator.

When presented with the strop, the survivor takes it firmly in hand and places it over his head and under his armpits. It is secured by adjusting the sliding toggle. When he is ready to be lifted he simply and clearly indicates this to the winch operator by looking up and giving a single 'thumbs up' signal. The operator, having satisfied himself that all is well, will then bring the survivor up to the aircraft and as the winch wire is wound in the survivor will keep his elbows to his side and hold the strop just above the toggle.

The standard procedure for all survivors on reaching the aircraft's cabin door level is to allow the winch operator and other aircrew to take over completely. The winch operator will reach out and turn the survivor away from the aircraft, put his arms around his waist (or seize the strop handling loop) to bring him aboard. At this stage, the operator may need to winch out some cable or call, over the intercom, for the pilots to take control of the winch and pay out cable at his command. When the survivor is safely in the cabin, he is extracted from the strop, placed on a convenient seat and strapped in.

During operational sorties, it is possible that circumstances will dictate the use of the single lift for a large number of survivors. In this case, it is necessary for the winchman to be lowered to the surface and to brief the survivors for a number of single lifts. It is standard practice for the winchman and last survivor to use a double lift.

The double lift. This is the standard method used by the Royal Air Force and HM Coastguard to rescue an uninjured survivor from the surface of the water, a life-raft/dinghy, deck of a ship or oil platform or anywhere over land.

In the cabin of the rescue helicopter running in to the rescue position the winchman and winch operator will work together to attach the Grabbit Hook; a NATO standard strop, earthing lead and the winchman himself are attached to the winch hook. As the helicopter nears the location, running into the overhead, the winchman and his kit are winched out and lowered to a position alongside the survivor.

Unless the survivor has a parachute still attached, the first job of the winchman on arrival is to secure himself to the survivor. This is carried out even before assessing that the survivor is not too badly injured to be rescued by the double lift method. A parachute must, however, be cut away first.

If the survivor is wearing a Service life-preserver or a parachute harness, the winchman can use the Grabbit Hook instead of the more cumbersome strop. This is used in heavy weather at sea when a rapid pick-up will prevent unnecessary exposure to the elements of the survivor and winchman. In the case of the parachute harness wearer, the winchman's first duty is to clear any vestige of the parachute canopy because to try and lift the survivor with this and its lines still attached to his harness would be most dangerous for him, the winchman and the crew of the rescue helicopter.

When the winchman is satisfied that all is correct and suitable for a double lift, he will signal the operator, who in turn checks that all is well and that the helicopter is in a safe position to commence the lift. As the winch wire is wound in, the winchman uses his legs to steady the survivor by putting him between and close to the helicopter, his main concern being to protect the survivor from contact with the airframe.

In Germany, this RAF Wessex HC 2 light support helicopter shows the double lift method of recovering a survivor from a forest location. (RAF/Barry Ellson.)

Generally, winch operators do not like the Grabbit Hook because it means that the survivor is more difficult to bring into the aircraft's cabin as he is suspended at a much lower position on the winch hook.

With the conventional double lift, the winchman should arrive at the helicopter's door facing inwards and the survivor facing outwards, protected against contact. The winchman pulls the survivor inboard, using his body to both shield and propel him into the cabin. Once unhooked from the winch, the survivor is seated and strapped in, the main door closed and the helicopter departs for hospital as needed.

The single lift with two strops. For certain injuries, medical advice suggests that survivors and patients should be winched into the rescue helicopter in the sitting position. This is especially true for appendicitis, one of the most common causes of medical evacuations

A Sea King's aircrew show how to recover a patient in a Neil Robertson stretcher. (Westland.)

from ships at sea by British rescue helicopters. The winchman loops a strop around the casualty's knees, making sure blood does not rush to his legs when he is pulled from the water, thus inducing shock. Shock has been known to kill in these conditions.

In some cases, the norm would be to use a stretcher but the nature of the wounds or illness can render this method unsatisfactory and even dangerous. For example, with immersion hypothermia, such as that likely to be experienced by aircrew who have parachuted into the sea, the vertical lift of a survivor in a double lift may cause blood to move to the lower limbs. This could be fatal. A double strop lift allows the survivor to be winched into the helicopter horizontally.

In addition, it is possible for a survivor in a two-strop rig to be lifted in the sitting position and this would benefit appendicitis and stomach wound casualties.

RAF winchmen in particular are trained to improvise during all rescue situations and there are times when a double lift with two strops has not been prepared for, leading to the use of a long lead strap as a jury-rigged second strop. This is usual only from dry locations.

The Neil Robertson stretcher lift. This stretcher was first issued to British rescue helicopter crews in the late 1960s and has proved to be invaluable as a device for rescuing injured civilians and military personnel alike. The Neil Robertson is especially useful for unconscious casualties.

Normal deployment is for the stretcher to be attached by its harness to the winch hook before the winchman attaches himself, thus allowing him to detach from the hook on the ground or ship's deck.

Because a casualty will take some time to be transferred into the Neil Robertson stretcher, the helicopter will move away from the rescue location to allow the winchman to work in relative peace and quiet. In this situation, he can communicate with the helicopter by hand-held radio and in the near future will be receiving an integrated helmet radio for all rescue situations.

A passenger-type life preserver is recommended for all stretcher winching over the sea and for transits back to hospital which are over water. It is usual to fix the life preserver to the stretcher for all but minor injuries.

On the deck of a ship, the winchman will usually be assisted by members of the crew to place and secure the survivor in the stretcher. On land, after a climbing accident, there is usually a companion available to assist but winchmen are trained to complete the work solo if circumstances dictate. The lifting harness is adjusted on the stretcher to ensure that the lift will be balanced. The helicopter is then signalled to return, either by radio or by using hand signals.

The stretcher harness and winchman

Neil Robertson stretcher in the stowed configuration for winching and carriage on the helicopter (1); at the incident location, the stretcher is opened out to allow the casualty to be placed on (2).

are attached to the helicopter's winch hook and the combination is now ready to be lifted into the helicopter. The lift proceeds in the normal way, except that the winchman will face the stretcher at all times and is careful to protect it from the main rotor downwash and contact with the side of the helicopter's airframe. The stretcher is kept in the fore-and-aft axis during this part of the recovery.

On reaching the cabin door level, the winch operator gives control of the winch to the pilots and prepares to bring the stretcher inboard. The winchman will turn the stretcher, with the aid of the winch operator and usually the use of the re-connected intercom for better communications, to bring the stretcher into the cabin head first.

The mountain rescue stretcher lift. Because Mountain Rescue Teams (MRTs) are often the first on the scene of a mountaineering or other upland rescue, the crews of all British search and rescue helicopters practise operating with the various equipment used by Royal Air Force and locally recruited teams. Four main types of MRT stretchers are encountered: MacInnes, Para Guard, Bell and Thomas. It is often inadvisable and impractical for a casu-

A Royal Navy crew recover a stretcher case from the deck of a ship.

CALLSIGNS AND RADIOS

SAR Helicopter Callsigns

Each search and rescue helicopter in the United Kingdom has its own callsign number which identifies its base location. The prefix for aircraft on emergency operations is 'Rescue' and for normal operations, including training flights, the aircraft is prefixed with its type designation.

For example, D Flight of 202 Squadron's first standby helicopter at RAF Lossiemouth is known as 'Sea King 137' or 'SKD 137' during normal flight operations but during a rescue mission the callsign changes to 'Rescue 137'.

The standard listing is:

Northern Rescue Co-ordination Centre (Pitreavie)

01-16	Fixed-wing aircraft (particularly the SAR Nimrod)
117-118	HMCG Sumburgh S-61N
119-120	HMCG Stornoway S-61N
121	Spare callsign
122-124	RAF Valley Wessex
125-127	RAF Coltishall Wessex
128-130	RAF Leconfield Sea King
131-133	RAF Boulmer Sea King
134-136	RAF Leuchars Wessex
137-139	RAF Lossiemouth Sea King
140-142	Northern Ireland operations
143-144	BP Petroleum Forties Field (North Sea)
145-146	Shell Brent Field (North Sea)
177-179	RNAS Prestwick Sea King

Southern Rescue Co-ordination Centre (Mount Wise)

51-65	Fixed-wing aircraft (Nimrod)
166-168	RAF Manston Sea King
169-171	RAF Chivenor Wessex
172-173	RNAS Portland Sea King
174-176	HMCG Lee-on-Solent S-61N
180-189	Spare
190-192	RAF Brawdy Sea King
193-199	RNAS Culdrose Sea King

Mountain Rescue Teams

These also have special callsigns which are usually prefixed by the word 'Alpine' and the current numerical listing is:

20 Stafford
21 Valley
22 Leuchars
23 Kinloss
24 Leeming
25 St Athan

Radio frequencies

It is vital that radio traffic is carefully controlled during a search and rescue operation. For this reason, international protocol has allowed the allocation of special frequencies to SAR operations. These frequencies are widely published in aviation, maritime and other 'must read' publications for those who make their business in the air or at sea.

A selected listing includes:

500 kHz	distress and calling
2182 kHz	Distress and calling
121.5 MHz	VHF(AM) distress (also known as aviation guard)
243.0 MHz	UHF(AM) distress
156.8 MHz	VHF(FM) (Channel 16) maritime distress
406.0 MHz	SARSAT (SAR Satellite)
5680 kHz	Primary day (all)
3023 kHz	Primary night (all)
5695 kHz	Primary day
3085 kHz	Primary night (UK)
244.6 MHz	Primary UHF (UK)
123.1 MHz	NATO Scene of Search
282.8 MHz	NATO Scene of Search
252.8 MHz	NATO SAR training

alty to be transferred from an MRT stretcher to the aircraft's standard Neil Robertson, so a working practice has been established to cater for the need to use a non-standard piece of equipment.

Problems could occur if the stretcher is collapsible, but by using the locking devices and a karabiner gate collar, any potential hazards are negated. If the stretcher is not rigged for helicopter winching it is normal practice to use a special four-legged nylon sling attached to the corners of the stretcher and gathered together with a karabiner to secure the sling to the winch hook.

Some HM Coastguard units are equipped with a modified Para Guard stretcher which has been cleared for direct winching into SAR helicopters.

The open-ended strop lift. For awkward rescues, such as those of a casualty on a cliff face in an insecure position, British rescue helicopter crews will use the open-ended strop technique. For this procedure one end of the strop is initially disconnected from the winch hook and used to secure the survivor as a priority.

Such potentially dangerous cliff rescues can be performed without the need for a full aerial reconnaissance and internal brief. It is vital, however, to pinpoint the survivor's position to allow for an approach to be made without hazard from the main rotor downwash. It requires considerable flying skills to bring the helicopter into a position where the winchman, suspended on the cable, is brought to the correct height immediately before reaching the survivor's position.

In such awkward positions, the winchman is trained to dismantle the strop assembly and to slide the open-ended line around the survivor and reconnect it on to the Grabbit or winch hook. It is possible that there will be no opportunity to re-assemble the strop assembly but winching can still safely take place in this situation. The winch operator will ensure that the strops are brought together at the cabin door.

The physical grip lift. Although very small children can be lifted face-to-face with the winchman and without the use of a strop, it is highly undesirable for anyone larger to be brought to the helicopter without a strop or other safety device.

The involuntary physical grip lift is potentially very dangerous and alarming for the winchman and survivor because it is unpredictable and because a frightened survivor could lose his strength and therefore his grip very rapidly.

If a survivor does grab at the winchman and become dependent on him, the winch operator will direct the flying pilot to bring the helicopter over the sea or to the nearest suitable place where a traditional strop lift can be carried out. SAR helicopter crews are taught that decisive flying is vital to the successful outcome of such an emergency and, if all else fails, the winchman is to use his legs to secure a survivor to prevent him becoming inverted and then present a very difficult problem to bring into the aircraft. The procedure has been carried out successfully but it is never tested during training.

The aircrew lift. All British military search and rescue helicopters will treat the rescue of military aircrew and other Service personnel as a priority. It is especially hazardous work, particularly if the aircrew survivor still has his parachute attached.

The potential hazard of parachutes and the winchman was graphically demonstrated in November 1980 when a Sea King from 202 Squadron's C Flight, then based at RAF Coltishall, was scrambled to pick up the pilot of a US Air

The aircrew lift is the standard method of recovery for military personnel and in this case is being carried out with a double lift.

Force A-10A Thunderbolt II fighter-bomber. He had parachuted into the sea in 5 m (15 ft) waves and 45 knot (85 km/h) winds. Master Air Loadmaster Dave Bullock and the American pilot, Lt Colonel William Olsen died when they became entangled in the parachute and the winch cable parted. This first fatal accident in the history of Royal Air Force and Royal Navy helicopter SAR operations led to the USAF modifying its parachute release mechanism and a call for all SAR helicopters to have secondary emergency winches. The latter has never come about.

All aircrew who have ejected from military aircraft are deemed to have back injuries, even if there is no evidence of such when the winchman reaches the scene. Over land, it is relatively simple to strap the survivor into the Neil Robertson stretcher but in the sea it is different. Great care is taken to lift the survivor by the double lift method and to transfer him to a stretcher inside the helicopter's cabin immediately afterwards for the transit to hospital.

THE WINCHMAN

The most visible member of the aircrew is the winchman. Helicopter winchmen are a blend of experience, courage and tenacity so necessary for a job which can require them to put themselves in jeopardy to save another's life.

Like all military search and rescue personnel, the winchman's primary training and role is devoted to military tasks which might include extracting an injured pilot from a crashed high-performance fighter aircraft. But from the very first days of helicopter SAR operations in the United Kingdom, the winchman found himself dealing directly with members of the public — stranded walkers, injured climbers or the victims of disaster at sea.

RAF helicopter winchmen are invariably drawn from serving support helicopter aircrewmen and loadmasters on transport aircraft, but these senior non-commissioned officers can also come from other flying departments of the Royal Air Force.

In the day-to-day routine of SAR operations, the winchman is responsible for the condition and availability of all the rescue equipment, including the medical supplies carried aboard the Sea King and Wessex helicopters.

All helicopters, but particularly SAR aircraft, carry their own survival equipment for the crew members and other passengers who might be aboard, for use should the helicopter make a forced landing away from base.

The specialist rescue equipment carried aboard all SAR helicopters includes the 'monkey strap' harness for security in the cabin, but ease of movement as well. Very pistols and cartridges for determining wind direction and signalling to other aircraft, ships and ground units are also carried. The winch is run out and checked for satisfactory operation immediately prior to take-off.

Irrespective of weather conditions, if the helicopter can fly then the winchman will risk his life to save another. Winchman Bill Payne swings into action from Rescue 137 over the snowy Cairngorms to aid an injured climber.

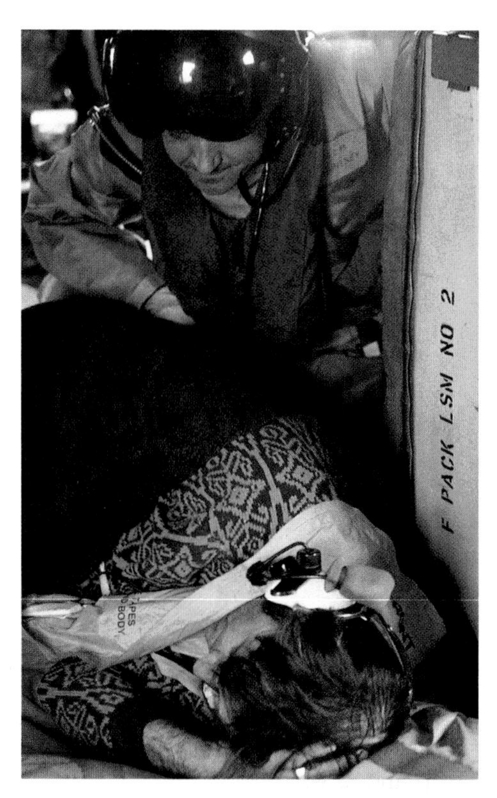

Right *A high level of first aid experience is taught to RAF SAR winchmen. Here Bob Poutney comforts an injured seaman winched aboard Rescue 137 for medical evacuation to Aberdeen Royal Infirmary.*

In the Mountains
Far right *Ian Bonthrone wears the standard clothing for search and rescue operations in the mountains — the Gortex shell jacket, with Gortex salopettes, 'yeti' gaiters and climbing boots. Because of the emergency equipment it contains — flares and a personal locator beacon — the winchman also wears the standard issue lifejacket. His rucksack contains a sleeping bag, ice axe, crampons and emergency rations for use if the helicopter cannot recover the winchman after he has left the aircraft.*

At Sea
The SAR winchman wears the standard yellow one-piece immersion suit complete with integral boots. In his standard issue lifejacket there are flares and a personal locator beacon. Ian Bonthrone is also wearing the bons'n's chair harness for attachment to the winch.

On return from a sortie during which the winch was used, it is run out to its full extent and thoroughly checked for faults. A winchman's life depends on its smooth operation.

At the scene of a rescue, if the winchman is likely to detach himself from the winch hook to effect the rescue, it is normal for him to carry a portable radio. For several years trials have been under way for the winchman to be fitted with an integrated helmet/radio to allow two-way communications with the helicopter even when on the winch.

The winchman is trained to cope with almost all emergencies as a first 'responder' and will often carry out the first aid treatment on a survivor to enable him to be stabilized for a lift into the helicopter. For this purpose, the helicopter has a first aid kit for the winchman to take down on the winch and has a variety of lifting gear, including a double strop and stretcher.

General Flying over Sea/Land
The basic dress is the standard, green one-piece immersion suit, known as the goon suit. It has sealed foot-pieces over which the winchman generally wears climbing boots. Again the standard issue lifejacket is worn with the bos'n's chair harness for winching out of the helicopter.

Far left *Bill Payne, dressed for mountain operations, brings a 'volunteer survivor' aboard Sea King 137 during a demonstration at Aviemore. SAR helicopters, as part of regular training sorties, will take part in local fêtes, galas and shows as part of a public relations effort.*

Left *Detached from the helicopter during routine training in Sutherland, winchman Dave Warmsley keeps in contact using the Pye radiophone. He is dressed in the summer rig of flying coverall, flying jacket and life-jacket.*

Right *Bill Payne.*

Middle right *Ian 'Bonnie' Bonthrone.*

Far right *Paul 'Chox' Barton.*

Right *Dave Aitkin.*

Far right *Bob Pountney (centre) with Paul Readfern (Flight Commander) and rad op/winch operator, Bill Reid (foreground), at a shift change briefing.*

Below *Looking aft from the Sea King's main cabin door, Bob Pountney checks that the tail rotor is clear of obstructions as the helicopter turns into wind for a scramble take-off into the Scottish Highlands.*

THE RADAR OPERATOR

Completing the standard RAF helicopter aircrew complement of four is the radar operator, who doubles as the winch operator. He is also winchman-trained and in long and difficult rescues can change places with the winchman to assist in operations outside the helicopter.

Radar operator duties are only carried in the RAF Sea King SAR helicopter as the Wessex does not have the provision of radar. The standard Wessex crew is three — pilot, winch operator and winchman.

Generally, the radar operator is responsible for the radar, navigation equipment and other instruments in the rear cabin of the Sea King. Recruitment is at officer or senior non-commissioned officer level and many operators have experienced tours on Shackleton airborne early warning and Nimrod maritime reconnaissance aircraft before being selected for search and rescue.

On reaching the scene of an incident, the radar operator becomes the winch operator. He carries out the vital role of directing the helicopter and is totally responsible for positioning in all three planes — height, left and right movement and forward and backward movement. He is responsible for the winchman's safety and can fly the helicopter by means of the auxiliary hover trim with automatic heading control. He also watches for obstructions during winching, such as a vessel's rigging, and in the mountains or near cliffs he is on the alert to minimize the risk of striking an obstruction.

As the helicopter approaches the winching point, the main cabin door is opened by the winch operator or winch-

Steve Larke checks the harness and strops before descending from the relative safety of Rescue 137.

Right *Steve 'Larky' Larke, in the role of winch operator.*

Middle right *Paul 'Gramps' Challice (with non-issue helmet!).*

Far right *Steve 'Griff' Griffin.*

Right *Bill Reid.*

Right *Pat Thirkell.*

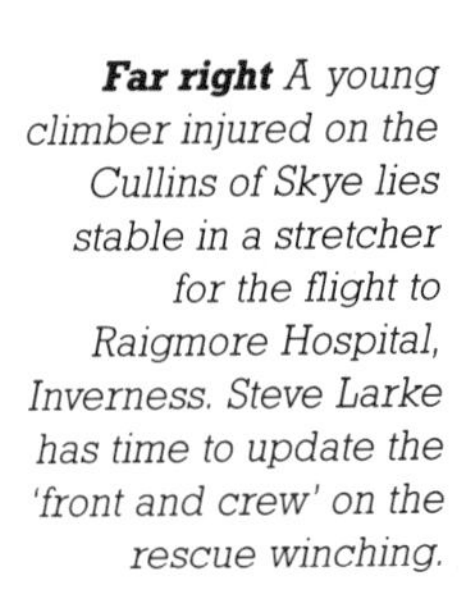

Far right *A young climber injured on the Cullins of Skye lies stable in a stretcher for the flight to Raigmore Hospital, Inverness. Steve Larke has time to update the 'front and crew' on the rescue winching.*

man. The former then begins to scan the scene for obstructions which will effect the helicopter manoeuvring into a position to winch. These will have been located on the initial reconnaissance of the site but it is vital that the pilot — sitting nearly 20 ft further forward — is aware of all nearby obstructions. Some of these hazards might only become apparent during the final run in to the rescue.

The winch operator briefs the situation using the neumonic of 3Hs, 3Es:

- **Hazards:** clear of birds, coils of rope and so on;
- **Height:** clear of masts by 5 ft minimum;
- **Heading:** into wind;
- **Entry:** move right to the overhead position;
- **Exit:** move left to start point;
- **Escape:** in case of emergency: dead ahead

During the winching operation, the winch operator passes a regular stream of information to the flying pilot, including manoeuvring instructions to keep the helicopter in the best position relative to the rescue and the wind conditions. If there are any obstructions on the port side of the helicopter, it is the job of the co-pilot to ensure safe clearance, allowing the winch operator to concentrate on the well-being of the aircraft and winchman on the wire below.

Although the radar operator will always take over the role of winch operator during a rescue, it is essential, according to RAF standard operating procedures, that the two roles are taught as one responsibility. The role of winch operator and winchman are also interchangeable but rarely, in an actual rescue, will the winch operator have to go down the wire and act as winchman.

However, the RAF Search & Rescue Wing trains its rear aircrew with both roles in mind.

In normal operations, the co-pilot is responsible for the operation of the Tactical Air Navigation System (TANS) and other navigational avionics. He also monitors all the communication frequencies and in the event of a systems failure with the TANS the radar operator is capable of navigating the helicopter back to base using the radar.

THE PILOTS

The Royal Air Force operates helicopters to support the British Army in the battlefield, for liaison and transport, as well as for search and rescue. Pilots for all these operational roles are trained in the United Kingdom to the same basic level.

Steve Hodgson (right) and Paul Berriff discuss a refinement to the filming in the rescue flight's operations room.

Helicopter pilot selection is made at the end of the trainee's basic flying training course after between 70 and 100 hours of flying the Jet Provost/Tucano fixed-wing training aircraft. During this period a common syllabus for all pilot training — fast jet, multi-engined or helicopter — is followed.

At the selection point, Group 3 pilots are posted to RAF Shawbury for Phase 1 rotary-wing training on the Aerospatiale Gazelle light training helicopter for 80 hours. The successful graduates from the basic rotary phase then move to Phase 2 on the Shawbury-based Wessex twin-engined helicopter. During this time, basic search and rescue techniques are taught to the pilots because most RAF helicopters, including the Wessex, Puma and Chinook battlefield support type have the capability of carrying out SAR missions should circumstances dictate.

Candidates for first tours on SAR helicopters — Wessex or Sea King — are then posted to RAF Valley for the SAR Training Unit's extended search and rescue course, flying the Westland Wessex.

Pilots who qualify from this course and are destined for the Wessex helicopters of No 22 Squadron will be posted to a Wessex Flight as first tour pilots. Those destined for the Sea Kings of No 202 Squadron will then spend a further five months at Royal Naval Air Station

Far left *Steve Martin.*

Middle left *John Prince and Simon 'Slug' Willson.*

Left *Don Strother, the US Coast Guard exchange pilot.*

Far left *John 'TC' Tennyson-Collins.*

Far left *Paul Readfern, Flight Commander.*

Left *A last visual check of the Sea King as Paul Readfern completes the outside pre-flight checks.*

Paul Readfern's Sea King 'front office' — a summertime overland training sortie.

Culdrose in Cornwall with the RAF Sea King Training Unit.

At the RAF SKTU, there is an intensive course of ground school, use of the Royal Navy's Sea King simulator and type conversation to the Sea King. During the period at Culdrose, the pilots will be trained in the SAR role but are unlikely to be called upon for SAR stand-by. The successful graduate from the SKTU is then posted to a Flight of 202 Squadron as a pilot.

It takes between 12 and 18 months for a first tour Sea King pilot to achieve operational captaincy but during his first few months with the Flight he will stand-by for operations, alternately flying the left-hand (co-pilot) or right-hand (first pilot's) seat for training. He will not be able to act as the captain of the aircraft on rescues until deemed fit to do so by the commanding officer of 202 Sqn.

On No 202 Squadron a 'first tourist' pilot will spend three years on the same Flight before being either re-posted to that unit for a second tour of three years or moving to another Flight to complete six years in the SAR role. Operational demands often contrive to alter such a programme, especially with commitments for Sea King aircrew in the Falkland Islands.

It is possible for an SAR pilot to be appointed the deputy flight commander towards the end of his second tour with No 202 Squadron and, although there is no standard rule, he could expect to be posted as a Flight Commander for his third tour on type.

The Flight Commander's slot need not be filled by a pilot and although it is always a position held by an officer, there are a number of navigators and radar operators who have carried out this task.

A support helicopter pilot, perhaps flying the Puma or Chinook, can be selected for transfer to the SAR world and will then undergo a conversion to the Sea King at RNAS Culdrose. It is normal for an experienced helicopter pilot, without an SAR background, to spend three years with his first SAR Flight.

ROYAL NAVY SEARCH & RESCUE

Although today the Royal Air Force provides the bulk of the United Kingdom's search and rescue helicopters, the Royal Navy's Fleet Air Arm was the first British armed service to experiment with helicopters and pioneered search and rescue.

Initially, Fleet Air Arm SAR was orientated towards the provision of helicopters to act as plane guards aboard the fixed-wing aircraft carriers and at Royal Naval Air Stations. Today, the role is integrated within the UK SAR set-up and the Royal Navy has specific areas of responsibility. These are primarily in the south-west of England, along the Dorset coast and the Clyde approaches in Scotland.

The Royal Navy formed the UK's first all-helicopter general-purpose unit in the late 1940s with the acquisition of the first Sikorsky Hoverfly and Dragonfly helicopters. The Dragonfly was then produced under licence by Westland and later modified for the SAR role.

During the Korean War, the Fleet Air Arm learned a great deal about air-sea rescue when the Dragonfly was operated on plane-guard duties, saving many aircrew from ditched, damaged aircraft.

In 1952/53, the first Dragonfly HR 3 helicopters began the first search and rescue operations in the vicinity of the local naval air stations and a great deal of experience was gained during the East Anglian and Dutch floods of 1953.

The RAF's Fighter Command briefly examined the Dragonfly, but it was the Royal Navy which pioneered the helicopter's use at Brawdy and Lossiemouth (now RAF stations with Sea King SAR flights) and RNAS Culdrose, still the home of Fleet Air Arm medium helicopter operations.

The success of the Dragonfly was built upon, especially, for shipborne use where the helicopter was a vital part of the aircraft carrier's inventory in the early days of operational jet aircraft flying. The far more adequate Whirlwind was introduced to SAR in November 1955 and the piston-engined version continued in widespread service for a further nine years. The Whirlwind could accommodate more survivors and had a greater endurance.

Again its operations were principally concerned with the rescue of downed aircrew during aircraft carrier and naval air station flying training. Some 20 of the Mk 3s were built for the Fleet Air Arm and a limited number of specially modified versions, the Mk 5, with a new tail cone were introduced a year later.

Like the RAF, the Royal Navy investigated the use of gas turbine-powered helicopters for search and rescue duties, especially in the Antarctic with the Ice Patrol Ship and for the Royal Naval Air Stations at Brawdy, Culdrose and Lee-on-Solent. The gas turbine power plant changed the profile of the Whirlwind to give it a bulbous nose but the resultant increase in power and safety more than compensated for the loss of good looks.

ROYAL NAVY
RESCUE
22
RESCUE
822
47-030

During the rundown of the Royal Navy's strike aircraft carrier force, the Fleet Air Arm relinquished command of two principal air stations at Lossiemouth and Brawdy, to RAF control. This had little effect on naval helicopter operations because the carrier-based anti-submarine warfare helicopters were redeployed to 'Tiger' class cruisers, Royal Fleet Auxiliaries and eventually the smaller 'Invincible' class light aircraft carriers.

From mid-1975, the UK Ministry of Defence brought SAR into the front-line operational capabilities of the Sea King squadrons at Culdrose and Prestwick. A Sea King was kept at readiness of no more than 120 minutes, day or night, at both naval air stations. By 1985, the Royal Navy was operating SAR helicopters on standby within the parameters of a 90 minutes readiness for Sea Kings at Prestwick and 15 minutes readiness for the Wessex HU 5s at Lee-on-Solent and Culdrose, as well as the Culdrose-based Sea Kings.

The phasing out of the Wessex helicopter from Royal Naval service in 1988 led to an increasing burden being placed upon the front-line and training Sea King anti-submarine warfare units. In addition to the ASW Sea King helicopters at Culdrose and Prestwick, the less sophisticated, daylight only, Westland Sea King HC 4 has now entered service with 772 Squadron. The Sea King Mk 4 is normally used for Royal Marine Commando assault and re-supply operations.

Following the privatization of the SAR operation at RNAS Lee-on-Solent in April 1988 and the withdrawal of the Wessex from Portland, a detachment from 772 Naval Air Squadron now provides cover in the Weymouth and Lyme Bay areas, flying the Sea King Mk 4.

Following the nationwide review of the SAR commitment in 1988, the readiness of SAR helicopters at Culdrose and Prestwick was shortened to 15 minutes by day, 45 minutes by night. For a while Prestwick continued at 90 minutes notice day and night, but from 1 August 1989 it has followed Culdrose's readiness times. This aligns the civil SAR tasking of the Fleet Air Arm with that of the Royal Air Force and HM Coastguard. The SAR service is provided by a primary aircraft with a second stand-by or reserve aircraft at each location.

These changes, linked to the RAF's replacement of the Manston-based flight by Sea Kings and the provision of an HM Coastguard S-61N helicopter at Lee-on-Solent, means that all gaps in British SAR cover in the English Channel have been eradicated and in fact the coverage has been enhanced considerably.

In the South-West Approaches and around the coast of the Republic of Ireland into the North Atlantic, Culdrose's Sea King HAR 5s share the work in really bad weather with RAF Brawdy. RNAS Prestwick can also provide a UK SAR coverage supplement for parts of Scotland and Northern Ireland.

Special equipment

Amongst the Fleet Air Arm's contribu-

Above *The Wessex was a stalwart helicopter in Fleet Air Arm service and its many roles included SAR coverage of the Portland Sea areas with 772 Naval Air Squadron. It is pictured here working with Weymouth lifeboat.* (Rolls-Royce/Peter Scott.)

Far left *In 1988, soon after 771 Naval Air Squadron at RNAS Culdrose received the Sea King HAR Mk 5, it commenced working up with local rescue services, including the Falmouth lifeboat.* (RN/Culdrose.)

A Royal Navy Whirlwind deploys SAR divers. Ark Royal *is in the background.*

tion to search and rescue flying has been the advent of the SAR diver, a trade developed after some serious losses from aircraft carriers during flying operations. The SAR diver is trained to stay with a stricken, ditched aircraft and go down with it to recover the aircrew. It is very simple to transfer the technique to more traditional SAR around the coast of the United Kingdom. Many holidaymakers, divers, sailors and yachtsmen owe their lives to the skill and bravery of SAR divers who have recovered them from trapped positions underwater.

The SAR diver has now been adopted by the US Navy for aircraft carrier operations although the RAF is satisfied that its needs are slightly different and it will continue to fly with SAR winchmen only.

Another equipment/technique export from the Royal Navy is the Sproule net pioneered in 1951/52. Although no longer used by the British forces it has been successfully developed in Canada and the United States for survivor recovery.

The net enables an inexperienced or injured survivor to be recovered to the helicopter's cabin by a simple net, dragged through the water whilst attached to the rescue winch.

A Westland-built Dragonfly helicopter equipped with an early development of the rescue winch.

RN SAR HELICOPTER SPECIFICATIONS

Dragonfly HR Mk 3

Manufacturer: Westland Helicopters Ltd; Crew: 1 pilot, 1 aircrewman; Cabin: 3 survivors; Maiden flight: 1952; Service: 1952-1960; Range: 300 nm (556 km); Max speed: 89 kts (166 km/h); Power plant: 1 × Alvis Leonides 50 (520 shp) piston engine; All-up weight: 5,871 lb (2,663 kg).

Whirlwind HAR Mk 3

Manufacturer: Westland Helicopters Ltd; Crew: 1 pilot, 1 aircrewman/winch operator, 1 winchman; Cabin: up 8 survivors; Maiden flight: 1954; Service: 1955-64; Range: 278 nm (515 km); Max speed: 86 kts (159 km/h); Power plant: 1 × Wright Cyclone R-1300 (700 shp) piston engine; All-up weight: 7,500 lb (3,402 kg).

Whirlwind HAR Mk 5

Data as for Whirlwind HAR Mk 3, except Service: 1956-60; and Power Plant: 1 × Alvis Leonides Major (750 shp) piston engine.

Whirlwind HAR Mk 9
Manufacturer: Westland Helicopters Ltd; Crew: 1/2 pilot(s), 1 aircrewman/ winch operator, 1 winchman/SAR diver; Cabin: up to 10 survivors; Maiden flight: 1965; Service: 1966-77; Range: 300 nm (556 km); Max speed: 92 kts (170 km/h); Power plant: 1 × Rolls-Royce/Bristol Gnome H-1000 (1,050 shp) turboshaft engine; All-up weight: 8,000 lb (3,629 kg).

Wessex HU Mk 5
Manufacturer: Westland Helicopters Ltd; Crew: 1/2 pilot(s), 1 aircrewman, winch operator, 1 winchman/SAR diver; Cabin: up to 16 seated survivors; Maiden flight: 1963; Service: 1963-88; Range: 416 nm (770 km); Max speed: 132 kts (245 km/h); Power plants: 2 × Rolls-Royce/ Bristol Gnome H-1200 (1,350 shp) gas turbines; All-up weight: 13,492 lb (6,120 kg).

Sea King HAS Mk 2
Manufacturer: Westland Helicopters Ltd; Crew: 2 pilots, 1 observer/winch operator, 1 sonar operator/winchman (plus 1 SAR diver as required); Cabin: up to 10 seated survivors; Maiden flight: 1976; Service: 1976-85; Range: 664 nm (1,230 km); Max speed: 144 kts (267 km/h); Power plants: 2 × Rolls-Royce Gnome H1400-1 (1,600 shp) turboshafts; All-up weight 21,000 lb (9,525 kg).

Sea King HC Mk 4
Manufacturer: Westland Helicopters Ltd; Crew: 2 pilots, 1 aircrewman/winch operator, 1 winchman/SAR diver; Cabin: up to 28 seated survivors but with SAR equipment fitted can carry 18 seated survivors; Maiden flight: 1973; Service: 1979-date; Range: 664 nm, (1,230 km); Max speed: 113 kts (210 km/h); Power plants: 2 × Rolls-Royce Gnome H1400-1 (1,660 shp) turboshaft engines; All-up weight: 21,000 lb (9,525 kg). This helicopter is generally used for commando support operators but has been modified for daylight SAR duties from RNAS Portland, Dorset. Portland's task for the Department of Trade is to provide one Sea King and one crew at 15 minutes notice during the day. Only military SAR is flown at night, using the flight control system in the Doppler mode. The aircraft is fitted with a maritime and air band VHF homer.

Sea King HAS Mk 5
Data as Sea King HAS Mk 2, except

After retirement from SAR duties, Westland Whirlwinds were used for pilot training at RNAS Culdrose. (RN/Culdrose.)

Sea King HAR Mk 5 recovering an SAR diver during a training exercise in the English Channel. (RN/Culdrose).

Maiden flight: 1980; Service: 1980-date.

Sea King HAR Mk 5

Data as Sea King HAS Mk 2, except that it entered service in 1988 at RNAS Culdrose and is optimized for SAR operations. This type has a very distinctive light 'whale grey' overall colour scheme with the Royal Navy's dayglo red fuselage and nose markings, identified by the 'Ace of Clubs' emblem of 771 Naval Air Squadron. It can carry ten seated survivors.

Sea King HAS Mk 6

Over the next three years, the Sea King Mk 6 will replace the Mk 5 throughout the Fleet Air Arm. This has already started with 819 Naval Air Squadron at Prestwick. The technical specification is the same as the Mk 5, the exception being that only eight survivors can be carried although the communications system has been updated. In some circumstances, the sonar could be used to assist in the location of wreckage and ditched aircraft.

Practising over the cliffs of the Dorset coast, this Portland-based Sea King HC Mk 4 is pictured training for cliff walking. In this case, only a short length of the 250 feet winch wire is necessary. (RN/Portland.)

The Culdrose SAR team stand in front of a Sea King HAR Mk5 and the emergency service vehicles needed for each and every rescue mission to be a success. (RN.)

Weymouth lifeboat and one of 772 Naval Air Squadron's Sea King Mk 4s practice single-lift personnel transfers. Note the horse collar-style strop being lowered from the helicopter. (RN/Portland.)

COMMERCIAL SAR HELICOPTER OPERATIONS

Although there was considerable press speculation surrounding the United Kingdom Ministry of Defence's examination of the unsolicited bid by Bristow Helicopter Company Ltd to civilianize or 'civilize' (the company's term for privatization) all United Kingdom SAR helicopter operations during 1987-88, the use of commercial helicopters for such operations is not a new phenomenon.

The advent of North Sea oil brought about a dramatic increase in the number of civilian-registered helicopters in the country. The sector which grew rapidly was the intermediate/medium size helicopters like the Sikorsky S-61N, a cousin of the ubiquitous Sea King. In addition, the number of smaller, light/intermediate helicopters, like the Bell 212 twin-engined type for inter-rig transport, also increased.

In 1971, the forerunner of today's commercial SAR contracts was launched with the Department of Trade (as it was then), on behalf of HM Coastguard, at RAF Manston in Kent. During the contract's duration, 668 sorties were flown and 108 people were rescued or transferred by the Whirlwind helicopters.

Almost simultaneously funded was a British European Airways Helicopters (later British Airways Helicopters, now British International Helicopters) Sikorsky S-61N on 60-minutes readiness for HM Coastguard at Aberdeen.

The helicopter was equipped with a detachable winch and could quickly be fitted to carry stretchers and resuscitation equipment. The operator was even able to supply some ex-RN and RAF winchmen/winch operators and several pilots undergoing SAR training. Like so many commercial companies operating helicopters in the North Sea, BEAH, like Bristow, was able to recruit highly trained service personnel who in turn could train the company's people.

A British Petroleum contract commenced in February 1978 for SAR services using Bristow Helicopters S-61N Mk IIs based at Aberdeen and offshore in the oil company's Forties oil field. This unit flew 179 sorties and rescued 780 people, including the single emergency evacuation of the crane barge *Hermod* with 527 being successfully transferred.

British European Airways Helicopters/British Airways Helicopters held the Aberdeen contract for about seven years but by the beginning of the 1980s the contract had moved to Sumburgh, on the southern tip of the Shetland Islands, and to the control of the Bristow company with its SAR-fitted helicopters.

Bristow had also been operating an inter-rig shuttle and casualty evacuation service for Shell Expro since 1979 using the Bell 212, hangared at Unst, in the Shetland Islands. The helicopter has been updated to carry Flight Path Control and Auto-Hover, as well as the specialist Forward Looking Infra-Red to spot survivors in the water. The service provides a rapid flying doctor facility and can be used to ferry injured or sick

HM Coastguard charters three Sikorsky S-61N Mk II helicopters from Bristow Helicopters to support operations in parts of Scotland and the English Channel. This S-61N is pictured exercising with an 'Arun' class lifeboat of the RNLI.

In the early 1970s, the UK Board of Trade chartered a number of Westland Whirlwind helicopters for SAR duties at RAF Manston. There is now a resident flight of RAF Sea King helicopters at Manston. (Bristow/ Malcom Pendrill.)

The Sumburgh-based S-61N Mk II during a winching demonstration.

personnel to the mainland. The helicopters are now integrated within the UK SAR service and can be called upon by the RCC at Pitreavie Castle, Dunfirmline. By the end of 1988, more than 330 sorties had been flown and more than 300 people rescued or evacuated.

Bristow was an obvious choice for HM Coastguard to launch a helicopter rescue service to fill in one of the major gaps in the military cover. In December 1983 negotiations were completed to commence a civil-registered and Department of Trade-funded search and rescue helicopter operation from Sumburgh, taking over the British Airways Helicopters contract.

The helicopter in use is the S-61N Mk II supported from the Bristow main base at Aberdeen. The helicopter proved its worth in November 1986 when, on a training flight from Sumburgh (Shetland Islands), the aircrew sighted the wreck of the British International Airways Boeing 234 tandem-rotor helicopter. Through careful and skilful flying the crew managed to locate and rescue the only two survivors. More than 230 other call-outs have been answered.

With the continued development of oil-related exploration operations and another gap in the UK cover in the Outer Hebrides, it was decided to station another helicopter at Stornoway.

In any case, Stornoway is increasing in importance to NATO as a forward operating base. However, it was decided to put the Stornoway operation out to tender in 1987 as the Royal Air Force's SAR operations were stretched with existing UK and Falkland Island commitments. The operation began in May 1987 and over 140 persons have since been successfully transferred to hospital for emergency medical attention or rescued from mountains and the water.

In 1988, however, there was a near disaster when the resident S-61N, callsign Rescue 119, crashed during a search and rescue operation for missing fishermen. The crew were successfully rescued by a Sea King from RAF Lossiemouth just 35 minutes later and the crew of four taken to Lewis Hospital in the Outer Hebrides. The wrecked helicopter was recovered and taken to Aberdeen. A subsequent enquiry reported that the S-61N's pilot lost his bearings whilst hovering at 200 ft over the sea and that the helicopter actually flew backwards into the water. The particular night-time conditions were very bad for helicopter operations, especially after a fault in the attitude direction indicator.

Also in 1988, the Royal Navy closed its SAR Flight at RNAS Lee-on-Solent at the mouth of Southampton Water, overlooking the Isle of Wight and the busy pleasure-boating areas of the nearby English Channel. Although a RAF Sea King (and a 22 Squadron Wessex HC 2) were temporarily posted there, the contract for the SAR cover from Selsey Bill, Sussex, to Weymouth Bay, Dorset,

was eventually let to Bristow Helicopters who again provided a single S-61N from 1 June 1988.

With this commercial SAR experience, Bristow Helicopters proposed to the UK Ministry of Defence that commercial contracts could replace all SAR helicopters around the British Isles. Bristow claimed that the Aerospatiale AS 332L Super Puma and the Sikorsky S-61N Mk II, modified with auto-hover, FLIR (Forward Looking Infra-Red) and a multi-frequency radio homing facility would be more effective than the Royal Air Force/Royal Navy Wessex and Sea King fleet.

Bristow proposed to base 14 Bell 212 helicopters around the UK coast to replace the Wessex, and 20 Super Pumas or S-61Ns to replace the Sea Kings. The Super Puma offered not only greater range but the ability to operate in icing conditions. The keys to the Bristow approach were competitive tendering and the ability of a civilian service to cut costs by more than 40 per cent. This claim by the company was never substantiated as no specification for the contract was ever agreed. Bristow told the UK Ministry of Defence that more than 1,600 people had been rescued by its helicopters, on contract to HM Coastguard, since 1971.

In the spring of 1988, it was announced that the SAR coverage would be maintained with military (primarily Royal Air Force) helicopters and contract civilian machines in parts of Scotland and on the South Coast.

Bond Helicopters, formerly known as North Scottish Helicopters, was not part of the privatization bid for commercial

UK CIVILIAN SAR HELICOPTER CONTRACTS AND EXPERIENCE

Rescue sorties flown and people assisted

SAR helicopter operator	Unit/base	Period of contract	Client	Number of sorties flown	Number of persons rescued/ transferred
Bristow Helicopters	RAF Manston	1971-74	Department of Trade and Industry	668	108
	Forties Oil Field	1978-83	British Petroleum	179*	780*
	Brent oil field/ Unst (Shetland Is)	1979-current	Shell Exploration	276	276
	Sumburgh	1983-current	Department of Trade and Industry	104	125
British European Airways (subsequently British Airways Helicopters)	Aberdeen, subsequently Sumburgh	1971-83	Department of Trade and Industry	143	262
North Scottish Helicopters (subsequently Bond Helicopters)	Forties Field	1983-current	British Petroleum	111	126
	Frigg Field	1983-current	Elf Petroleum		

*Note: Statistics include the evacuation of the *Hermod* crane barge in December 1979 with 13 Bristow aircraft flying 25 sorties (in up to Force 12 conditions) and evacuating 527 men.

31 March 1989

A Bond Helicopters SA 365N Dauphin 2 helicopter of the type used for the Forties and Frigg Fields' rescue services. (Bond/Paul Stickland.)

search and rescue operations, but the company does operate the Aerospatiale SA 365N Dauphin 2 for offshore-based SAR.

The company has operated the offshore medical evacuation and SAR service for British Petroleum in the Forties Field and for Elf Petroleum in the Frigg Field since 1983. The primary role of these helicopters is the inter-platform transport of men and materials. The aircrew are, however, SAR trained with winchmen available offshore, thereby giving the helicopters a day SAR capability.

COMMERCIAL SAR HELICOPTER SPECIFICATIONS

Model 212

Manufacturer: Bell Helicopter Textron; Purpose: intermediate weight commercial and military support helicopter; Crew: 2 pilots (Instrument Flight Rules operations), 1 winch operator, 1 winchman; Cabin: 12 seated survivors or 4 stretchers; Maiden flight: 16 April 1969; Service entry: 1970; UK operators: Bristow Helicopters, British International Helicopters; Radius of action: 215 nm (398 km) max fuel; Max speed: 132 knots (245 km/h); Operational speed: 100 knots (185 km/h); Service ceiling: 14,200 ft (4,328m); Length overall: 57.275 ft (17.45m); Height overall: 12.83 ft (3.91 m); Rotor diameter: 48 ft (14.63 m); Hover Out of Ground Effect (take-off power): 9,300 ft (2,835 m); Power plant: 1 × Pratt & Whitney of Canada PT6T twin pack (1,800 shp take-off, 1,600 maximum continuous power); Empty weight: 6,110 lb (2,771 kg); Maximum all-up weight: 11,200 lb (5,080 kg).

S-61N Mk II

Manufacturer: Sikorsky Aircraft; Purpose: long-range offshore support helicopter; Crew: 2 pilots, 1 winch operator, 1 winchman; Cabin: 24 seated, 19 seated survivors or 6 stretchers; Maiden flight: 11 March 1959; Service entry: 1971 (North Sea); UK operators: Bond Helicopters (when known as North Scottish Helicopters), Bristow Helicopters, British International Helicopters; Radius of action: 287 nm (532 km) with auxiliary tanks, 217 nm (402 km) using standard tanks; Max speed: 150 knots (278 km/h); Operational speed: 120 knots (222 km/h); Service ceiling: 12,500 ft (3,810 m); Length fuselage: 59.4 ft (18.1 m); Length overall: 72.9 ft (22.22 m); Height overall: 19.0 ft (5.79 m); Rotor diameter: 62 ft (18.9 m); Hover Out of Ground Effect: 3,800 ft (1,158 m); Power plants: 2 × General Electric CT58-140-2 turboshafts (1,500 take-off, 1,250 maximum continuous power); Empty weight: 12,510 lb (5,675 kg); Maximum all-up weight: 20,500 lb (9,300 kg).

Super Puma

Manufacturer: Aerospatiale, Helicopter Division; Purpose: medium offshore support helicopter; Crew: 2 pilots, 1 winch operator, 1 winchman; Cabin: 12 seated survivors or 4 stretchers (AS 332 L1 version); Maiden flight: 13 September 1978; Service entry: 1980; UK operators:

Bond Helicopters, Bristow Helicopters, British International Helicopters; Radius of action: 340 nm (630 km); Max speed: 150 knots (278 km/h); Operational speed: 144 knots (266 km/h); Service ceiling: 15,088 ft (4,600 m); Length fuselage: 53.44 ft (16.29 m); Height overall: 16.4 ft (4.92 m); Rotor diameter: 51.18 ft (15.6 m); Hover Out of Ground Effect: 7,544 ft (2,300 m); Power plants: 2 × Turbomeca Makila 1A1 turboshafts (1,877 shp take-off, 1,588 shp maximum continuous power); Empty weight: 9,745 lb (4,420 kg); Maximum all-up weight: 18,960 lb (8,600 kg).

Dauphin 2

Manufacturer: Aerospatiale, Helicopter Division; Purpose: light/intermediate offshore support helicopter; Crew: 2 pilots, 1 winch operator, 1 winchman; Cabin: 10 seated survivors or 2 stretchers (SA 365C1 version); Maiden flight: 24 January 1975; Service entry: 1977; UK operators: Bond Helicopters; Range standard fuel: 245 nm (455 km); Max speed: 170 knots (315 km/h); Operational speed: 138 knots (257 km/h); Service ceiling: 15,910 ft (4,850 m); Length fuselage: 36 ft (11 m); Height overall: 11.4 ft (3.5 m); Rotor diameter: 38.3 ft (11.7 m); Hover Out of Ground Effect: 2,790 ft (850 m); Power plants: 2 × Turbomeca Arriel turboshafts (630 shp take-off power, 579 maximum continuous); Empty weight: 4,189 lb (1,900 kg); Maximum all-up weight: 7,495 lb (3,400 kg).

The S-61N, although many of the North Sea airframes are older, is claimed to have significant advantages over the Sea King. Bristow Helicopters believes that the former has a larger cabin volume although it is slightly bigger than the Sea King in overall dimensions, but not enough to make a significant difference in tight environments, such as mountain flying. However, it has less payload (although it can take a greater bulk), less range, no search radar and less tail rotor authority (that is, it has poorer control in cross-wind situations).

Bristow's SAR S-61Ns have the Louis Newmark LN450 Flight Path Control and Auto-Hover system, jointly developed for the S-61 with Bristow. This is a digital system which receives information from several sensors including the primary Doppler 71, attitude gyros, four accelerometers and dual radio altimeters.

This data is processed by the LN450 computer to provide commands to the Louis Newmark LN400 Automatic Stabilizer Equipment which is also incorporated into the helicopter to provide it with a modern duplex control system which gives good stabilization after a single system failure. The commands are based on the flight 'mode' selected by the pilot which includes specific SAR flight modes, giving automatic hover as well as general navigation 'en-route' modes.

Another claimed advantage is the Forward Looking Infra-Red (FLIR) which

In the offshore hangar in the Forties Field, Bond Helicopters maintain an impressive equipment supply for the Dauphin 2 rescue service.

The standard Bristow/HM Coastguard S-61N Mk II cockpit arrangement showing the weather radar and automatic flight control system. (Bristow/Marcus Taylor.)

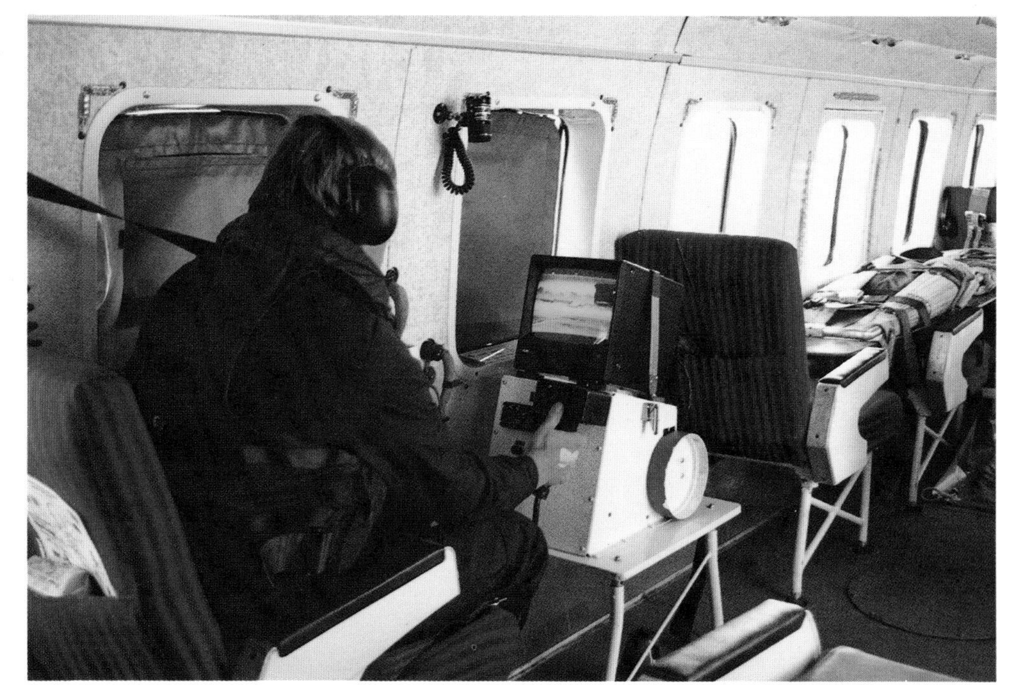

The FLIR (Forward Looking Infra-Red) installation aboard the Bristow/HM Coastguard SAR helicopter; note the Neil Robertson stretcher positioned on the seats. (Bristow/Marcus Taylor.)

is used by other nations to increase significantly the likelihood of detecting a survivor in the water, particularly when no personal locator beacon has been deployed. At night and in some adverse weather conditions, the FLIR can be an addition to the human eye, but it is degraded by rain and is not considered successful in poor visibility. RAF SAR crews have now been equipped with night vision goggles because the military have yet to be convinced that the FLIR system is the best alternative to the human eye.

The FLIR system works by means of detection and display on a monitor in the cabin of the helicopter and this shows differences in temperature of the scene being viewed by the FLIR camera. The camera body is mounted below the nose of the helicopter on a gimbal controlled from within the aircraft. It is able to highlight very small temperature differences and has been proved to detect a human head in the water from, Bristow Helicopters say, 'normal search attitudes and ranges'. This capability should be equally applicable by day or night.

The third specialist system on the S-61N is the Bendix RDR 1400C colour weather and mapping radar. This is rated to be one of the most modern, advanced capability, multi-mode civilian radars in the world but on the S-61N only scans 30 degrees either side of the nose (against the Sea King's 360 degrees coverage). It has been optimized by Bristow for searching for small targets in rough seas where its processing capability allows the highlighting of targets against a background of sea clutter. It does, however, miss targets outside its arc and directly ahead.

It incorporates the choice of two weather modes and three search modes. In the weather modes, the receiver gain is preset and cannot be changed by the aircrew in the search modes, giving the best possible gain in all display resolutions. Additionally, in search modes on ranges below 20 nm (37 km), the transmitter pulse is changed to enhance target resolution. This enables the radar to distinguish objects spaced as close as 0.04 nm (or 80 yards) on the shorter range search modes. Besides the more usual display ranges of 240 nm (445 km) down to 2 nm (3.7 km), the RDR 144 1400C also allows the selection of full-scale display ranges of 1 and 0.5 nm (1.8 to 0.9 km) — especially useful during search and rescue operations because they keep the target from becoming lost in the clutter at the vertex of the display. The radar, like that of the Sea King, incorporates a beacon mode whereby it can interrogate, receive and display signals from fixed X-band transponder beacons on all ranges.

Another claimed advantage of the S-61N is the proximity of the cabin door and the flying pilot's seat on the right-hand side of the cockpit make winch co-ordination easier than from the rear door Sea King. It is smaller than the Sea King's door which makes stretcher entry very difficult. The Sea King's barn door allows anything to be dragged aboard and the RAF maintain that a single person in control during winching is very important.

MOUNTAIN RESCUE TEAMS

In the United Kingdom there are 74 civilian mountain rescue teams (MRTs) and six Royal Air Force teams. The civilian teams operate under the jurisdiction of the police. The police are responsible for all incidents in the mountains and the MRTs act as their agents.

TEAMS IN THE BRITISH ISLES AND THEIR CALL-SIGNS

1 Lake District Mountain Accident Association

Team	Call-sign
Cockermouth MRT	CHARLIE
Coniston MRT	CONISTON
Eskdale OBMS	ESKIMO
Furness MST	FURNESS
Kendal MSRT	MINTCAKE
Keswick MRT	KESWICK
Kirby Stephen MRT	BOGTROT
Langdale/ Ambleside MRT	LANGDALE
Millom FRT	MIKE
Patterdale MRT	PATRICK
Penrith MRT	PENNINE
Ullswater OBMS	BOUNDER
Wasdale MRT	WHISKY
Lake District NPR	PARK

2 Mid-Pennine Mountain Accident Panel

Team	Call-sign
Bolton MRT	BOLTON
Bowland-Pennine MRT	TROUGH
Calder Valley MRT	CALDER
Holme Valley MRT	HOLME VALLEY
Rossendale FRT	ROSSENDALE
Lancashire Police	MIKE BRAVO DELTA

3 North East Search and Rescue Association

Team	Call-sign
Cleveland SRT	VIKING
North of Tyne SRT	KEY
Northumberland National Park FRT	CURLEW
Scarborough & District SRT	MOORJOCK
Upper Teesdale & Weardale FRA	TEESDALE

4 North Wales Mountain Rescue Association

Team	Call-sign
Aberdyfi OBS	OSCAR
Aberglaslyn Hall OPC	GLASLYN
Clwyd RT	CLWYD
Llanberis MRT	PERIS
Moelwyn MRT	MOELWYN
Ogwen Valley MRO	OGGI
Plas-y-Brenin NMC	SIABOD
Rhinog MRT	RHINOG
SARDA (Wales)	AVALANCHE
Snowdonia National Park Wardens	SNOWFLAKE

5 Peak District Mountain Rescue Organizations

Team	Call-sign
Buxton MRT	BUXTON
Derby MRT	DERBY
Edale MRT	DERWENT
Glossop MRT	GLOSSOP
Kinder MRT	KINDER
Oldham MRT	OLDHAM
Woodhead MRT	WOODHEAD
Derbyshire County Council Rangers	RANGER
National Trust	ACORN
Peak District NPR	PEAKLAND

6 Search and Rescue Dog Association

SARDA (England)	SEARCH DOG

7 South Wales Mountain Rescue Association

Brecon MRT	ZEBRA
Bridgend MRT	BRAVO
Lontown MRT	BLACKS
Morlais MRT	MORLAIS
SARDA (South Wales)	DINGO
South Wales CRO	DRAGON

8 South West England Rescue Association

Avon Rocks RT	SHED
Dartmoor Rescue Group	DART
East Cornwall Mine RG	MINER
Mendip Rescue Organization	HUNTER
Cheddar Gorge Cliff RT	SCEPTRE
Gloucestershire Ambulance Service Cliff Rescue Team	DEAN
Devon and Cornwall Constabulary	QUEBEC BRAVO CHARLIE
Severn Auxiliary RA	SARA

9 Yorkshire Dales Rescue Panel

Cave Rescue Organization	CRO
CRO Base — Settle	CRAGDALE
Swaledale FRO	SWALE
Upper Wharfdale FRA	FELL

MOUNTAIN RESCUE COMMITTEE OF SCOTLAND

1 Central Police

Killin MRT	KILLIN
Lomond MRT	LOMOND
Ochil Hills RT	OCHIL

2 Dumfries and Galloway Constabulary

Biggar SAR Group	BIGGAR
Galloway SAR Group	GALLOWAY
Moffat Hill RT	MOFFAT

3 Grampian Police

Aberdeen MRT	ICE
Braemar MRT	BRAEMAR

4 Lothian and Borders Police

Borders SAR Association	REIVER
Borders SAR Association Tweed Valley MRT	TWEED

5 Northern Constabulary

Assynt MRT	ASSYNT
Cairngorm MRA	CAIRNGORM
Dundonnel MRT	DUNDONNELL
Glencoe MRT	GLENCOE
Gleneig MRT	GLENEIG
Glenmore Lodge MRT	GLENMORE
Kintail MRT	KINTAIL
Lochaber MRT	NEVIS
Skye MRT	SKYE
Torridon and Kinlochewe MRT	TORRIDON

6 Search and Rescue Dog Association

SARDA (Scotland)	DOG

7 Strathclyde Police

Arrochar MRT	ARROCHAR

8 Tayside Police

Tayside MRA	TAYCIV
Tayside Police MRT	TAYPOL

NORTHERN IRELAND MOUNTAIN RESCUE CO-ORDINATING COMMITTEE

Royal Ulster Constabulary MRT	EVEREST

SERVICE ORGANIZATIONS

RAF Kinloss MRT	ALPINE KILO
Leeming MRT	ALPINE TANGO
Leuchars MRT	ALPINE LIMA
St Athan MRT	ALPINE SIERRA
Stafford MRT	ALPINE HOTEL
Valley MRT	ALPINE VICTOR
RAF Helicopters Operational Training	RESCUE HELICOPTER

Key to abbreviations:
CRO Cave Rescue Organization
FRA Fell Rescue Association
FRO Fell Rescue Organization
FRT Fell Rescue Team
MRO Mountain Rescue Organization
MRT Mountain Rescue Team
MST Mountain Search Team
MSRT Mountain Search & Rescue Team
NMC National Mountaineering Centre
NPR National Park Rangers
OBS Outward Bound School
OBMS Outward Bound Mountain School
OPC Outdoor Pursuits Centre
RA Rescue Association
RG Rescue Group
RT Rescue Team
SARDA Search & Rescue Dog Association
SRT Search & Rescue Team

Call out

On receiving an emergency call, the police telephone the team leader of the nearest mountain rescue team and give details of the incident. During this first telephone call an action plan is formulated between the police and the MRT. Depending on the information available to the police from the first emergency caller, the team leader will decide whether to call out all the mountain rescue team immediately or to call only a small number.

The incident's first informant will be interviewed by the MRT leader and the police to obtain an accurate location, description of casualty, any injuries and, if possible, weather conditions at the scene. This information will speed the type of search or rescue operation to be carried out.

For searches during darkness a small number of the MRT may set out with the rest of the team called later for a search at first light. Where a casualty is on a rock face the most experienced climbing members of the team will be in the

The Lochaber MRT in action, bringing out a severely injured walker for onward transport to hospital by rescue helicopter. For full details of this incident, see Job No 58 11 September 1988.

Winchman Bill Payne counts members of the RAF Kinloss MRT as they board the helicopter.

Rescue 137 lands alongside the RAF Kinloss MRT communications vehicle during a search near Newtonmore.

Pilot Steve Hodgson (right) and RAF Kinloss MRT team leader Tommy Taylor (blue anorak) survey the mountains around Newtonmore before beginning a search for an overdue skier.

Doctor Alistair Macgregor is briefed by winch operator Pat Thirkell before being winched out of Rescue 137 to a skier who had fallen to his death in the Cairngorms. Dr Macgregor is medical officer to the Mountain Rescue Committee of Scotland and medical adviser to the Glenmore and Cairngorm MRTs.

A member of the Glenmore MRT leads winchman Dave Aitken to an injured climber in the Cairngorms as Rescue 137 stands off. Dave Aitken is carrying a portable Entinox unit and first-aid kit; a portable VHF radio can be seen on his left. Entinox is a pain-killing gas administered through an oxygen mask.

first advance party. The others will follow with, if necessary, back-up equipment. Persons reported overdue are given an opportunity to 'walk out' by the MRT, allowing time for the police to check cafés and car parks in the area. There is no sense in risking an MRT for an unncessary search.

In the early stages of an incident, helicopter assistance will be considered. It can sometimes take time for a helicopter to transit to the scene, so a call to the Rescue Co-ordination Centre (RCC), at Pitreavie in Scotland or Mount Wise in Plymouth, will be made as soon as the severity of the situation is known. The RCC will scramble the nearest rescue helicopter. Also search dogs may be required so the nearest SARDA team may be called.

The RCCs are also the co-ordinating authority for the RAF MRTs. They, like the rescue helicopters, are available every day of the year and can be called out to assist the civilian teams. At weekends, the RAF teams exercise in the mountains and are often 'on scene' when an incident occurs. Even so, they will work and co-operate with the local civilian team to the best advantage of the casualty. Whilst away from base the RAF MRTs always keep in radio contact with the appropriate RCC and frequent sitreps (situation reports) are passed.

All mountain rescue teams have close liaison with local doctors who they can call upon to assist in an emergency. Indeed, some doctors are team members and will often be included on the first call-out.

MRT procedures

An advance party of around six members will set off to the location, taking with them a first-aid kit, climbing equipment (if necessary), a casualty bag and radio communications equipment. This advance party usually consists of the

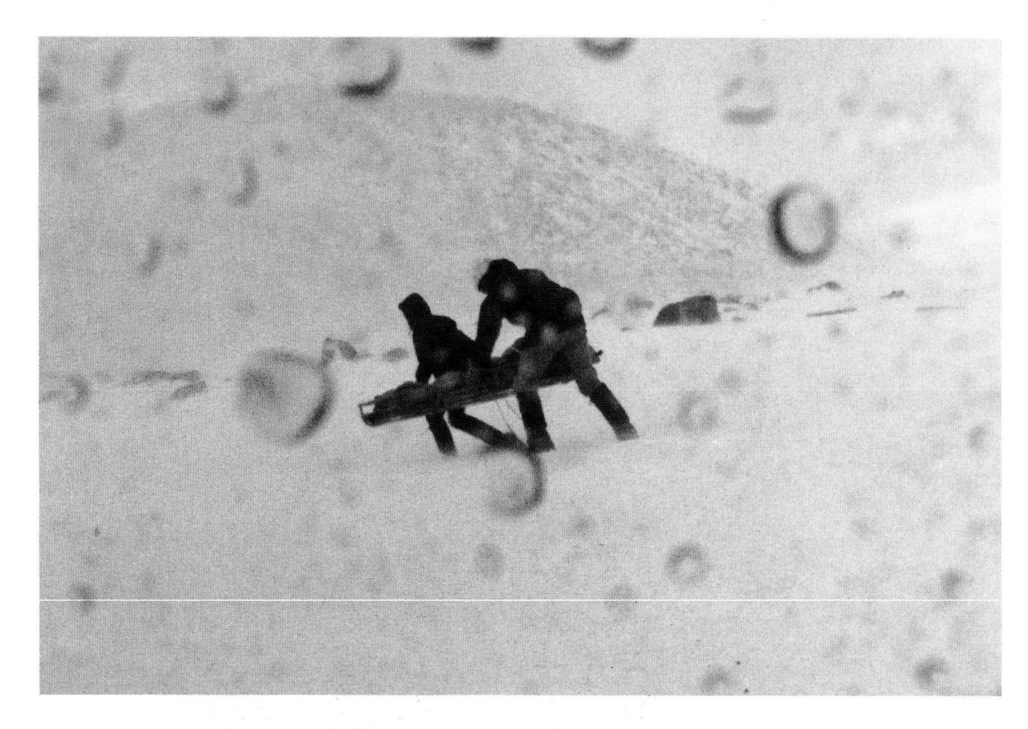

In blizzard conditions members of the Glenmore MRT carry a Stokes Litter stretcher to a suitable helicopter recovery point.

most experienced team members who can quickly get to work to reach the casualty. Once 'on scene' the team must be able to carry out immediate life-saving assistance and report by radio to base with an accurate position, the patient's condition and request back-up if necessary.

The advance party will be followed by the main rescue team which usually consists of a dozen or more members who will be carrying stretchers, more advanced medical equipment and, if required, further climbing equipment. Often a third rescue team will set out, their task being to relieve other members of the advance and main teams as well as acting as support for large operations. For example, the third team might rendezvous with the main party coming down the mountain and take over with stretcher carrying.

Each rescue party will be headed by a group leader who is responsible for the organization of his team. At all times, the elements of the teams are in radio contact with each other as well as base control, which can be set up anywhere, but usually at the nearest point of vehicular access. In some places, the base is a defined centre, such as Glenmore Lodge in the Cairngorms. If the terrain makes radio communication difficult, then relay points will be set up on high ground to form an unbroken radio link. Good radio communication is essential at all times.

Use of helicopters

When a rescue helicopter is scrambled it will fly to a rendezvous point designated by the MRT, usually near the mountain rescue base. On landing at the base the winchman will leave the aircraft to obtain further information from the team leader or co-ordinator.

If the incident dictates a large search area, with several other units involved, then the helicopter is shut down and the complete crew leave the aircraft for a thorough briefing. Alternatively, if the incident is serious and an advance res-

cue team is already on scene, then the helicopter would fly straight to its location. If night is imminent then again the rescue helicopter's captain may want to 'have a look' to see if he can spot and assist or rescue the casualty before flying on to the rescue base to collect the MRT. Obviously, flying at night in mountains has increased risks, especially when vision is limited to the illumination of the helicopter's searchlights.

Normally after a short briefing the rescue helicopter will lift an advance party to the incident or search location. Sometimes the advance team will make its own way to the incident while the helicopter is in transit. Whenever possible the helicopter will land near the position of the casualty to allow the MRT to leave the aircraft and reach the casualty with the minimum of delay. This action is not always possible, however, and landing on adjacent to a casualty is the exception rather than the rule, especially in the mountains.

It is more normal for the MRT and its equipment to be winched down from the helicopter because the terrain does not allow a safe landing. After depositing the MRT the rescue helicopter will normally leave the immediate area and return to the MRT base, either to pick up more team members or shut down. This conserves fuel, is less tiring for the aircrew and in some cases is desirable because of noise, which could cause an avalanche in certain snow conditions.

The rescue helicopter waits for the casualty to be assessed and made ready for helicopter recovery. Radio contact with the MRT is maintained at all times.

Most of the mountain rescue team bases have dumps strategically placed to replenish the rescue helicopter's fuel tanks. If the rescue helicopter's remaining fuel endurance is limited, refuelling takes place prior to the casualty being taken to hospital. During rescue operations in the mountains the helicopter's handling characteristics are improved with a light fuel load but often more fuel is required for the transit.

Regular training visits are made to all the MRTs by rescue helicopter crews. It is important that every team member knows his way in, out and around the helicopter as well as being competent in winching techniques and operation. Speed is often of the essence on a mountain rescue incident, not necessarily because of the patient's injuries but more than likely bad weather. Individual communications around the helicopter can be difficult because of engine noise.

The rescue helicopter, working in mountain conditions, is often operating to

Members of the Pitlochry MRT are briefed about the Sea King helicopter by Pat Thirkell, radar/winch operator, during a visit to RAF Lossiemouth. Such visits are encouraged to ensure familiarity between MRTs and helicopter crews during a rescue operation.

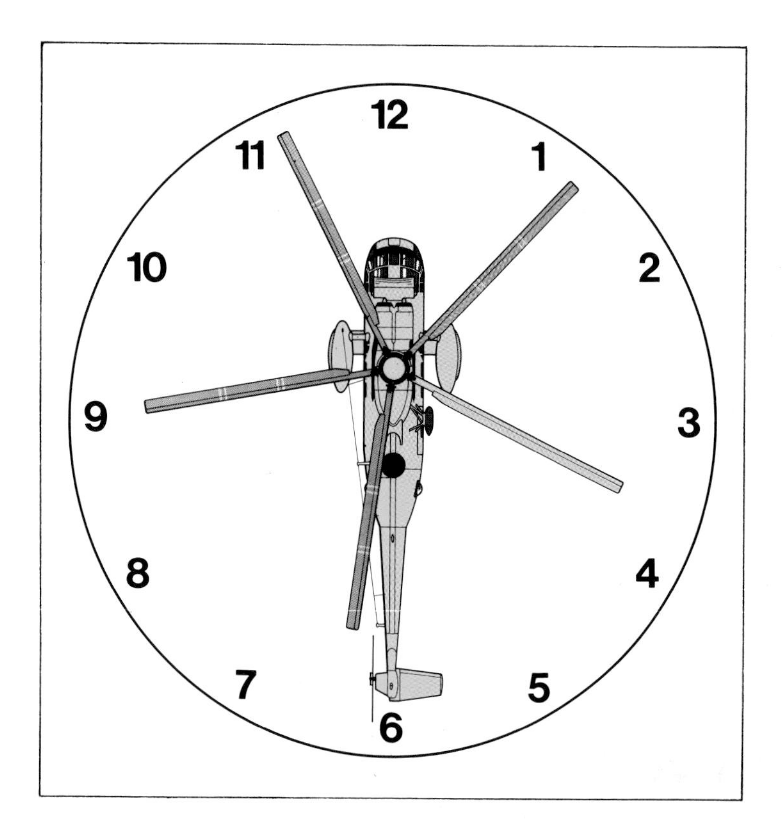

its limits in ice, wind and poor visibility and therefore MRTs must be expert in helicopter operations — their lives, and others', depend on it.

The rescue team member must also be able to talk the helicopter into position by radio. It is very difficult for the crew on board a helicopter to see small figures on a rock face but it is easier for the team on the ground to see a large yellow helicopter. A 'clock code' is used (see diagram): the nose of the helicopter points towards 12 o'clock and the tail to six o'clock. The words 'high' and 'low' are also added to this code to give an indication of the elevation of the object being identified. A distance can also be added, for example: 'the casualty is in your 12 o'clock low, range one mile'.

So, as the rescue helicopter approaches a target, the information passed from the ground would be continued: 'one o'clock low, three hundred metres, two o'clock, three o'clock'. At this

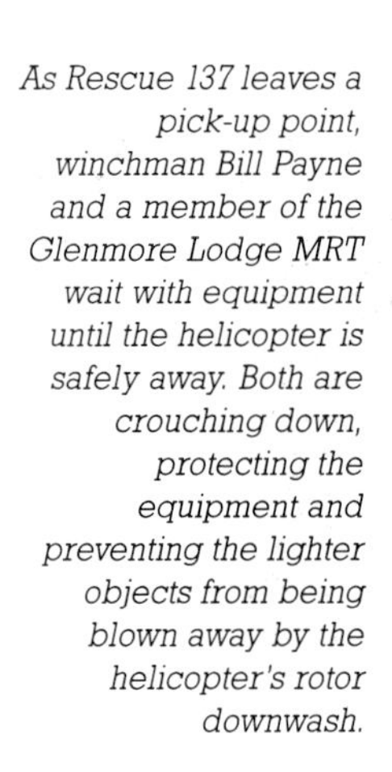

As Rescue 137 leaves a pick-up point, winchman Bill Payne and a member of the Glenmore Lodge MRT wait with equipment until the helicopter is safely away. Both are crouching down, protecting the equipment and preventing the lighter objects from being blown away by the helicopter's rotor downwash.

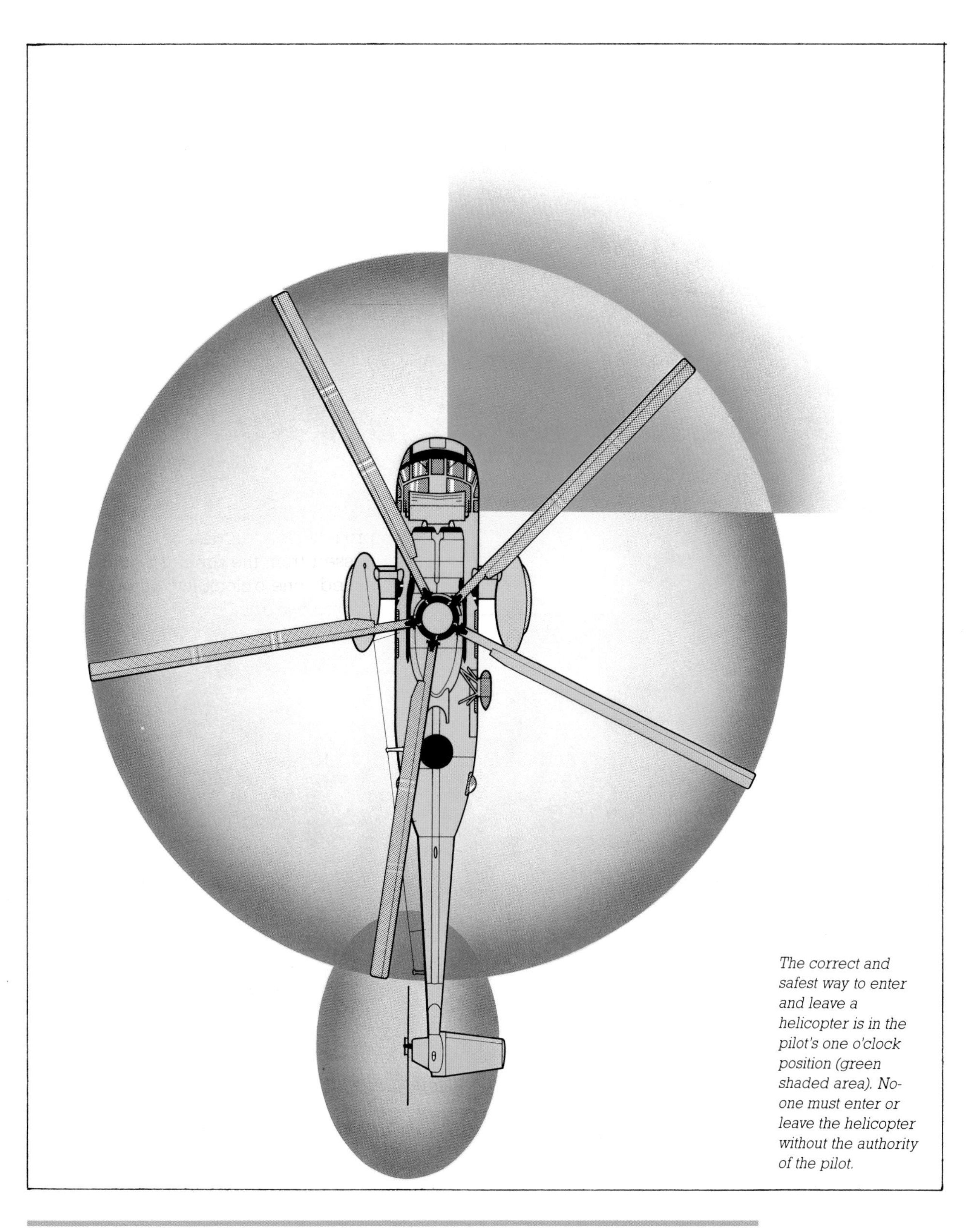

The correct and safest way to enter and leave a helicopter is in the pilot's one o'clock position (green shaded area). No-one must enter or leave the helicopter without the authority of the pilot.

point the helicopter's main cabin door, on the right-hand side, would be alongside the target position.

There is a right and wrong way to enter and leave a helicopter (see diagram). There have been many accidents with people walking into tail rotors and with main rotor blades 'sailing down' to near ground level, especially during rotor start and shut down. There have also been accidents with people walking into the rotating main blades of a helicopter standing on an incline, and passengers are always taught to exit the area of the main rotor disk downhill.

Usually the MRT will kneel in a group at the pick-up point allowing the helicopter to manoeuvre into position. No one must approach the helicopter without permission from the pilot or crewman in the rear who, when ready, will give the signal for the team to enter the aircraft. The equipment carried by MRTs could cause damage to the helicopter, so special attention must be given to radio aerials, ice axes and crampons before entering the aircraft. Rescue helicopters that operate frequently in mountain terrain are fitted with special mats which prevent the spikes on crampons penetrating the metalwork of the helicopter.

Mountain incidents

Each year more and more people head off into the mountains of Scotland, England and Wales, encouraged by ease of access due to improved roads, the teaching of outdoor pursuits in schools and other organizations, the growing coverage on television and radio programmes as well as the proliferation of adventure sports magazines. This exodus to the hills has also led to an increase in mountain accidents.

Scottish Crown Office statistics indicate that over the period 1979-1984 deaths on mountains in Scotland were four times more frequent than the next largest group of sport and leisure-related deaths. The fatality rate in Scotland (deaths as a proportion of accidents) was around 20 per cent over the period 1974-1986. This is equivalent to that found in Switzerland and the Chamonix Valley area of France, but contrasts with a lower rate of four per cent found in England and Wales.

Scottish incidents

A study of Scottish incidents by Dr Alistair Macgregor (Medical Officer, Mountain Rescue Committee of Scotland) highlighted a number of implications:

1 There should be increased awareness of the fact that the most common cause of injury is a simple slip or stumble while hill walking.

2 Too many winter accidents are the result of a failure to wear, or be competent in the use of, crampons or ice axe.

3 More publicity required to encourage mountain users to wear adequate protective clothing.

4 The use of a helmet for winter hill walking should be considered.

5 The public should be made aware that taking risks creates a risk for rescue personnel.

6 Helicopters are an essential part of the rescue process, greatly decreasing the time required to transfer the casualty to hospital.

7 Avalanches are a major cause of winter mountain accidents in Scotland.

An awareness of the frequency and causes of avalanches in Scotland should be appreciated by all mountain activists.

Mountain rescue signals

RAF Mountain Rescue Teams use a code of signalling in emergencies.

The Mountain Rescue Committee recommends the following simplified versions of the RAF code.

MESSAGE	FLARE	LIGHT, SOUND OR SEMAPHORE
1. Help wanted here	Red	Six long flashes/notes in quick succession repeated after a minute's interval. SOS. three short, three long, three short — repeated.
2. Message understood	White (from rescue party)	A series of three long flashes/ notes repeated at one minute intervals.
3. Position of rescue base	White (or yellow)	Steady white or yellow light, or car headlights (if possible pointing upwards).
4. Recall to rescue base	Green (used only at rescue base)	A succession of notes on horn, bell or whistle. A succession of white or yellow lights switched on and off. Or a succession of thunderflashes.

International alarm signals in the mountains

Yes

Red flare or fire

Square of red cloth

No

We need help

We don't need anything

MOUNTAIN RESCUE TEAMS

Mountain Rescue Committee of Scotland Regional Distribution of Incidents 1988

	North Highlands	West Highlands	Ben Nevis	Glencoe including Buachaille	Other Central Highlands	Cairngorms	Southern Highlands	Skye	Islands other than Skye	Southern Uplands	Acc 88 regions	Acc 89 regions
Rescues with casualties	14	10	18	20	13	15	27	5	5	3	131	136
Injuries	14 (1)	7 (1)	16 (3)	22 (6)	13 (3)	11 (2)	27 (3)	4 (1)	5 (1)	2	121 (21)	122 (20)
Exhaustion, etc	1 (1)	4	18	1	1 (1)	3	4	1	—	1	34 (2)	11
Illness	—	2 (1)	1	1	—	2	3 (1)	—	—	1	10 (2)	16 (7)
Cragfast	3	—	3	5	6	—	1	—	—	—	18	18
Separation	1	—	—	—	—	2	3	1	—	—	7	8
Lost	—	—	3	—	2	4	4	—	—	—	13	18
Overdue or benighted	8	5	6	—	2	3	6	3	1	—	34	39
False alarms	2	1	2	4	1	2	3	1	—	—	16	18
Non-mountaineering incidents	3	2	—	—	4	—	2	1	—	2	14	16
Non-mountaineering casualties	1 (1)	1	—	—	3 (3)	—	—	1 (1)	—	—	6 (5)	8 (5)
Total incidents	31	18	32	29	28	26	47	11	6	5	233	253
Total casualties	16 (3)	14 (2)	35 (3)	24 (6)	17 (7)	16 (2)	34 (4)	6 (2)	5 (1)	4	171 (30)	157 (32)

( ) = fatalities

MOUNTAIN RESCUE COMMITTEE

Mountain Incident Report 1988 (England and Wales)

	Lake Dist	NE Eng	Yorks Dales	Mid Pennine	Peak Dist	North Wales	South Wales	SW Eng	Total 1987	Total 1988
Rock climbing	15 16(1)	2 2	5 5		11 12	19 22(2)	2 3	4 4	55 59(3)	58 64(3)
Snow/ice climbing	5 5	1 5(2)				9 10(1)			10 17(1)	15 20(3)
Fell-walking April-Oct	99 109(8)	8 8	9 13(2)	5 6(1)	25 25(5)	31 35(2)	10 12(1)	3 5(1)	197 223(23)	185 208(20)
Fell-walking Nov-March	53 62(6)	4 4	3 3	8 9(1)	6 6(2)	15 19(3)	3 3	1 1	84 109(10)	93 107(12)
Searches Injured	5 8(3)	7 7(3)	1 1		2 3	3 4(2)		3 8	11 14(1)	21 31(8)
Searches Non-injured	30 77	16 20	4 5	3 3	6 17	16 32	7 15	9 35	87 183	91 204

Note: *upper figures of each pair indicate number of incidents lower figures show number of casualties figures in brackets indicate fatalities*

	Lake Dist	NE Eng	Yorks Dales	Mid Pennine	Peak Dist	North Wales	South Wales	SW Eng	Total 1987	Total 1988
Crag-fast	11	1	1		2	15	1	5	28	36
Non-injured	30	1	1		2	28	1	7	48	70
Non-mountain	5	4	2	8	4	8	5		32	36
	5(1)	6	2	11(3)	4(1)	12(5)	5(2)		51(12)	45(12)
Totals — Incidents	223	43	25	24	56	116	28	25	504	540
People involved	312(19)	53(5)	30(2)	29(5)	69(8)	162(15)	39(3)	60(1)	700(50)	754(58)
RAF Rescue	25	1	2	1	3	42	3	3	86	80
Helicopter Search	6	1			1	12		6	22	26
SARDA	23	3	2	9	8	15	3	11	65	74

MAIN CAUSES OF INCIDENTS

England and Wales 1988

Cause		Lake Dist	NE Eng	Yorks Dales	Mid Pennine	Peak Dist	North Wales	South Wales	SW Eng	Total 1987	Total 1988
Slips (fell walking)	Footwear Satisfactory	40	5	2	4	10	22	6	4	75	93
	Smooth Sole or Unsuitably Shod	25	3	7	3	7	14	2	1	64	62
Slips (fell walking snow/ice)	No Ice Axe	15					4			8	19
	+/or Crampons	12					8			9	20
	Suitably equipped	12					8			9	20
Falls (rock climbing or abseiling)	Roped	8		2		1	6		1	20	18
	Solo	6	2	2	1	5	7			13	27
Falls (snow/ice climbing or abseiling)	Roped	3					1			2	4
	Solo	3	1				2			3	6
Belay or runner failure	Climbing	3	1	1		2	1	1	1	10	10
	Abseiling	1		1	1	2	2			5	7
Rockfall		5			1	5	1	1		9	13
Avalanche		4	1						5	—	5
Inexperience incompetence, ignorance resulting in exposure exhaustion or 'lost'	April to October	47	16	7	4	13	34	7	14	168	142
	November to March	22	5	4	2	11	26	5	9	70	84
Suicide		1	2		1	1				3	5
Attempted suicide							1	3		7	4
Lightning strike		2								—	2

HER MAJESTY'S COASTGUARD

When an incident occurs at sea around the United Kingdom's 6,000 miles of coast, on cliffs or in estuaries, it is the members of Her Majesty's Coastguard (HMCG) who initiate and co-ordinate the civil search and rescue operation. They are also responsible for an area stretching out 1,000 miles into the North Atlantic.

Coastguards were first established in 1822 to combat the high levels of smuggling around the British Isles. In those days, fishing boats would come into harbour with brandy casks slung under their keels, sailing ships were found with false bows or false bottoms and tobacco was even woven into hawsers. The saving of life was only a small part of the coastguard's job compared with saving money for the nation's Revenue.

By the mid-19th century, smuggling was much less widespread and in 1856 responsibility for the service passed from the Board of Customs to the Admiralty. Finally, in 1923, the service was passed on to the Board of Trade and the coastguards took on their present day role of life-saving. Now it is the Department of Transport who is responsible for HMCG.

In a maritime emergency, HMCG can call for assistance to the rescue facilities of the Royal National Lifeboat Institution (RNLI), the helicopters of the Royal Air Force and Royal Navy, their fixed-wing aircraft and ships, as well as merchant ships, commercial aircraft and ferries. International co-operation in the North Sea and English Channel is also important.

Showing two sides of HMCG's work. The summer holiday-maker with his plastic dinghy which drifted out into the North Sea and the wreck of the trawler, Navina, *with the coastguard unit standing by after the crew had been rescued by RAF Search & Rescue helicopters.*

HMCG operates its own cliff rescue teams, a fleet of inflatable general-purpose boats for inshore emergencies and three rescue helicopters. These, chartered from Bristow Helicopters, are based at Stornoway (Outer Hebrides), Sumburgh (Shetland Isles) and Lee-on-Solent (Hampshire). Details can be found on page 164.

HM Coastguard also assists the United Kingdom Department of Transport with the control of pollution at sea, using an extensive communications network. HMCG is usually the first authority to learn of these incidents and can rapidly call upon spray-equipped tugs and aircraft to combat the threat. A marine pollution unit fast-response mobile communication unit is usually manned by coastguards and centrally based at Hull to travel to any part of the United Kingdom when a pollution threat occurs.

HM Coastguard network. The network is based on six search and rescue regions, each under the control of a coastguard regional controller who operates from a Maritime Rescue Co-ordination Centre (MRCC). These regions are further sub-divided into districts and controlled by a Maritime Rescue Sub Centre (MRSC), the responsibility of a district controller.

These stations keep a constant watch day and night and are situated at strategic positions around the coastline.

Within each district are a number of sector coastguard stations. These are operated by a sector officer who also manages auxiliary coastguard stations within his area. Neither the sector nor auxiliary stations keep a constant 24-hour watch. However, in emergencies they can be manned immediately.

Her Majesty's Coastguard is manned by 500 regular officers and 7,000 auxiliary coastguards. Most of the regulars work in the MRCCs, MRSCs and sector stations. The auxiliary coastguards are part-time volunteers from all walks of life who can be called upon at any time from home or at work.

Maritime Rescue Co-ordination Centres/Maritime Rescue Sub-Centres. MRCCs and MRSCs are responsible for co-ordinating all maritime search and rescue operations. Operations rooms keep a constant radio watch on the international maritime dis-

A typical HM Coastguard marine rescue unit of auxiliary coastguards with their Land-Rover 90 and trailer. The equipment on display shows the range of life-saving gear which is available; note that the auxiliary in the centre wears the crown on his sleeve to designate that he is auxiliary-in-charge.

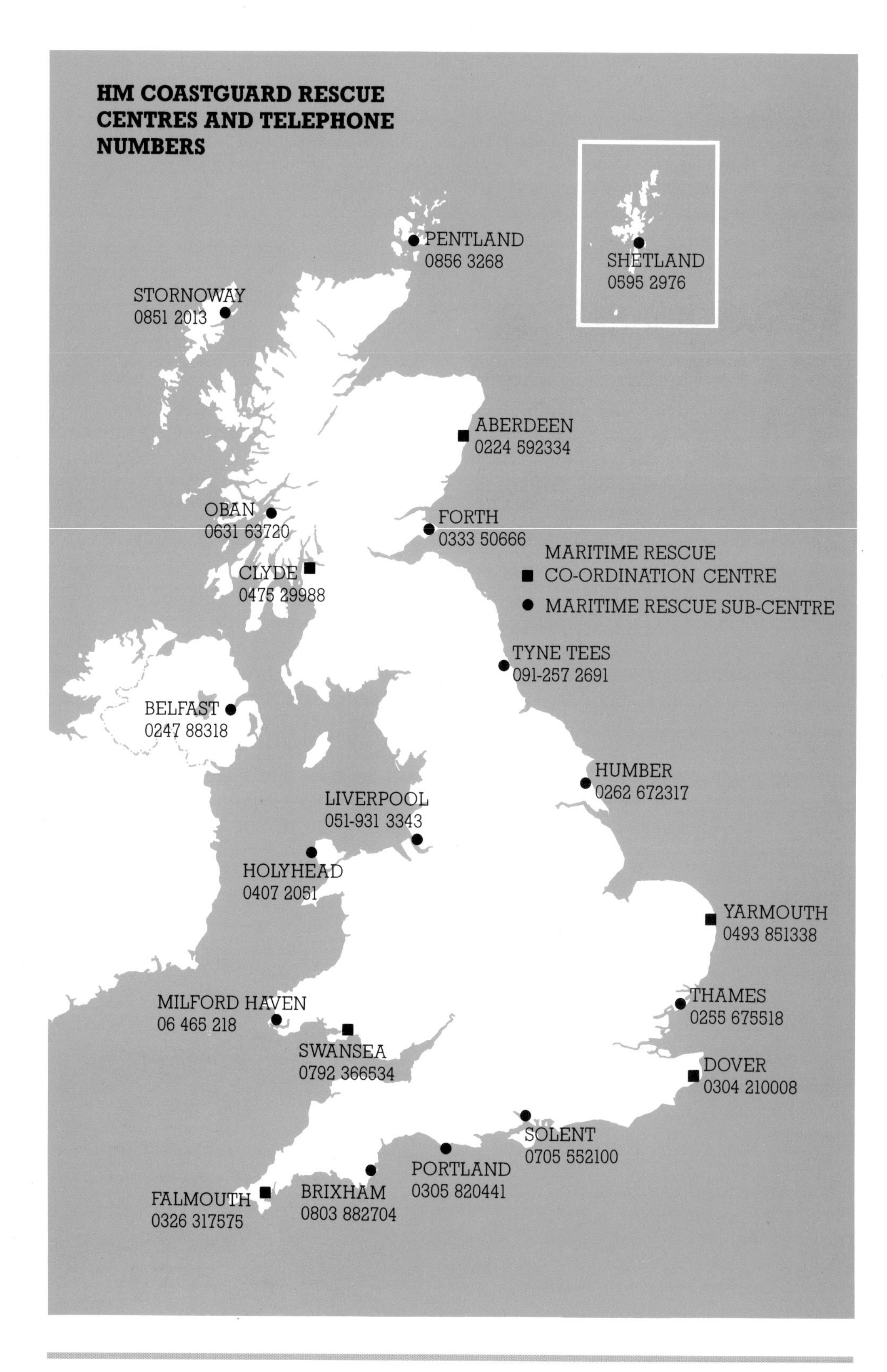
HM COASTGUARD RESCUE CENTRES AND TELEPHONE NUMBERS
PENTLAND 0856 3268
SHETLAND 0595 2976
STORNOWAY 0851 2013
ABERDEEN 0224 592334
OBAN 0631 63720
FORTH 0333 50666
MARITIME RESCUE CO-ORDINATION CENTRE
MARITIME RESCUE SUB-CENTRE
CLYDE 0475 29988
TYNE TEES 091-257 2691
BELFAST 0247 88318
HUMBER 0262 672317
LIVERPOOL 051-931 3343
HOLYHEAD 0407 2051
YARMOUTH 0493 851338
MILFORD HAVEN 06 465 218
THAMES 0255 675518
SWANSEA 0792 366534
DOVER 0304 210008
SOLENT 0705 552100
PORTLAND 0305 820441
FALMOUTH 0326 317575
BRIXHAM 0803 882704

Auxiliary coastguards come from all walks of life. Dr David Peebles Brown is one of the team at Hessle on the River Humber.

tress frequencies as well as answering 999 emergency telephone calls to the coastguard. Each of these control centres has emergency planning and press briefing rooms, plus telex and facsimile facilities to speed communications.

Computers also assist in the planning of search areas. By calculating wind and tide changes, computers can work out search patterns for both surface and air rescue units.

The operation rooms have their own radio consoles which are also linked to a network of remote aerials situated on high ground around the district. This enables the stations to monitor VHF radio communications over a wide area. On-site VHF antennas are also used for direction finding (DF), enabling the operation rooms to pinpoint the location of any maritime VHF transmission virtually anywhere within UK coastal waters.

The centres have direct landline links with British Telecom Coast Radio Stations (CRS), Rescue Co-ordination Centres (RCC), police and port operation rooms.

Falmouth MRCC is the sole UK control centre for maritime satellite distress communications. These calls are routed through to Falmouth from the UK coast earth station at Goonhilly Down in Cornwall, which is part of the INMARSAT global satellite system.

Falmouth also receives distress information from the SARSAT/COPAS satellite system which monitors maritime and aeronautical distress beacons worldwide.

The Coastguard MRCC or MRSC will be the first to receive information about an incident at sea or on the cliffs by radio message, telephone or telex. This can be anything from a sinking supertanker to a small child cut off by the tide who requires assistance. The news can arrive by various means:

By radio it can be in the form of:

- a MAYDAY call (grave and imminent danger)
- a PAN call (urgent help required but not in imminent danger)
- a MEDICAL ADVICE call (injured or ill person on board ship)

It can be received by telephone link from a coast radio station which has

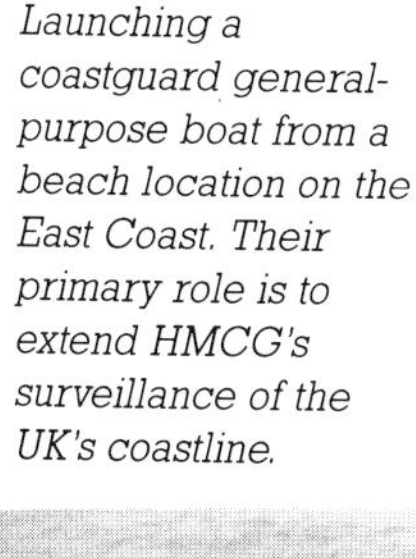

Launching a coastguard general-purpose boat from a beach location on the East Coast. Their primary role is to extend HMCG's surveillance of the UK's coastline.

A general-purpose inflatable craft training with a rescue helicopter of HM Coastguard.

received a long-distance radio distress call.

Or it can come in by the telephone 999 system or by direct link from police or port operation rooms.

The coastguard officer will then decide which assets are required to effect a rescue. He can call upon passing ships, lifeboats, helicopters, fixed-wing aircraft and other coastguards to assist.

Sector stations. Each sector station is operated and managed by a sector officer. Unlike his counterpart at a MRCC or MRSC, the sector officer carries out most of his duties by mobile patrol. He liaises with local emergency services, supervizes the training and management of his local auxiliary teams and gives lectures to schools and clubs. The sector officer will direct operations at a maritime incident, for example a cliff rescue, a beach search or where a ship has run aground. He will call upon his auxiliary teams to assist both with communications and rescue as required.

A sector station is equipped with a mobile rescue unit. These vehicles, usually Land Rovers, carry extensive rescue equipment enabling the sector officer and his auxiliaries to deal with many types of maritime emergency. The vehicles are fitted with a multi-channel VHF radio which allows the mobile team to talk to lifeboats, helicopters, ships and the coastguard rescue centres.

Some sector stations have their own rigid inflatable boats to enable patrols of the cliffs and beaches to be carried out efficiently. These craft can be called out to assist in rescue work where necessary.

Auxiliary coastguards. The backbone of the service is the auxiliary coastguard. They are dedicated men and

Typical of the rescue equipment carried by HMCG Land-Rovers is the rescue winch, used for such diverse tasks as cliff rescue and boat recovery.

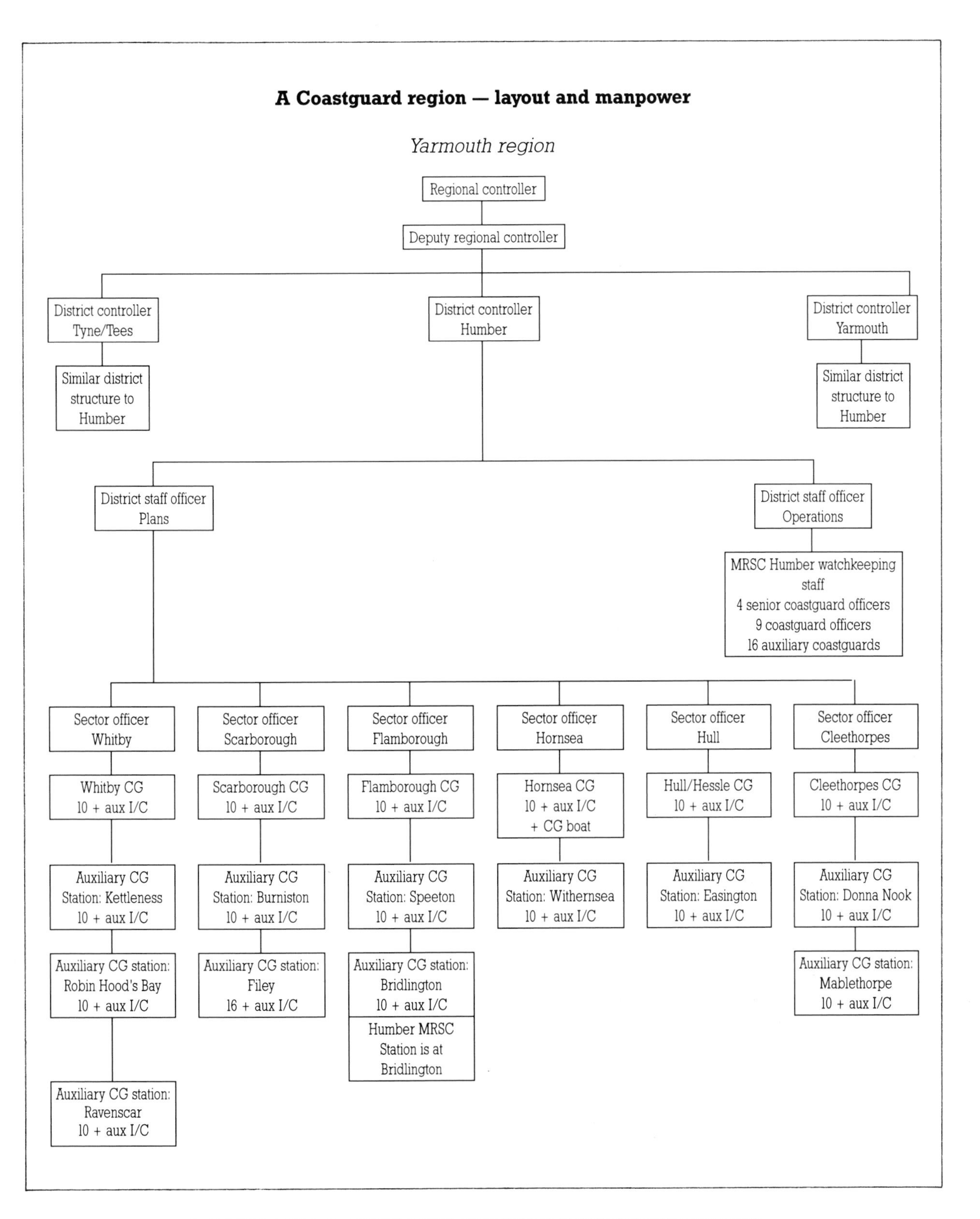
A Coastguard region — layout and manpower
Yarmouth region
Regional controller
Deputy regional controller
District controller Tyne/Tees
Similar district structure to Humber
District controller Humber
District controller Yarmouth
Similar district structure to Humber
District staff officer Plans
District staff officer Operations
MRSC Humber watchkeeping staff
4 senior coastguard officers
9 coastguard officers
16 auxiliary coastguards
Sector officer Whitby
Whitby CG 10 + aux I/C
Auxiliary CG Station: Kettleness 10 + aux I/C
Auxiliary CG station: Robin Hood's Bay 10 + aux I/C
Auxiliary CG station: Ravenscar 10 + aux I/C
Sector officer Scarborough
Scarborough CG 10 + aux I/C
Auxiliary CG Station: Burniston 10 + aux I/C
Auxiliary CG station: Filey 16 + aux I/C
Sector officer Flamborough
Flamborough CG 10 + aux I/C
Auxiliary CG Station: Speeton 10 + aux I/C
Auxiliary CG station: Bridlington 10 + aux I/C
Humber MRSC Station is at Bridlington
Sector officer Hornsea
Hornsea CG 10 + aux I/C + CG boat
Auxiliary CG Station: Withernsea 10 + aux I/C
Sector officer Hull
Hull/Hessle CG 10 + aux I/C
Auxiliary CG Station: Easington 10 + aux I/C
Sector officer Cleethorpes
Cleethorpes CG 10 + aux I/C
Auxiliary CG Station: Donna Nook 10 + aux I/C
Auxiliary CG station: Mablethorpe 10 + aux I/C

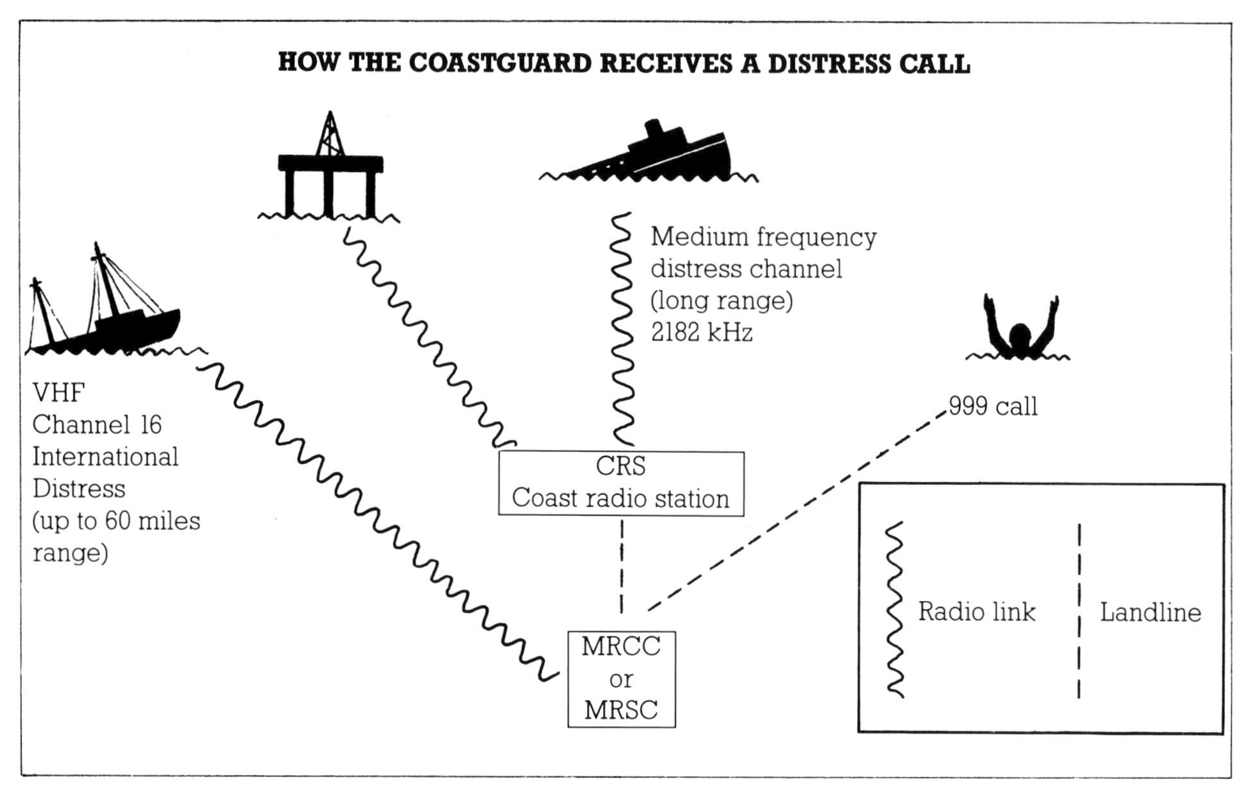
HOW THE COASTGUARD RECEIVES A DISTRESS CALL
Medium frequency distress channel (long range) 2182 kHz
VHF Channel 16 International Distress (up to 60 miles range)
999 call
CRS Coast radio station
MRCC or MRSC
Radio link
Landline

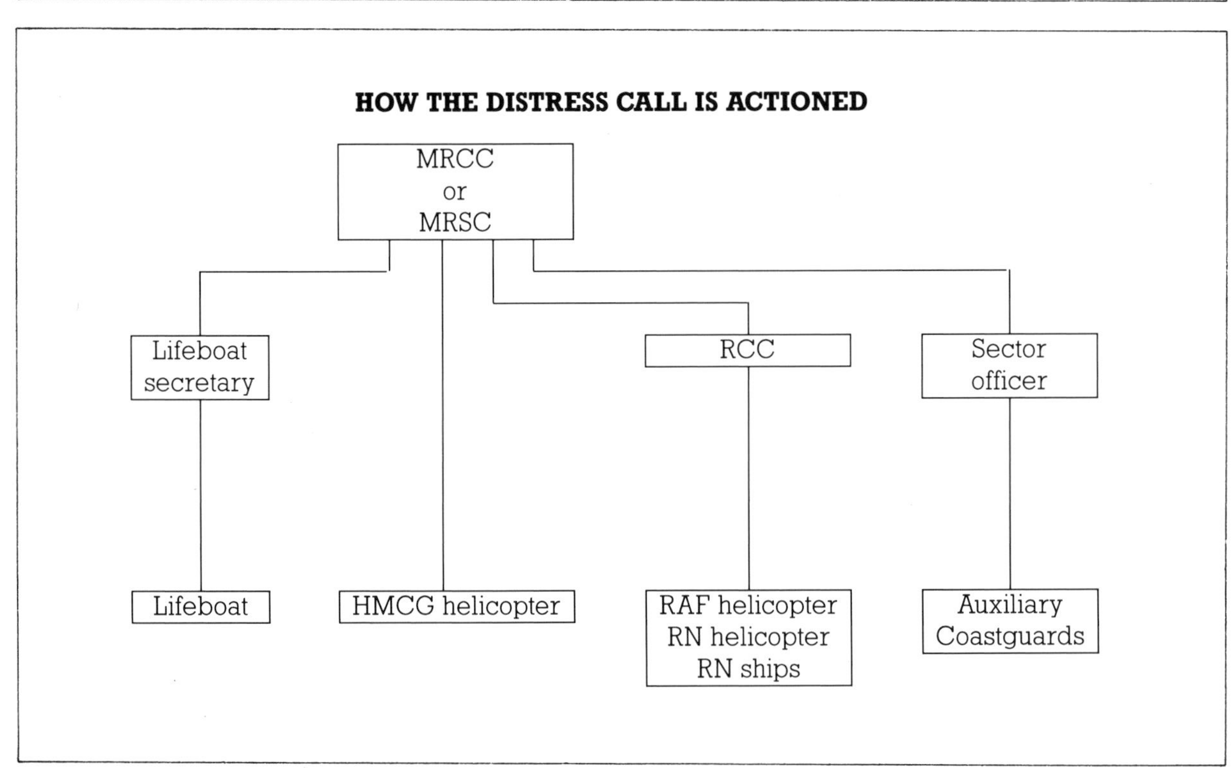
HOW THE DISTRESS CALL IS ACTIONED
MRCC or MRSC
Lifeboat secretary
RCC
Sector officer
Lifeboat
HMCG helicopter
RAF helicopter RN helicopter RN ships
Auxiliary Coastguards

women who give up their own time to participate in rescue teams, mobile patrols or carry out radio and visual watchkeeping at coastguard stations. These auxiliaries are part-timers, come from all sections of the community and can be called out at any time of the day or night, either by a sector officer or directly from a MRCC or MRSC, to assist in search and rescue operations.

Each auxiliary unit is managed by the auxiliary-in-charge. The auxiliaries are often the first at the scene of an incident and quickly have to assess the situation to ascertain if assistance from other coastguards, lifeboats or helicopters is required.

The auxiliary coastguards work closely with the sector officer and carry out his role when he is absent. They train regularly in all aspects of maritime safety and distress, navigation, first-aid and cliff rescue techniques.

There are also reporting members whose home or workplace is situated in a position where they can observe and give first-hand information of a likely incident. Another sector of the auxiliary team is the 'auxiliaries afloat'. Their activities at sea, both pleasure and com-

An auxiliary coastguard checks a wrecked car, driven into the River Humber, for survivors. Note the safety line.

One of the UK's busiest coastguard cliff rescue teams is based at Flamborough Head, Yorkshire. The pictures show an auxiliary coastguard preparing to go down a cliff face, putting on his bosun's chair and safety harness. Right, moving down the cliff with a specialist cliff rescue stretcher to an injured walker.

A casualty is carried to a waiting ambulance by Flamborough auxiliary coastguards.

mercial, give them the opportunity to report incidents by radio to the MRCC or MRSC and they can also be called by the controlling coastguard station to assist other vessels which may be in distress nearby.

Maritime distress radio frequencies
There are three international maritime radio distress frequencies:

500 KHz: W/T — wireless telegraphy
2182 KHz: R/T — radio telephony
156.80 MHz: R/T also known as Channel 16

All MRCCs and MRSCs keep constant watch on VHF Channels 0 and 16.

VHF Channel 0 is HMCG's own radio frequency and all coastguard stations, mobiles and hand portable radios are fitted with this channel enabling communications direct with operation rooms without interruption to the dedicated distress frequencies. All the RNLI lifeboats, RAF and RN helicopters are also fitted with this channel.

VHF Channel 67 (156.375 MHz) is used by HM Coastguard as a working frequency for radio communications other than distress traffic.

British Telecom coast radio stations (CRS) receive and acknowledge distress and urgency calls from ships on 500 KHz and 2182 KHz. These channels are on the medium frequency band (MF) and have a greater transmission range than VHF. When an emergency call is received on these frequencies by the CRS, it is immediately passed on to the nearest coastguard rescue centre for action.

Distress and urgency calls. A distress or urgency message has priority over all other radio transmissions and all radio telephony calls of this type should be made on VHF channel 16 or 2182 KHz. Wireless telegraphy (morse) calls are transmitted on 500 KHz.

To assist in speedy and efficient rescue operations and to let the land-based co-ordinating authority, as well as other vessels, know how best to deal with the emergency, calls are identified as:

DISTRESS CALL — I am in grave and imminent danger
CALL:-
Mayday, mayday, mayday (three times) and then give:
Mayday name and callsign
position
nature of distress
type of boat
persons on board
intentions (eg abandoning ship)

URGENCY CALL — I require urgent help but not in imminent danger
CALL:-
Pan, pan, pan and give:
name and callsign
nature of urgency
position
intentions

The coastguard or coast radio station will then reply and organize the appropriate action.

THE LIFEBOAT SERVICE

The Royal National Lifeboat Institution (RNLI) is a voluntary organization which exists to save life at sea. Since its foundation in 1824 more than 118,000 people have been rescued by lifeboat within the British Isles.

The RNLI, on 24-hour call, has the lifeboat service necessary to cover search and rescue requirements out to 30 miles from the coast of the United Kingdom and the Republic of Ireland. There are 203 lifeboat stations with 263 lifeboats (offshore and inshore) and 98 lifeboats in the relief fleet.

The RNLI was founded by Sir William Hillary and is the oldest national lifeboat service in the world. Hillary established the first lifeboat stations on the Isle of Man, and personally won the Institution's gold medal for gallantry three times in the Douglas lifeboat.

The early lifeboats were powered by

Fraserburgh's latest lifeboat is the 17-knot 'Tyne' class vessel, a low profile boat which is ideal for the stormy seas around the north-east coast of Scotland. This small Scottish fishing port has lost three lifeboats this Century.

FV Galatea *of Peterhead photographed from an escorting lifeboat during a severe storm in the North Sea. The fishing vessel was successfully recovered to port.*

men using oars and in 1890 the first steam-powered lifeboats went into service. Experiments with petrol engines started in 1904 but in 1932 the diesel engine was introduced. Now all offshore lifeboats are fitted with twin diesel engines.

Until the 1970s the lifeboat service received, on average, between 300 and 500 calls a year. But recently there has been a dramatic increase in service launches. Now the lifeboats are being launched on 4,000 emergency calls a year. The increase is due mainly to the explosion of recreation activities on and by the sea, although calls to commercial and fishing vessels have also increased.

The lifeboat fleet. To fulfil the RNLI's commitment to be able to launch a lifeboat at any time of day or night regardless of tidal condition and the varied coastline, many types of lifeboat are needed. Some of the larger lifeboats can only lie afloat while others are only suitable for slipway launching.

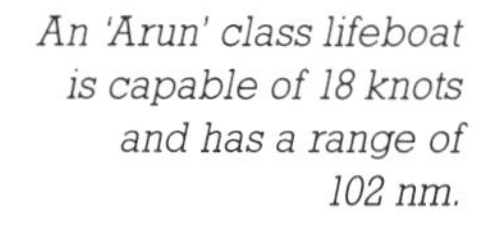

An 'Arun' class lifeboat is capable of 18 knots and has a range of 102 nm.

RNLI LIFEBOAT PROFILES

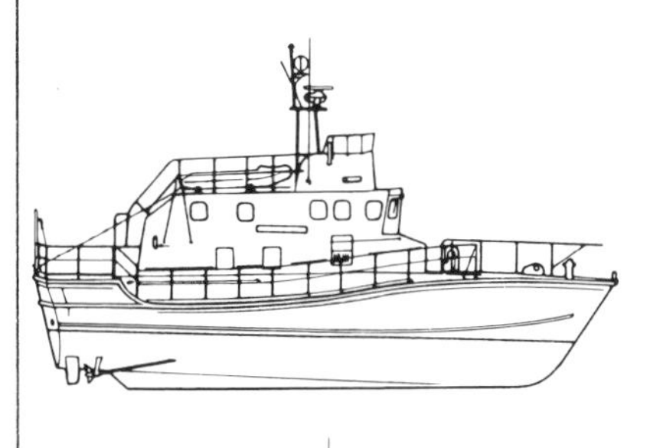

ARUN
Length: 15.86-16.47m/ 52-54ft
Speed: 18.2 knots
Range: 102 n miles

THAMES
Length: 15.25 m/50ft
Speed: 16.9 knots
Range: 95 n miles

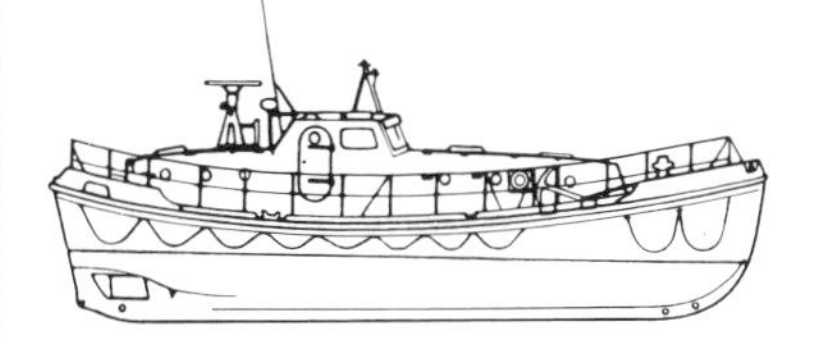

SOLENT
Length: 14.8 m/48ft 6in
Speed: 9.25 knots
Range: 120 n miles

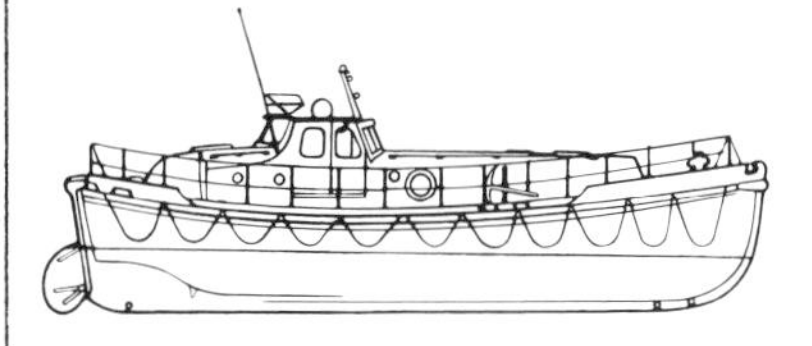

WATSON
Length: 14.34 m/47ft
Speed: 8.7 knots
Range: 115 n miles

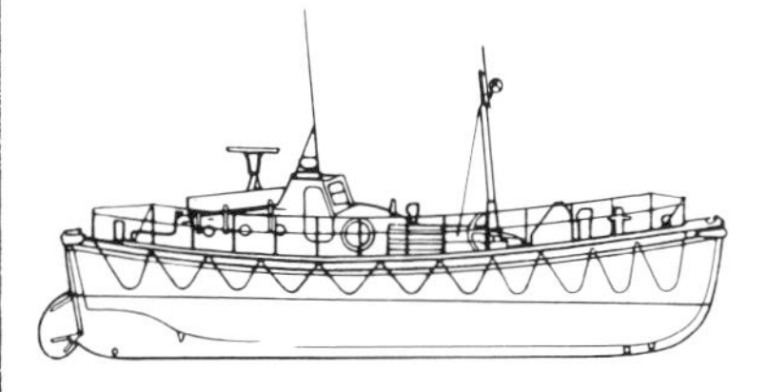

WATSON
Length: 14.26 m/46ft 9in
also 14.34 m/47ft
Speed: 8.8 knots
Range: 143 n miles

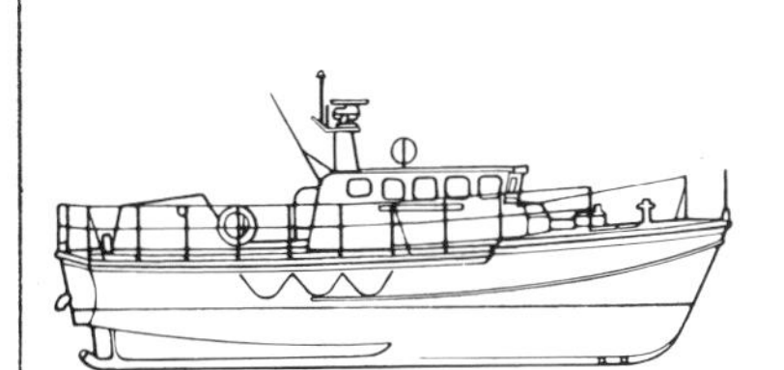

TYNE
Length: 14.34 m/47ft
Speed: 17.6 knots
Range: 116 n miles

WAVENEY
Length: 13.42 m/44ft
Speed: 15.4 knots
Range: 97 n miles

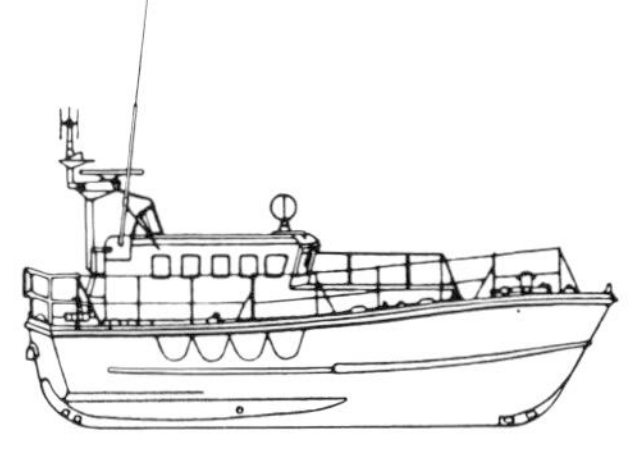

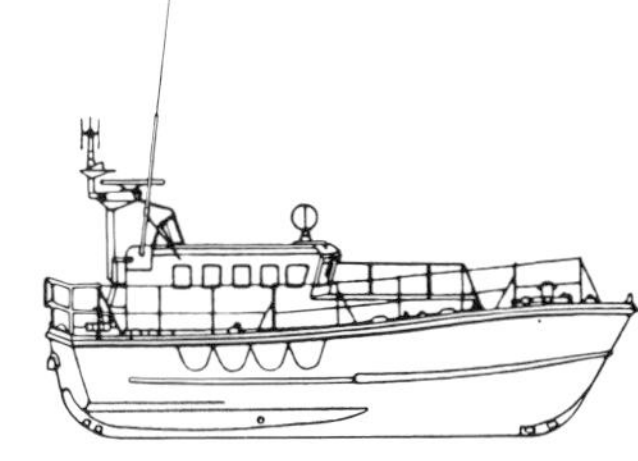

MERSEY
Length: 11.57 m/38ft
Speed: 17.5 knots
Range: 180 n miles

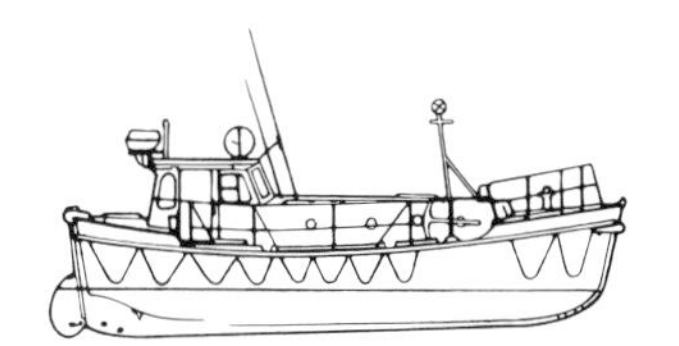

ROTHER
Length: 11.29 m/37ft
Speed: 8.0 knots
Range: 65 n miles

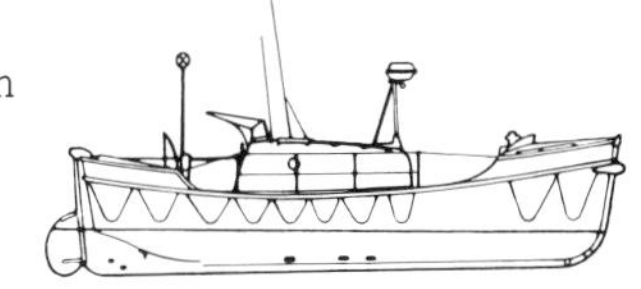

OAKLEY
Length: 11.29 m/37ft
Speed: 8.0 knots
Range: 65 n miles

BREDE
Length: 10.07 m/33ft
Speed: 18.6 knots
Range: 62 n miles

ATLANTIC
Length: 6.41 m/21ft
Speed: 29 knots
Range: 50 n miles

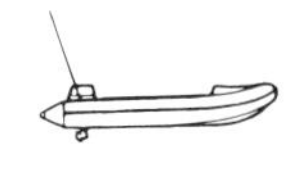

C CLASS
Length: 5.33 m/17ft 6in
Speed: 30 knots
Range: 90 n miles

D CLASS
Length: 4.88 m/16ft
Speed: 25 knots
Range: 60 n miles

The RNLI's policy is to operate its fleet of lifeboats so that they can reach a casualty up to 30 miles from the shore within four hours, although some of the fast lifeboats can achieve this distance within two hours. From this point they can continue to search or stand-by a vessel for a further four hours.

The lifeboat fleet consists of 128 large lifeboats ranging from 33 to 54 ft (10 to 16.5 m) in length and more than 133 lifeboats of between 16 and 21 ft (4.9 to 6.4 m). To house the boats there are 203 lifeboat stations with some having both the large offshore boats and inflatable craft on station.

For close inshore work inflatable craft are ideal. They were first introduced in 1963 because of the dramatic increase in emergencies near the shore. They have a much quicker response time than the larger boats and can gain access to virtually any part of the coast. The top speed of these small craft can exceed 30 knots which is twice that of the larger counterparts. They are the perfect rescue boat for swimmers in difficulties, a cliff faller, persons cut off by the tide and for assisting pleasure craft. The inflatable is made of nylon coated with neoprene/hypalon which can withstand contact with rocks, piers and other craft without causing serious damage.

The coxswain can work the lifeboat from below in the wheelhouse or, as illustrated here, from the flying bridge.

Running a lifeboat. The lifeboat stations of Britain and Ireland are divided into seven operational areas, each under the supervision of an Inspector of Lifeboats. Other area staff consist of engineers, hull surveyors and electronic engineers who are responsible for overseeing the maintenance of the lifeboat fleet. The lifeboats are regularly surveyed and serviced and periodically go 'off station' for overhaul. When this occurs a similar type of lifeboat from the reserve fleet takes over.

Each lifeboat is run by a volunteer committee who supervize the management of the station. The honorary secretary of each station is responsible for authorizing the launch of the lifeboat.

Each lifeboat carries a crew of six, all volunteers except the mechanic who is employed by the RNLI on a full-time basis. His job is to ensure the lifeboat and all its equipment is well maintained and at sea he monitors the engines as well as acting as radio operator. The coxswain and the rest of the crew come from all walks of life. Traditionally lifeboat crews were made up from local fishermen but today they are being replaced by builders, shopkeepers, teachers and many other professions. Apart from a crew to man the lifeboat, shore parties are necessary to assist in the launching and recovery of the boat.

Launching the lifeboat. The coastguard normally requests the lifeboat honorary secretary to launch the lifeboat. However, the secretary and the coxswain can launch their own boat 'on their own initiative' if they so desire. Traditionally lifeboat crews were summoned to the boathouse by the firing of two maroons

but nowadays pocket radio bleepers are used to scramble the crew.

Some of the lifeboats, like the Arun, Thames and Brede class, lie afloat while others can be slip-launched or pushed out on a carriage by a fully waterproof Talus tractor unit.

As soon as it has been launched the lifeboat will contact the coastguards on VHF channel 0 and pass them a list of the crew members on board. The coastguards will pass back any further information they have received from the incident.

While at sea the lifeboat listens out on VHF channel 0 and channel 16. In a distress situation all vessels and the coastguard will work communications on channel 16 and for long-range incidents the lifeboat can work on 2182 KHz — the international distress channel on the medium frequency — with the coast radio station and HMCG. The latest lifeboats are fitted with VHF DF equipment which means they can 'home in' and accurately pinpoint the vessel in distress. Plotting a course onboard a lifeboat can be extremely difficult in bad weather so it is often left to the coastguard to assist with chartwork.

Lifeboats versus helicopters. Whenever an emergency call is received about a person or vessel in difficulties at sea, the nearest lifeboat will be launched. In the event of a rescue helicopter being scrambled, the lifeboat will still proceed because although a helicopter can often be on the scene faster than a lifeboat and is able to make safer approaches, it is limited in endurance. Often when a helicopter has been scrambled it may have to turn back because of worsening weather conditions and in fog helicopters can only remain on the ground.

Lifeboats can stay at sea for long periods, they can carry more survivors, they have the capability to tow and can operate in all weather conditions both by day and at night.

Both lifeboats and helicopters work very closely together and on many incidents work as a team. They regularly have joint exercises where they practice their abilities in search and rescue techniques.

Cost of the service. The RNLI depends on voluntary contributions for its income. In 1989 it cost £36 million to run the service. The lifeboatmen receive a small allowance to compensate for loss of earnings when they are at sea. This is £5 for the first hour and £1.70 for each hour afterwards, and this is subject to income tax.

Lifeboats under 10 metres (33 ft) in length cost between £9,000 and £45,000 for the Atlantic 21 type. The larger boats cost between £350,000 (for the Mersey), £560,000 (for the Tyne) and £570,000 (the Arun).

Aith
Lerwick
Stromness
Kirkwall
Longhope
Thurso
Wick
Stornoway
Lochinver
Invergordon
Buckie
Macduff
Fraserburgh
Peterhead
Barra Island
Mallaig
Aberdeen
Montrose
Arbroath
Broughty Ferry
Oban
Anstruther
Kinghorn
North Berwick
Helensburgh
Dunbar
Queensferry
St. Abbs
Tighnabruaich
Eyemouth
Islay
Largs
Berwick-upon-Tweed
Arran (Lamlash)
Troon
North Sunderland
Campbeltown
Craster
Amble
Portrush
Girvan
Newbiggin
Arranmore
Red Bay
Blyth
Cullercoats
Stranraer
Kippford
Tynemouth
Silloth
Sunderland
Port Patrick
Crinidon Dene
Kircudbright
Hartlepool
Bangor
Workington
Teesmouth
Staithes and Runswick
Donagnadee
St. Bees
Redcar
Whitby
Portaferry
Ramsey
Scarborough

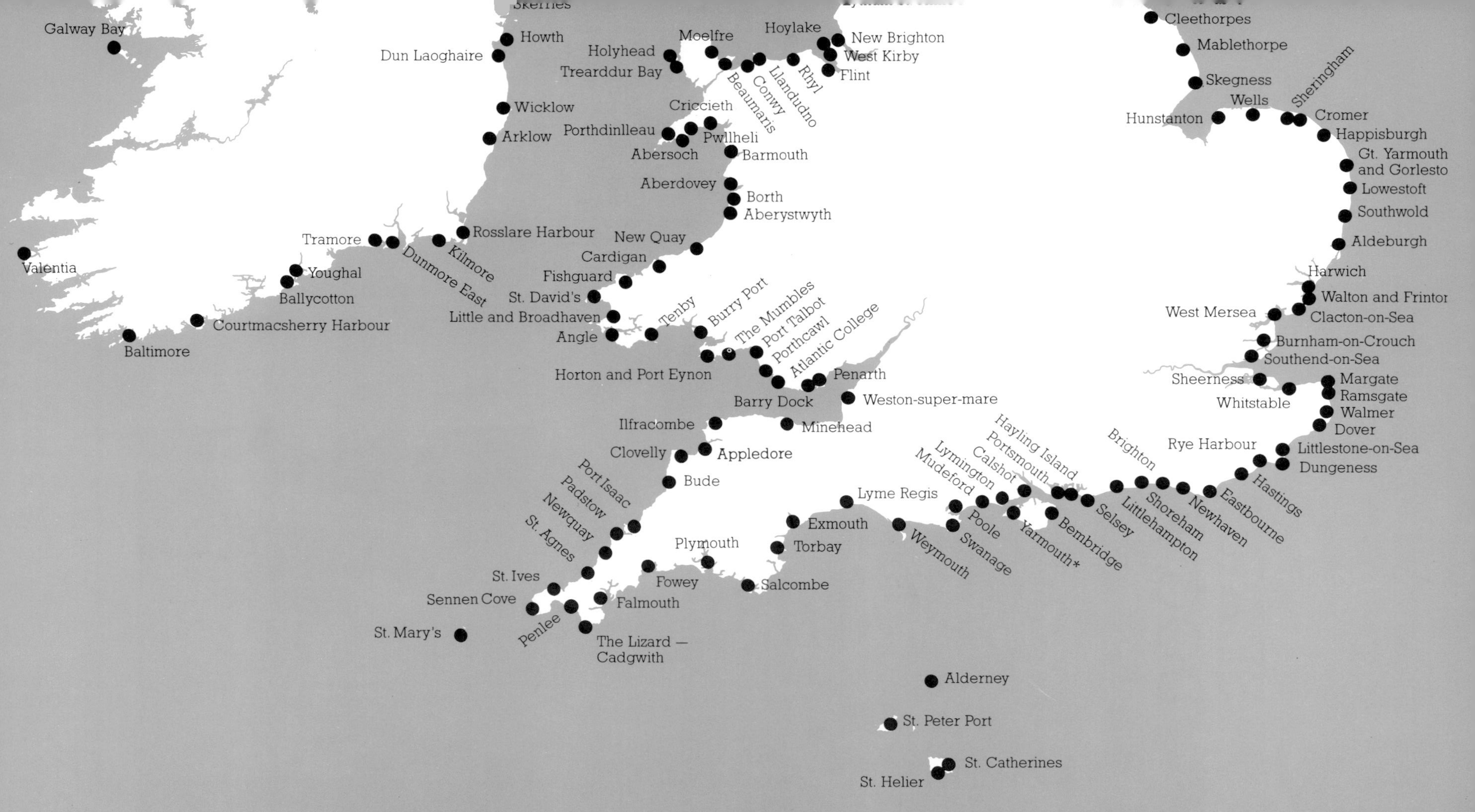

Galway Bay
Valentia
Baltimore
Courtmacsherry Harbour
Ballycotton
Youghal
Tramore
Dunmore East
Kilmore
Rosslare Harbour
Arklow
Wicklow
Dun Laoghaire
Howth
Holyhead
Treарddur Bay
Moelfre
Beaumaris
Conwy
Llandudno
Rhyl
Hoylake
New Brighton
West Kirby
Flint
Criccieth
Porthdinlleau
Pwllheli
Abersoch
Barmouth
Aberdovey
Borth
Aberystwyth
New Quay
Cardigan
Fishguard
St. David's
Little and Broadhaven
Angle
Tenby
Burry Port
The Mumbles
Port Talbot
Porthcawl
Atlantic College
Horton and Port Eynon
Barry Dock
Penarth
Weston-super-mare
Ilfracombe
Minehead
Clovelly
Appledore
Bude
Port Isaac
Padstow
Newquay
St. Agnes
St. Ives
Sennen Cove
Penlee
St. Mary's
The Lizard — Cadgwith
Falmouth
Fowey
Plymouth
Salcombe
Torbay
Exmouth
Lyme Regis
Weymouth
Swanage
Poole
Mudeford
Lymington
Calshot
Portsmouth
Hayling Island
Yarmouth*
Bembridge
Selsey
Brighton
Littlehampton
Shoreham
Newhaven
Eastbourne
Hastings
Rye Harbour
Littlestone-on-Sea
Dungeness
Dover
Walmer
Ramsgate
Margate
Whitstable
Sheerness
Southend-on-Sea
Burnham-on-Crouch
West Mersea
Clacton-on-Sea
Walton and Frintor
Harwich
Aldeburgh
Southwold
Lowestoft
Gt. Yarmouth and Gorlesto
Happisburgh
Cromer
Sheringham
Wells
Hunstanton
Skegness
Mablethorpe
Cleethorpes
Alderney
St. Peter Port
St. Catherines
St. Helier

SEARCH & RESCUE DOG ASSOCIATION

One of the most valuable assets available to a search team is the search and rescue dog. The dogs and their handlers are members of a unique organization called SARDA — Search and Rescue Dog Association.

These dogs are capable of doing the work of 20 men during a search operation across rough country and open hillsides. The rescue dog is specially trained to find people on the airborne scent which is given off by the human body, and they can find people buried under snow or hidden by rocks and undergrowth. The scent from a 'casualty' can be carried up to 300 metres (330 yd) on normal air currents.

The origin of the rescue dogs goes back to the 17th Century when those of the famous St Bernard Hospice, situated 3,000 metres (nearly 10,000 ft) above sea level on the Great St Bernard Pass between Switzerland and Italy, were first used to find travellers. Dogs were initially introduced to the Hospice to act as guards but after a time the monks began taking the dogs with them on rescue missions. Their value in guiding lost travellers and breaking trails through the deep snow was soon recognized by the monks. One particular dog, Barry, became famous after saving more than 40 lives.

The St Bernard was the first breed to be used for rescue work but in the First World War dogs were trained by the Red Cross to locate wounded soldiers on the battlefield. During a lull in the fighting the dogs would home in on the human scent emanating from the soldiers. In the Second World War they were used to find people buried under the rubble of devastated buildings, particularly in the blitzed cities of the United Kingdom. Again the dogs used the scent of humans, carried in the air, as location targets.

The training of dogs to locate avalanche victims was started by the Swiss Alpine Club (SWC) after the Second World War. The Club began to incorporate the dogs in the Swiss Rescue Service and a training programme was devised. This initiative by the SWC has led to the present system of dialling the number 11 on any telephone in Switzer-

Sgt John MacLean and his dog Dirk (right) and PC Alexander Fraser, with Ross, scramble to Rescue 137 to be lifted to the Five Sisters area of Kintail to search for an avalanche victim. The dogs were instrumental in finding the body of the missing climber. Both police officers are based at Inverness and are members of SARDA. For further details, see Job No 104.

land to bring the rescue dogs into action. A team can be summoned to the scene of an accident in a matter of minutes. Dogs and handlers are flown in by Alouette helicopters or ski-equipped Pilatus aircraft. There are now over 500 trained avalanche dogs in the European Alps.

Rescue dogs were introduced to the United Kingdom by international mountaineer Hamish MacInnes, leader of the Glencoe Mountain Rescue Team. In 1963 Hamish was invited by the International Red Cross to attend a training course for avalanche dogs in Switzerland. He was so impressed by what he saw that on his return home he arranged a training course for six dogs and handlers in Scotland. He realized that avalanche training could be adapted so that dogs could search in the United Kingdom during the summer as well as the winter months. The first training course run by Hamish MacInnes was so successful that it led to the formation of the Search and Rescue Dog Association.

The UK dogs are required to be more versatile than some of their Continental European counterparts and capable of maintaining search interest for long periods over rough mountainous terrain. Their primary aim is to locate a casualty who might be lying injured or unconscious.

In the British Isles there are six SARDA units with over 70 fully trained dogs which are made available for each of the UK mountain rescue teams. These dogs and handlers can be called upon for tasks varying from a search for overdue walkers to locating buried victims after an avalanche.

Dogs are selected and trained from a very early age. They must have a good scenting ability, a stable temperament and be intelligent. Handlers must take them on to the hills and mountains in all weather conditions so that they become accustomed to working in such an environment.

A very stringent selection process determines which animal will eventually become a rescue dog. The various search and rescue dog associations hold courses each year to select the best animals and they are graded into two categories: 'novice dog' and 'rescue dog'. The selection panel consists of senior officials of the regional SAR dog associations.

After a preliminary course it is usual for only 50 per cent of the entrants to succeed in passing to the second stage. This is a course, lasting five days, which decides the dogs to be chosen for operational work. These animals are then classed as novice dogs. After a further year of advanced testing, they attain the grade of rescue dog. Throughout the training period both dog and handler are assessed as a team.

A search dog must be competent in seeking out the source of human scent, be able to give its handler the location of a casualty and be skilful enough to carry out a search pattern. The dog and handler team must also be competent in

Search and rescue dogs are used extensively in mountain searches. SARDA in conjunction with the Royal Air Force, has developed a special dog harness for helicopter operations. Note particularly the light stick on the forward part of the dorsal harness strap.

upland snow conditions, especially in Scotland, and have a certain amount of climbing experience. It takes continuous training to bring a dog up to a standard where it can be involved in search and rescue operations for real.

On the instruction 'seek', the dog must be able to find a casualty some distance from the handler, and when it locates a 'target' it must 'speak' (bark loudly). This signifies that the target has been found. The handler must also be able to observe tell-tale signs in the dog's behaviour when it makes a find. These include general excitement, erect ears and a tail held high.

In winter it is important to activate search dogs and have them working as soon as possible, especially after an avalanche. To be buried under snow is similar to being placed in a deep freeze. The victim rapidly cools down and the body scent diminishes. The dog and handler first start their search in the most likely area where the casualty is thought to be located and it is important that other teams allow the dog an opportunity to look for its victim over ground or snow that has little or no other human scent on it.

SAR dogs are habitual helicopter passengers, including travelling up into the hovering aircraft by winch with a handler. In this case, it is Steve Ross (from Forres, near RAF Kinloss) with his dog and mountain rescue equipment.

The rescue dog can carry out a search much quicker than a conventional search party, and for example in an avalanche area a rescue dog can accomplish a search in 30 minutes that would otherwise take a 20-man probe team about four hours to implement.

In darkness, the SAR dog can search more efficiently than its human counterpart because a victim's scent is often more detectable at night, in the cooler air. For night searches, rescue dogs are fitted with a chemical light stick attached to their harnesses which emits a flourescent green glow enabling the handler to keep sight of his dog over a long distance.

All the SAR dogs are fitted with a special harness enabling them to be winched in and out of SAR helicopters. Helicopter transportation is the quickest way to move a rescue dog/handler team into a search area. If a dog team is available for a search, it usually takes priority over anyone else in the helicopter and is always taken first to the scene. During training the rescue dogs are given the opportunity of training with SAR helicopter crews to familiarize the dogs with the noise, smell of aviation fuel, feel of winching and layout inside the helicopter's cabin.

A fully trained rescue dog will become extremely excited once he hears the sound of an approaching helicopter — to him it signals the start of an interesting job. The dog's abilities can, and very often do, save life.

'THAROS'

When he declared the Multi-functional Support Vessel *Tharos* operational in 1980, His Royal Highness, Prince Philip, Duke of Edinburgh described the vessel as 'the most expensive fire engine in the world with a vital role to play in the safety of North Sea oil production'.

On the night of 6 July 1988, an explosion and fire ripped apart the North Sea oil rig, Piper Alpha. Alongside Piper Alpha at the time was MSV *Tharos*; her unique features and facilities were tested to their limits and helped save the lives of the 63 men who survived the Piper inferno.

When international oil companies are awarded licences to explore for oil and natural gas in the North Sea, the UK Secretary of State for Energy's directive insists that adequate safeguards must be provided to ensure that a major blowout or an uncontrolled leakage of oil or gas be controlled in such a way as to minimize any spillage and to ensure the safety of a structure and its personnel.

As part of the oil companies' fulfilment of these requirements, a number of Multi-function Support Vessels (MSVs) were constructed. Their operational concept is to be 'on scene' within 36 hours of an emergency arising. Two of these vessels are MSV *Tharos* (operated by Occidental Petroleum, and the centre of operations during the Piper Alpha disaster) and MSV *Stadive*, under the control of Royal Dutch Shell with British Petroleum having a 25 per cent stake and the ability to call upon its services in an emergency.

Apart from being capable of giving emergency assistance in severe weather, supporting firefighting and pollution control, MSVs act as diving and underwater support vessels. They have comprehensive engineering and maintenance facilities on board and are self-propelled, each fitted with four 3,000 horsepower thrusters capable of moving the vessels at speeds up to 7 knots (13 km/h). The 30,000 ton *Tharos* can be operated by one man using a joystick control box.

Both vessels are constructed on a conventional semi-submersible drilling rig hull giving a high platform and good stability in rough seas. Dynamic positioning enables them to remain in a fixed position, by feeding the vessel's satellite position into a computer which automatically makes corrective adjustments to the four thrusters so that a constant position can be maintained.

Impressive equipment

MSV *Tharos* was built in Japan at a cost of US$100 million and included in the package is a comprehensive fire-fighting suite. Oil trouble shooter Paul 'Red' Adair helped to develop the vessel's fire-fighting facilities, which include water cannon capable of throwing 40,000 US gallons of water per minute over a horizontal distance of 73m (240 ft) Sixteen fire monitors are fitted, with one mounted on the boom tip of the giant Clyde crane.

In typical North Sea conditions, MSV Tharos *on station, showing the vessel's semi-submersible construction and heavy duty crane.* (Occidental Public Affairs.)

Tharos can also pipe 20,000 Imp gallons of water per minute on to a platform to assist fire-fighting teams. It is equipped with a 24m (80 ft) fire boom fitted with a grab claw which is capable of a 20 ton pull. The boom is able to withstand the intense heat of an oil or gas fire and can remove debris from vital areas. In addition, it can be used to stem the flow of oil from a wild well. A 19m (62 ft) extending footbridge on *Tharos* and a 43m (140 ft) access tower on the *Stadive* can be used to board stricken rigs.

Both *Tharos* and *Stadive* have drench systems capable of cooling themselves down when exposed to excessive heat. This is achieved by screening and covering the parts exposed to the heat with sea water from jets and deluge nozzles. Through a detergent oil dispersal system. *Tharos* can pump 10,000 gallons of detergent a minute through two monitors.

Specialist facilities

Tharos has an extensive self-contained hospital facility for almost 90 people, who can be treated for the effects of exposure, hypothermia, shock and burns. The hospital is equipped with a mini-operating theatre, resuscitators and patient monitoring equipment including electrocardiograph and defibrillator units. The intensive care unit consists of 23 beds and enough medical supplies are on board to treat over 300 persons without re-supply.

A comprehensive communication centre is installed enabling the MSVs to contact other installations, standby vessels, HM Coastguard and helicopters by radio, telex, telephone and computer

links. *Tharos* has two blastproof control centres from which it is said any emergency can be handled. They can be sealed to give protection from gases produced by hydrocarbon fires.

A comfortable life-style is provided for the men working on board the Multifunctional Support Vessels. Hotel accommodation is provided for 301 personnel on board the *Tharos* in one-, two- and four-man air-conditioned cabins each with a toilet and shower. As well as a galley, mess room, laundry and recreation rooms there is even the luxury of a movie room which shows a different feature film each day. A sauna and duty-free shop (but no alcohol) also keeps the crew happy.

Operational role

Apart from working above the surface, the MSV fulfils its functional task by constant monitoring and maintenance of underwater pipelines and installations. Both *Tharos* and *Stadive* have saturation diving systems, which allow divers to live in reasonable comfort for periods of up to one month while working each day to depths of 305m (1,000 ft). An important feature is the miniature submarine or Mobile Diving Unit (MDU) which locks on to the divers' compression chamber at the beginning of a working shift and carries them to the work site around the oil platform, or pipeline, before returning them to the compression chamber at the end of a shift. With an adequate number of men in the compression chamber an underwater shift system can be operated around the clock using this method.

Each of the MSVs have large helidecks which are operated independently of the main control centres. Here a radio operator keeps in contact with all the inbound and outbound helicopter traffic. Next to the helideck is a hangar where the vessel's own helicopter is housed. Full fire-fighting and support facilities, including fuel, are carried.

Days after the Piper Alpha explosion, MSV Tharos *continues to spray water on to the burning platform. Note the heavy-duty crane in use and the helideck used to transfer casualties by helicopter during the Piper emergency.* (Occidental Public Affairs.)

The Lossiemouth-based film crew (left to right): Steve Phillips, Caroline Houghton, Ross Neasham, Paul Holmes, Andrew Dearden and Paul Berriff, all dressed in Berghaus protection wear.

Paul Beaver (centre) after flying in Rescue 137 during the first 'reconnaissance visit' in July 1987. Left to right: Bill Payne (winchman), Simon Willson (co-pilot), Harry Watt (captain) and Paul Challice (radop/winch operator).

HOW THE SERIES WAS MADE

Months, sometimes years of planning go into making a successful television documentary series. Although, with action documentaries like RESCUE, the exact sequence of scenes or programmes and even the eventual format of the series are not possible to determine at the beginning, the producer and his team have to plan for every detail.

The birth of RESCUE goes back, at least in part, to 1985 when Paul Berriff, then working on his highly acclaimed *Animal Squad* series about the RSPCA, met Paul Beaver, then editor of *Helicopter World*. They were introduced through a mutual friend, Jerry Grayson, the Operations Manager of Castle Air Charters (who provide the helicopters for *Treasure Hunt*). Jerry, previously a Royal Naval SAR pilot, and Paul Berriff had worked together on a BBC Nationwide programme, *Rescue Flight*, while Paul Beaver was known to Jerry through his helicopter journalism.

Detailed planning for a single documentary programme at RAF Lossiemouth began in 1986. However, it was not until a long weekend spent with No 202 Squadron's D Flight that the two Pauls realized that the variety and subject matter of the 150-plus operations a year at Lossie would be ideal for a major television series.

Surprisingly enough, it took several attempts to interest the Royal Air Force's public relations organization that it would be of great benefit to the Service. Luckily, it did not take long to convince Scottish Television that the series had merit for network screening in the United Kingdom and possibly overseas.

Paul Berriff (producer/director/cameraman) took on a team of Martin Harris (Film Editor), Mark Hutchinson (Assistant Film Editor), Caroline Houghton (Production Assistant), Andrew Dearden (cameraman), sound recordists Mike Riley, Ross Neasham and Steve Phillips, Paul Holmes (assistant cameraman) and Paul Beaver (researcher/technical adviser). The crew lived at RAF Lossiemouth for twelve months from April 1988 to March 1989, during which time, working on a shift basis, they covered 120 scrambles.

In order to achieve the kind of close involvement which Paul Berriff's style of documentary requires, the crew lived side-by-side with the Rescue Flight. A portable office was made available by the Station Commander, alongside the Operations and Crew Room of the Flight which enabled close liaison and meant that there was no time lost when the scramble bell sounded.

In fact, the film crew, dressed and equipped as aircrew, were fully integrated into the scheme of things within days of arriving at RAF Lossiemouth. The film crew's training included dinghy, wet dunker, survival and aircraft safety drills — little did Paul Berriff and Ross Neasham realize that all the training would be invaluable when Sea King 138 crashed on to a Scottish mountainside in

Right *Producer/director/cameraman Paul Berriff dressed in his survival clothing for the filming of the series RESCUE.*

Far right *Steve Phillips with his sound recording equipment in his place in the Sea King's main cabin.*

January 1989!

In the normal course of events only the rescue helicopter's winchman would expect to go out of the aircraft on operations, but the film crew also had to take opportunities to film on the ground. To protect them against the elements the Royal Air Force provided standard safety equipment, but Berghaus, the world's leading mountain clothing manufacturers, kitted out the film crew with the latest protection wear.

To achieve actuality realism for the series it was essential that all dialogue on the helicopter's intercom, ground-to-air between the Rescue Co-ordination Centre, HM Coastguard and helicopter and all other relevant communications were recorded. Small modifications to the Sea King's intercom system were authorized to allow the sound recordists to plug into the system and tape conversation. Even the scramble phone didn't escape the crew's attention!

As soon as the film crew arrived at the helicopter — for every training or operational sortie — the tape recorders were switched on. Sound recording tape is less expensive than film stock and it proved invaluable for dialogue purposes when the programmes were later edited at Lossiemouth and back at Martin Harris's Leeds office.

In all, 500 rolls of Kodak-Eastman colour 16mm television film and 600 rolls of sound tape were used — that's a total length of 38 miles of film and 102 miles of sound tape! Many television profes-

sionals regard this as a low figure for action documentaries but it is a mark of the professionalism of the team that its operation was so cost-effective.

The Royal Air Force, for flight safety reasons, would not allow a camera to be attached to the helicopter's airframe, so all the footage, even the air-to-air material, was shot with hand-held Eclair and Aaton cameras. To assist with the filming of night operations, Osprey Electronics of Aberdeen supplied the Pocketscope, a special night vision lens which could be attached to the television camera. As viewers saw during *Avalanche*, the lens made all the difference to night shooting.

Both Paul Berriff and Andrew Dearden, strapped to the helicopter's deckhead by a despatcher harness, had literally to hang out of the cabin door to film the actual rescues underway. So professional was their action that at no time did the film crew interfere with the smooth operation of the RAF aircrew. In fact, the cameramen developed a technique of tracking back, still filming, into the beam seats as the casualty was brought in through the cabin door, to leave the working space free for the winch operator and winchman.

However, several times during the filming all the film crew experienced the need to stop filming and help the aircrew. During the filming of the sequences used in *Water Falls*, Paul

Mike Riley and Paul Berriff load the filming equipment into the Sea King helicopter. Great care was taken to carry only the gear essential for filming and personal survival in the event of an emergency.

Ross Neasham (sound recordist) and Andrew Dearden (film cameraman) being winched into a location by Sea King.

Berriff, a former lifeboatman and trained HM Auxiliary Coastguard, took it in turns with the winchman and winch operator to try to revive the drowned casualty. The film crew also gave assistance during the rescue of survivors from Piper Alpha.

Paul Berriff's particular skills and abilities were put to almost the ultimate test on a stormy night in October 1988, when he led the successful attempt to rescue a climber on The Old Man of Stoer, a 300 feet high rock stack off the north-west tip of Scotland. Both the rescue helicopter and the local lifeboat were unable to reach the man, but Paul, dressed in RAF survival gear and assisted by the Assynt MRT, reached the man and recovered him through heavy seas.

At a meeting of the Royal Humane Society on 7 March 1989 it was resolved that the Society's Silver Medal be awarded to Paul Berriff for 'having, on 27th October 1988, at great personal risk, saved the life of a man from drowning in heavy seas at the base of The Old Man of Stoer, Stoerhead, Lochinver, Sutherland'. The citation was signed by HRH The Princess Alexandra.

RESCUE has established a number of firsts, including the first major documentary series by an independent production company for Scottish Television to network throughout the United Kingdom and the first television series to commence film editing on site (Martin Harris moved part of his office to a room made available by the Station Commander in one of RAF Lossiemouth's hangars).

Martin Harris, the programme's film editor (left) and producer/cameraman Paul Berriff on the helicopter dispersal at RAF Lossiemouth.

The scene of Paul Berriff's dramatic and award-winning rescue during the filming of the series — The Old Man of Stoer.

GLOSSARY OF SEARCH & RESCUE TERMS

a/c aircraft
ATC air traffic control
brace . . . brace emergency call on intercom, meaning prepare for impact
casevac casualty evacuation
circuit breakers (CCBs) fuses for electrical systems
clock code using clock face to give direction, with 12 o'clock being dead ahead
committed a time in the helicopter's flight, usually in the hover and using high power, when if one engine fails there is insufficient power in the second to keep the helicopter in the air; it will go down with only moderate control to cushion the landing
co-pilot second pilot
Decca medium-range navigation system
DF Direction Finding
DME distance measuring equipment
double lift two-person hoist (winchman and survivor)
endurance fuel in helicopter equivalent to a time in minutes during which it can remain airborne, at a consumption of 1,000 lb fuel per hour, ie 3000 lb is equivalent to three hours endurance
external power engine start power supply
first pilot captain of the aircraft
FLIR Forward Looking Infra-Red
flot gear flotation gear (to keep helicopter afloat)
FM marine radio (HMCG/fishermen)
FRT Fell Rescue Team
goon suit see **immersion suit**
GSU Group Standardization Unit (an inspection team)
HAR Helicopter, Air Rescue (Wessex/Sea King)
harness bosun's chair used to lift winchman
HC Helicopter, Cargo (Wessex)
HF high frequency (radio) for long-range communications
hi-line transfer method of winching from constricted scene
'hoist to pilot' passing control of winch to pilot
HMCG Her Majesty's Coastguard
HP cocks high pressure fuel cocks
immersion suit part of aircrew safety clothing
INMARSAT INTernational MARitime SATellite
job euphemism for SAR mission
KHz kilohertz
master caution indicator for system malfunction
MAYDAY international distress call
medevac medical evacuation
mission crew see 'rear crew'
MRCC Maritime Rescue Co-ordination Centre
MRT mountain rescue team
NAR no action required
NATO North Atlantic Treaty Organisation
off-state no helicopter available
Omega global navigation system
on scene arrival at the incident
Opeval operational evaluation (random annual test by GSU)
PLB personal locator beacon
POB persons on board
point of no return position along route beyond which helicopter can no longer land at origin and must land elsewhere
QFE airfield pressure setting (altimeter reads zero at touchdown)
QNH regional pressure setting (altimeter reads zero at sea level)
radop radar operator
RAF Royal Air Force
RCC Rescue Co-ordination Centre
'rear crew' crew at the rear of the helicopter
RNAS Royal Naval Air Station
RNLI Royal National Lifeboat Institution

R/T Radio Telephone (speech)
RTA Road Traffic Accident
SAR search and rescue
SARDA Search & Rescue Dog Association
SARSAT Search And Rescue Satellite
SARTU SAR Training Unit
sitreps situation reports
SKTU Sea King Training Unit
stab automatic flight control system
State 2 military in-flight emergency
strop used to lift survivor
Ts & Ps temperatures & pressures (helicopter engines/transmission)
TANS Tactical Air Navigation System
UHF ultra high frequency (military ATC radio)
USAF United States Air Force
USCG United States Coast Guard
VHF very high frequency (civilian ATC radio)
WIFA well intentioned false alarm
winchman airman lowered from the helicopter
winch operator crew member who controls the winching
W/T Wireless Telegraphy (Morse code)